Pearl Harbor Reexamined

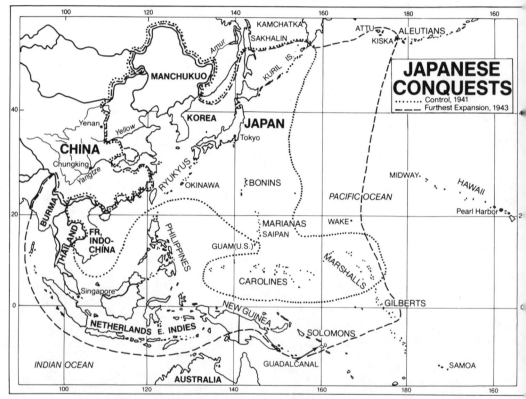

Source: Woodbridge Bingham, Hilary Conroy, and Frank W. Iklé, *A History of Asia,* 2d ed. Boston: Allyn and Bacon, 1974.

Pearl Harbor Reexamined

Prologue to the Pacific War

Edited by Hilary Conroy
and Harry Wray

 University of Hawaii Press · Honolulu

© 1990 University of Hawaii Press
All Rights Reserved
Printed in the United States of America
95 94 93 92 91 90   5 4 3 2 1

Library of Congress Cataloging-in-Publication Data

Pearl Harbor reexamined: Prologue to the Pacific war /
edited by Hilary Conroy and Harry Wray.
     p.   cm.
   Includes bibliographical references.
   ISBN 0–8248–1235–2 (alk. paper)
   1.   Pearl Harbor (Hawaii), Attack on, 1941.   I.   Conroy, Hilary,
1919–   .   II.   Wray, Harry, 1931–   .
D767.92P398   1989   89–37487
940.54'21—dc20   CIP

University of Hawaii Press books are printed
on acid-free paper and meet the guidelines
for permanence and durability of the Council
on Library Resources.

*To Charlotte and
to the memory of
Harry's sister Mary*

Contents

Acknowledgments

The editors thank the contributors to this volume for their cooperation and patience during the time it took to prepare the manuscript for publication. Our original intention was to include the Pearl Harbor story as part of the *Japan Examined* volume, which was published by the University of Hawaii Press in 1983. In the process of review and analysis, however, it was decided that the original format of the essays with only minimal documentation was unsuitable to the handling of a historical problem as intense and complex as the startup of the Pacific War. Hence, in revising the essays for inclusion in the present volume, we inflicted difficult demands on our contributors. Gary Dean Best was especially helpful with this problem. Our thanks, too, to Charlotte Conroy for assistance with the editing and to Conroy grandson Steven Ushioda for word-processing the list of suggested readings.

Chronology

1894–1895   Sino-Japanese War, ending in victory for Japan, ceding of Taiwan to Japan, and Treaty of Shimonoseki (1895). Kwantung Peninsula (southern Manchuria) at first ceded to Japan but returned to China after Triple Intervention protest and threat by Russia, France, and Germany (1895).

1899–1900   Japan a party to Open Door Notes promising respect for China trade and "entity."

1910   Japan annexes Korea, after taking control there after Russo-Japanese war (1904–1905).

1915   Twenty-One Demands on China. Japan obtains many special privileges in China, especially in Manchuria.

1922   Washington Conference agreements to "freeze the Pacific." Japan agrees. Promises China uninhibited opportunity to form stable government.

1928   Chinese nationalists (Nanking government) declare Manchuria a part of China (the three Eastern provinces).

1928   Kellogg-Briand Pact, outlawing war as an instrument of national policy.

1930   London Conference extends Washington Conference agreements; Japan signs, amid rumblings from ultranationalists; Premier Hamaguchi wounded in assassination attempt.

1931   Manchurian (Mukden) Incident (September 18).

1932   Murder of Premier Inukai; end of Party government in Japan.

1933   Establishment of Manchukuo; Japan withdraws from League of Nations.

1936   Tokyo mutiny by "young officers." Put down by "Control group" (February 26).

1936   Sian Incident leads to "United Front" (Nationalist-Communist) in China (December).

1937 China (Marco Polo Bridge) Incident (July 7–8). Japan attacks North China.

1937 Japanese take and "rape" Nanking (December). FDR quarantine speech.

1938 Nationalist Chinese government to Chungking.

1939–1944 Stalemate in China war; U.S. aid to Chungking.

1940 Japanese "puppet government" (Wang Ching-wei) established at Nanking.

1940 Japan enters Tripartite (Axis) alliance with Germany and Italy (September).

1937–1941 Three Konoe cabinets in Japan.

1940 Admiral Nomura sent as (peacemaking) ambassador to Washington (December).

1941 "John Doe Associates" active as peacemakers in Washington.

1940–1941 Increasing Japanese pressure on Indochina and Dutch East Indies. Mounting tension with United States.

1941 Japan-USSR Neutrality Pact (April). Germany invades USSR (June 22).

1941 Matsuoka, architect of Axis alliance, ousted from Konoe cabinet (July).

1941 United States freezes Japanese assets, cuts trade (August).

1941 Ambassador Nomura (and Premier Konoe[?]) seek summit conference with FDR. Hull (and Hornbeck) refuse to allow it. Hull demands prior acceptance of Open Door principles (Summer).

1941 Konoe resigns. General Tōjō takes premiership in Tokyo (October).

1941 Pearl Harbor attack plans laid (Fall). Nomura continues negotiations in Washington; Kurusu joins him, both apparently ignorant of Pearl Harbor attack plans. Hull and Nomura search for *modus vivendi*.

1941 Churchill urges Roosevelt to support China (November 24).

1941 Hull's note to Tokyo reiterates demand that Japan accept "principles," including withdrawal from China (November 26).

1941 Pearl Harbor attack (December 7; December 8, Tokyo time).

Introduction

HILARY CONROY AND HARRY WRAY

In the nearly fifty years since Pearl Harbor, there have been dozens of books on the subject but no definitive study. The closest is the work of Gordon Prange, published posthumously by his former students, Donald M. Goldstein and Katherine V. Dillon. In the preface to *At Dawn We Slept: The Untold Story of Pearl Harbor* (New York, McGraw Hill, 1981), the first volume of Prange's projected tetralogy, his editors refer to the author's "magnificent obsession" with the subject. It was indeed that. Prange and his editors deserve credit for making his immense and indefatigable research available to general readers and scholars alike. However, as his editors admit, "even in the context of a multivolume study, Prange never nourished the illusion that his would be the last word on the subject" (*At Dawn We Slept*, p. xiii).

This is certainly true, for in his "magnificent obsession" Prange incorporated a few minor obsessions that color his work. One is a tendency to become friends with all the Pearl Harbor actors, especially the Japanese perpetrators. Prange's is a problem characteristic of military history. In his enrapturement with the chesslike strategy and tactics of war, Prange failed to reflect sufficiently on its terrible cost in terms of human life and property and on the tremendous importance of the avoidance of war and the need to explore why leaders and governments fail to achieve it at memorable military crossroads.

Prange assumed the inevitability of the war, but, were Pearl Harbor and the Pacific War in fact unavoidable in the context of the times? The question is a crucial one, and, although the present volume is not entirely an exercise in peace research, it nonetheless approaches the Pearl Harbor-Pacific War problem from a broad perspective. We hope that this collection will shed the light of half a century's research by more than a dozen scholars on the various aspects of an elusive problem.

The essays that follow reexamine Japanese and American diplomacy in view of the Pearl Harbor attack, including to some extent the involvement of other nations. This reexamination seeks to answer such questions as the following: Were American and Japanese policies before Pearl Harbor realistic in terms of the problems and needs of the respective nations, or were they unrealistic, biased, mismanaged, or even absurd? Were they prudent or imprudent? Could U.S. and Japanese leaders have avoided or delayed the war if they had altered their positions? A great deal? A little? Why did they fail to do so? Were there those in the American and Japanese governments at the time who recommended wiser policies than those taken? If so, why were these policies not pursued? Or are these "wiser policies" only available by hindsight? What role did domestic politics or relations with other nations—Britain and China for the United States, Germany and Italy for Japan—play in limiting the freedom of diplomatic maneuver of the principals?

Harry Wray begins by providing a general historical perspective. Following Wray's analysis of Japanese-American relations and perceptions from 1900 to 1940 is an essay by Akira Iriye, which emphasizes that domestic conditions limited the range of Japanese policymakers far more than that of their American counterparts. Such issues as oil supply and relations with China were much more vital to Japan than to the United States. Iriye suggests that American leaders missed many opportunities to influence domestic conditions in Japan and to promote a climate for peaceful resolution of the issues of the time. In the third essay Gary Dean Best carries this critique of American policy further by arguing that President Roosevelt from the beginning, and in disregard of some of his more knowledgable advisors, elected to stress his "ancestral connection with China" in favoring China in Sino-Japanese relations, and that Secretary of State Hull was a "mediocrity" who was "on the defensive" in the Roosevelt cabinet and who toadied to Roosevelt's predilections on matters of East Asian diplomacy.

John K. Emmerson, who was living in Tokyo as a young career diplomat and was in close touch with Ambassador Joseph Grew there in the pre-Pearl Harbor years, agrees with this critical view of the FDR-Hull attitudes in his, the fourth, essay. He argues that Grew, the American expert on Japan, insofar as there was one, was not listened to, whereas Stanley Hornbeck, "whose only experience in Asia had been a teaching stint in China," gave the advice that was followed. This included a vetoing of a proposed Pacific summit between President Roosevelt and Premier Konoe, even though, Emmerson says, quoting Grew, that Konoe in a secret meeting with Grew had "conclusively and whole-heartedly" accepted Hull's principles.

Ikei Masaru, Japanese scholar, also feels that American diplomacy was "mismanaged" in the 1930s, beginning with the Manchurian (Mukden) Incident of September 18, 1931, to which he traces developments leading to the Pacific War. Diplomacy was too soft in 1931 when "the United States did not recognize the seriousness of the [Mukden] incident," but it was too hard in 1941 when a "more cautious attitude toward Japan" might have postponed or avoided war.

Hosoya Chihiro then elaborates on the hard-liner, soft-liner issue in American diplomacy in the months preceding Pearl Harbor. He argues that the "hard-liners," led by Stanley Hornbeck, hoped and expected to "deter" Japan with oil and trade embargoes and other "hard-line" policies but miscalculated the "psychology of the Japanese people and especially of the middle echelon military officers" associated with the "samurai do-or-die spirit." There was a "predisposition to make critical decisions in the face of taking extremely great, even illogical risks . . . [i.e.,] death rather than humiliation."

Lest we begin to think that all the essays fault the United States, it should be noted that Jonathan Utley, Michael Barnhart, and Alvin D. Coox defend Roosevelt, Hull, and even Hornbeck for being "realistic" about Japan's warlike intentions. Utley argues that Hull's actions, not his words, should be attended to; they indicate that Hull was indeed a realist. Utley observes that Hull's eyes were on Southeast Asia more than on China and that he was not merely enamored with "saving" China. In fact, he realized that the Japanese were bogged down there, and he hoped the strain of the war in China would bring down the militarists in Japan. War did not come because Hull was too legalistic or moralistic, says Utley, but because Japan and the United States had "irreconcilable differences."

Michael Barnhart argues that "Hornbeck was right" in his hard-line assessment of Japan. Although cables from the American embassy in Tokyo (Ambassador Grew) pleaded for caution and softness in U.S. diplomacy, Hornbeck "saw things differently. The [Japanese] military had risen to power not out of some dark conspiracy or temporary aberration but because all Japanese political leaders, including civilians, agreed with the military's aims. . . ." The United States had to "put up or shut up." Hornbeck's policies, where they were followed, "served American interests well."

Alvin D. Coox defends Roosevelt, Hull, and other U.S. leaders
against the charge that they invited the Japanese attack as a "back
door" into the war in Europe. "After all," he says, "it was Admiral
Yamamoto Isoroku, the Japanese Combined Fleet Commander, who
devised the Pearl Harbor raid in utmost secrecy, not Roosevelt." Japanese scholar Fujiwara Akira emphasizes in his essay that Japan deliberately entered the Pacific War "as the clear-cut nation's will." Pearl
Harbor was planned, and the coming of the war was not accidental or
something that grew out of incidents or skirmishes, as was the case
with Japan's involvement in China. "Even a summit conference"
would only "postpone" war.

Traditional interpretations of this period have argued that the
prospects for peace with Japan were permanently dashed by Japan's
signing of the Tripartite Pact with Germany and Italy on September
27, 1940. This pact recognized Japan's leadership in greater East Asia
and a future world dominated by the United States, Russia, Germany, and Japan. Ikei Masaru maintains that the United States overreacted to it. Akira Iriye, Hata Ikuhiko, Norman Graebner, and
Conroy agree that the signing of the Tripartite Pact had great repercussions, but they differ in their assessments of its import. Hata
maintains that its signing was "a point of no return on the road to
Pearl Harbor." Graebner and Iriye conclude that after its signing
Americans saw a linkage between the wars in Europe and East Asia.
In that context, China became an ally who, in Graebner's cynical
words, could not be allowed to suffer any longer the consequences of
appeasement. In his view Japan was now left with only two alternatives: to terminate the war on U.S. terms or to fight an endless war on
the mainland. Graebner argues that the American decision to support China even to the point of justifying war in the Pacific was a
departure from the pre-1940 policy of the United States.

On another point Professor Utley is in sharp disagreement with
several essayists, particularly Tsunoda Jun, dean of Japanese diplomatic historians and an adviser to several Japanese prime ministers on
foreign policy matters. The issue is the value of a summit conference
between Prime Minister Konoe and President Roosevelt, which had
been requested by the former on August 9, 1941. Utley defends
Hull's veto of a summit by saying it could accomplish nothing but
mischief.

One of the major reasons American policymakers failed to take
Japanese peace proposals seriously is that they had already concluded

that the Japanese were treacherous and insincere. To be accused of insincerity is a grievous insult in the Orient. In his essay Tsunoda Jun angrily argues that Prime Minister Konoe's bid was completely genuine. Konoe was willing to stake his very life on a summit. Professor Graebner's paper also argues for the view of Ambassador Grew (our representative in Japan) that Washington should have been more flexible on such things as agreeing to a Roosevelt-Konoe meeting.

Sachiko Murakami's contribution is from her doctoral dissertation on "Japan's Thrust into French Indochina, 1940–1945" (New York University, 1981). Her untimely illness and death prevented her from focusing her very interesting conclusions on the main question of this volume, "Was the Pacific War inevitable?" However, we present an edited version of her conclusion to bring about such focus with minimal reconstruction. The body of her dissertation, which presents a huge amount of evidence of Japanese ambivalence, internal argument and disagreement, and worried hesitation with regard to Indochina, is somewhat ambivalent on the question of whether the Pacific War was inevitable.

One of her chapters (Chapter 2), entitled "Don't Miss the Bus," shows how newspaper sensationalism, reporting of German victories in Europe in the spring of 1940, and the propaganda efforts of German Foreign Minister Joachim Von Ribbentrop and the German ambassador to Japan, Eugene Ott, did stir up considerable public pressure on the Yonai cabinet to get on "the omnibus of German victory," but the rest of her dissertation indicates that this by no means made Japan's "thrust" into Indochina a foregone conclusion. Despite this she states in her concluding paragraph: "It can be said in the last analysis, therefore, that French Indochina was caught in the inevitable collision of the opposing policies of the United States and Japan concerning China and the Pacific." This is quite emphatic. However, since Murakami's subject is the Indochina phase, we shall regard it as conclusion only in saying that more, indeed much more, than Japan's Indochina incursion was needed to make the Pacific War inevitable, if indeed it was.

What emerges from these essays are four major debates. One is about whether war could have been avoided. A second controversy centers on the latest date at which a solution was possible; some of the essayists argue that war could have been avoided up until November 26, 1941. A third issue is whether responsibility for the deadlock lay with the United States, the Japanese, or our allies. The fourth is about whether Hull acted wisely in assuming that Japan could not be deterred from her expansionist course. On the latter point both Graebner and Conroy show that Admiral Nomura Kichisaburō accepted his appointment as ambassador to the United States in January 1941 only after he had been assured by Konoe that the highest naval authorities sincerely sought improved relations with the United States. They support their contention by noting that the second Konoe cabinet resigned on July 12, 1941, for the specific purpose of replacing pro-Axis Foreign Minister Matsuoka Yōsuke with Admiral Toyoda Teijirō, an opponent of the Axis alliance. Despite these actions, however, Hull stubbornly persisted in the view that Japan was committed to aggression.

Norman Graebner's essay argues that China, not Southeast Asia, was the stumbling block but that Japanese efforts to negotiate resulted only in the continued assertion of principles by the United States. In contrast to Utley, Graebner believes that Japanese actions in Southeast Asia were undertaken not to obtain Southeast Asia but to achieve Japan's will in China. American embargoes only drove the Japanese deeper into Southeast Asia to block U.S. aid to China and to obtain desired raw materials. For this reason Japan always showed a willingness to return to pre-July 16, 1941 conditions if the United States would end its trade embargo of that date.

Graebner argues that, whereas the Japanese kept coming forth with proposals, the United States refused to engage in any pragmatic horse trading. For example, on November 20, Special Ambassador Kurusu and Ambassador Nomura presented a formal proposal, a *modus vivendi,* that Graebner maintains had the effect of repudiating the Tripartite Pact. The two ambassadors offered a Japanese withdrawal from southern Indochina and an eventual withdrawal from all of Indochina if the United States would resume normal trade relations and adopt a hands-off policy toward China.

It is regarding this point that the essay by David Klein and Hilary Conroy adds significantly to the essays by Graebner, Utley, and Tsunoda. The Klein-Conroy paper maintains that American interpretations of British and Chinese messages on November 25–26 regarding the American *modus vivendi* on November 24 dashed the prospect of avoiding war. They indicate that the Roosevelt administration's decision to scuttle the *modus vivendi* and to issue a general note by Hull emphasizing principles may have killed the last opportunity for peace. Time had run out. November 26, 1941, was the last day allocated by the Tōjō government for peace efforts. A point of no return had been reached.

In the final essay Waldo Heinrichs gives a "global" reason for this, namely that FDR and Hull, from the midsummer of 1941 on, were stalling on Japanese peace overtures while tightening the embargo on Japanese oil. Why? So that Japan would not dare attack the Soviet Union from the Siberian side, thus allowing Moscow to use Siberian forces to hold off Hitler in Europe.

Obviously these are complicated matters. Let us proceed, therefore, to the essays before attempting to answer whether the Pacific War was inevitable, a question to which a definitive answer may not be possible.

Pearl Harbor Reexamined

1. Japanese-American Relations and Perceptions, 1900–1940

HARRY WRAY

FORTY years after the Japanese attack on Pearl Harbor historians can perceive with less passion and greater clarity the basic causes for the Pacific War. Even the attack on Pearl Harbor, which led President Franklin D. Roosevelt to claim that December 7, 1941, (December 8, Japan time) would remain forever "a date which will live in infamy," seems less treacherous in retrospect. When the Japanese launched surprise attacks in the Sino-Japanese War of 1894–1895 and the Russo-Japanese War of 1904–1905, the contemporary Western press objectively praised these well-executed strikes as brilliant tactical maneuvers. American military authorities in the 1920s and 1930s carried out maneuvers based on simulated Japanese attacks on Pearl Harbor that were surprisingly similar to the real one. Furthermore, the Japanese assault, destructive as it was, was launched to destroy specific military targets. Although the Japanese bombed civilian populations in China, these attacks were not on the massive scale of the subsequent indiscriminate bombings of civilian populations by Germany, Great Britain, and ultimately the United States. The worst examples of the latter were undoubtedly the atomic bombings of Hiroshima and Nagasaki, which some might consider revenge for Pearl Harbor.

We now know that the underlying causes of the Pacific War, as with all wars, were complex and remote as well as immediate and direct. Few scholars would deny that Japanese foreign policy and military expansion, especially in the 1930s, were important factors. Today, however, as a result of more objective and sophisticated studies, most non-Marxist scholars no longer simply equate Japan with the totalitarian Nazi regime in Germany or facilely support the conspiracy theses of the Tokyo Military Tribunal days. (David Bergamini is a notable exception.) Nor do they simply label Japan the overt aggressor while portraying the United States as an innocent victim.

Such characterizations were, at best, half-truths. They encouraged
Americans to accept an overly simplistic and distorted view of Japan.
This was neither good history nor a contribution to an understanding
of the problems of diplomacy.

It is clear today, more than forty years after Pearl Harbor, that the
fundamental causes of the Pacific War go back to the turn of this century. International relations were then characterized by power politics, aggressive nationalism, and Western colonialism. These forces
worked to enlarge the empire, glory, and wealth of the individual
nation-state. Western diplomacy legitimized such conquests via
international law and foreign policy based on such concepts as geographic propinquity, white man's burden, manifest destiny, Monroe
Doctrine, balance of power, spheres of influence, power vacuum, and
a racist version of Social Darwinism. Japan quickly learned to emulate
this international outlook to justify its own expansionism. Japanese
leaders also felt the insecurities that accompany the achievement of
major power status and a newly acquired psychology of imperialism.
By 1900, through power politics and the rationale of Western imperialism, almost all of Africa and the Near East, and all of South, Southeast, and East Asia except for Thailand, Japan, and China had
become European colonies. In 1898, via the Spanish-American War,
the United States also acquired overseas possessions in the Pacific.
Japan accepted such a world and became an apt pupil of the West.
Through the Sino-Japanese War of 1894–1895, the Russo-Japanese
War of 1904–1905, the annexation of Korea in 1910, and the opportunistic annexation of German territories in the Pacific and in China
(Shantung province) during World War I, Japan had become a major
Asiatic power.

On the road to imperialism Japan learned its lessons well. Japanese
leaders presumed that imperialism was the equivalent of being modern and civilized. They reasoned, incorrectly, that Asian imperialism
in Asia would be acceptable in the eyes of their Western models.
Japan saw itself as a "respectable imperialist,"[1] and was disappointed
by the signs that its expansionist behavior was not universally
accepted by the Great Powers.

The Japanese also soon became aware that power, rather than international law, ultimately determined the fate of a nation. One Japanese liberal, Fukuzawa Yukichi, had written insightfully that "one
hundred volumes of International Law are not the equal of a few can-
nons."[2] Another Japanese opinion maker, the influential writer Toku-

tomi Sohō, wrote bitterly, after Japan was forced by Germany, France, and Russia to retrocede the Liaotung Peninsula to China in 1895:

> Say what you will, it had happened because we weren't strong enough. What it came down to was that sincerity and justice didn't amount to a thing if you were not strong enough.[3]

Subsequently, the Japanese learned that power was its own justification.

A final factor played into the Japanese mode of thought. They developed the same "pathology of insecurity" as their Western mentors regarding the acquisition of an empire, namely, that the annexation of any new territory led inevitably to anxieties.[4] Militarists argued that more territory should be acquired in strategic areas to protect Japan's overseas empire. They also argued that greater funding for an expanded army and navy were essential to the empire. Eventually, this kind of thinking created an encirclement mentality that led to irrationality in domestic and foreign affairs. Militarists and ultranationalists argued that an encircled and persecuted Japan must break its way out by expansion. When Japan did so in the 1930s and was criticized by the Anglo-American powers, many Japanese further confused cause and effect. They failed to see that their escalation of expansion in China, and later in Indochina, was the cause of Western censure. Instead, they saw Western criticism and economic sanctions as justification of their encirclement thesis.

How did Japan initially become committed to an imperialist continental foreign policy? We can see now that a turning point came in 1905. Japan's gains from the Russo-Japanese War on the Asian continent had committed her to an active role there. That decision easily could be construed to violate the American Open Door policy as well as the interests of all the major powers with spheres of influence in China. More important, it put Japan on a collision course with a growing Chinese nationalism. It prompted Japanese militarists to seek more Chinese territory to protect past conquests.

China deserves our special attention because it became a source of alienation between the United States and Japan. By 1898 it had become a semi-colony of other countries. Many Chinese, such as Sun Yat-sen and later the Communists, paradoxically believed that a colonial status under one nation was preferable to being ruled by a host of imperial powers, none of which was responsible for the welfare of the

Chinese people. Only the fear of each occupying power that China might be dominated or swallowed up by a rival saved China from extinction as a sovereign state. Furthermore, Western actions between 1895 and 1898 carved up the Chinese melon into spheres of influence. Although China was far from being conquered in actual substance, a prostrate China, the "sick man of Asia," had lost her ability to act decisively against her oppressors. Her weakened condition incited more greed and fear.

Each imperialist power feared that it would be placed at a disadvantage in the balance of power by a rival's seizure of further Chinese territory. These conditions incited anxiety and contempt in Japan. Could Japan sit by and complacently allow Western powers to increase their influence next door? The insistence of Germany, France, and Russia in 1895 (the Triple Intervention) that Japan must return one of the fruits of her victory over China in 1895, the Liaotung Peninsula, because of their professed solicitude over the territorial integrity of China now seemed to be a sanctimonious shedding of crocodile tears. It was obvious to the Japanese that the Western countries applied a double standard of international conduct when it came to protecting their national interests.

China's cause was also aided by the expansion of the United States. By the end of the nineteenth century the American annexation of Hawaii and the Philippines established the United States as a Pacific power. China became of strategic importance to American leaders, although more in theory than in fact. Although the United States never really acted to uphold the Open Door policy until the late 1930s, Americans on an emotional level began to identify with East Asian interests and to see themselves as protectors of an abject China. From that perspective the United States began—especially after the Japanese gains in the Russo-Japanese War (1904–1905)—to view Japan as a potential threat. The "Yankee of the East" was no longer an admired friend, but a rival. That feeling was reciprocated in Japan where many viewed the American assumption of China's cause with apprehension and believed incorrectly that the United States had not really acted as an honest broker in Portsmouth. Because the Japanese government did not take its subjects into its confidence, the Japanese people were led to expect more gains from the Russo-Japanese War than what actual military conditions at the end of the war merited. In such ignorance they felt cheated by civilian diplomats of their own country who, they charged, had been duped, ostensibly, by President Theodore Roosevelt.

A mixture of sentimental feelings for the underdog by the American public and a desire by the American establishment to exploit China commercially led Secretary of State John Hay to proclaim an Open Door policy in 1900. The U.S. government secured verbal statements from all the powers that they believed in preserving China's territorial integrity (already a travesty) and in maintaining the commercial equality of other nations within their respective spheres of influence, but none of them was willing to sign a binding treaty to that effect. Undaunted, Secretary Hay announced to an uncomprehending American public that the Open Door policy was in effect. In reality, it had little weight, but in the American populace's mentality it became a cornerstore of East Asian policy and an emotional shibboleth. Similar to the Kellogg-Briand Non-Aggression Pact of 1928 (which turned out to be a "worthless piece of paper") the Great Powers talked of abiding by an Open Door policy for China but violated their words in practice. In the meantime, however, the myth developed in the American mind that the United States was China's protector against a predatory Japan and the evil nations of the Old World.

After 1900 the Japanese increasingly argued that China's disintegration, weakness, and geographic propinquity entitled Japan to special interests in China. By virtue of the Root-Takahira agreement of 1908 and the Lansing-Ishii agreement of 1917, the United States seemed to be recognizing special Japanese rights based on territorial contiguity, actions that violated the spirit of its own Open Door policy and misled Japan. To make matters worse, Japanese elementary school children began to read, in the 1910 and 1918–1922 editions of their textbooks, about Japan's responsibility to preserve peace in East Asia. Japanese teachers called attention to Japan's economic interests in China, especially Manchuria. The post-Manchurian textbooks did not shrink from proclaiming what amounted to a Japanese Monroe Doctrine for East Asia. Japanese students easily inferred that the U.S. presence in China served as an obstacle to Japan. The seeds of the *Greater East Asia Co-Prosperity Sphere* were being planted before the 1930s and 1940s. Myths confused the Japanese public's perception of reality in the same way that the Open Door policy served American citizens.

During World War I, and in the immediate years thereafter, Japanese-American relations were strained further. President Woodrow Wilson believed that Japan's entry into World War I, and its Siberian intervention during Russia's civil war, were opportunistic and greedy, as they were. By the first action, at little cost, Japan joined the Allied powers, thus taking advantage of the West's preoccupation with war in Europe to seize German possessions in the Pacific and Shantung province on the mainland of China. Japan's excessive twenty-one demands on China of 1915 threatened the complete loss of Chinese sovereignty and demonstrated the level of Japanese ambition. Had China accepted all the demands, it would have become virtually a Japanese protectorate. Japanese troops did not withdraw from Shantung until 1922, despite President Wilson's demand for China's self-determination. Japan regarded its prize as the spoils of war, especially when no Western nation, including the United States, indicated that it would withdraw from China or abrogate the unequal treaties. Wilson assisted in the growth of Chinese nationalism and indirectly assisted in exacerbating relations between Japan and China. In the United States opinion was aroused against Japan—thus serving fears of a yellow peril. Likewise, to Wilson, the landing of large numbers of Japanese troops in Siberia, in cooperation with the American objective of rescuing Czechoslovakian troops, seemed like a case of overkill. The obvious objective of some Japanese expansionists to add Eastern Siberia to the Japanese empire through this intervention led to heated debate within the Japanese government and deep anxiety in Washington, D.C. Not until Japan withdrew its troops from Siberia in 1922 and from Northern Sakhalin in 1925 did the American fears subside. To many Americans, however, the Japanese had seemed a little too clever. Suspicions grew, and misperceptions and distortions on both sides abounded.

To some Japanese the American attitude seemed hypocritical and unrealistic. By her entry into World War I, Japan had aided in the defeat of Germany by the Allied powers. Was it not part of the game that Japan had learned from the West that she should be rewarded? Why, the Japanese asked, were not the Open Door policy and Wilson's self-determination of nations applied to Africa and to South and Southeast Asia? Why should they be applied only in China at the expense of Japan? As far as Japanese militarists and ultranationalists were concerned, developments in nearby Eastern Siberia were vital to Japan. A Japanese holding there was seen as a buffer for Japan vis-a-vis the Soviet Union and a safeguard against the spread of infectious Communism. The Americans seemed to them patently racist and hypocritical by preaching self-determination and an Open Door policy and at the same time refusing to pressure Great Britain and France to withdraw from their Afro-Asian colonies and from European Russia. Why also should the United States be concerned over Russian territory, since the Bolshevik government had withdrawn from the war? The Japanese fiercely resented the flagrant discrimination against Japanese settlers in California and other Western states. Insult was added to injury when Wilson would not agree to a statement of racial equality in the Covenant of the League. Japanese pride was further wounded by the Immigration Act of 1924, which prohibited further Japanese immigration.

After World War I, the era of crude territorial imperialism was over. The League of Nations, multilateral diplomacy, and the Versailles Treaty system sought to perpetuate the status quo. The rules of the game had changed. To Japanese ultranationalists and militarists it seemed as if the "have" nations of Great Britain, France, and the United States sought, through international agreements such as the Washington Naval Limitations Conference of 1921–1922, to preserve their gains while preventing Japan from expanding its empire to achieve greater autonomy. These Western nations seemed to have become suspiciously sanctimonious, conservative, and self-righteously devoted to international law. In this context, the "hot-headed" superpatriots began to win new converts with their arguments that Japan, a "have-not" nation, was denied its legitimate interest in nearby Asia and its need to find a way to extricate herself from economic recession. Japan became restless and politically fragile. Sympathy for other "have-not" nations, e.g., Italy and especially Germany, increased. During the 1920s, however, cooler heads prevailed with the argument that the Treaty of Versailles and the Washington Conference treaty system better served Japanese interests.

As a result of the Japanese decision to cooperate with the Anglo-American powers, relations between Japan and the United States were basically good during the 1920s. To a considerable extent the cordial relationship resulted from the American withdrawal into a policy of isolationism and the Japanese decision to join the League and to cooperate with the post-Versailles system of the victorious allies. During the period 1920–1931, Japan accepted the Wilsonian rules and Anglo-American domination. On the surface the Japanese also acquiesced to a reduction of armaments, the denial of force as an instrument of foreign policy, and the avoidance of interference in the domestic affairs of neighboring countries.

Actually, no country had a better record of sacrificing narrow national interests in those years than Japan. Part of the motivation came from a growth in Japan of peaceful internationalism, pacifism, and liberalism. These trends to some extent stemmed from the ascent of civilian-controlled political parties (which ever so briefly subdued the military) and Japan's faltering economy. Realistic Japanese perceptions of the nation as a secondary power lacking in essential self-sufficiency also motivated them to seek amity and international good will. Accordingly, Japan withdrew from Siberia, Northern Sakhalin, and the Shantung province. She participated responsibly but unspectacularly in the League of Nations and pledged herself to comply with the Kellogg-Briand Non-Aggression Pact (1928). Because of her own interpretation of the Open Door policy—as seen in the Lansing-Ishii agreement of 1917—Japan's anxiety regarding China was allayed until the assumption of power by Chiang Kai-shek's nationalist government in 1928. Before then Japan had abandoned aggressive gunboat diplomacy in China for the more subtle economic imperialism that she learned from the West and now practiced so assiduously in Korea and Taiwan. Japan had yielded also to U.S. and British pressure at the Washington Naval Conference of 1921–1922. Japan rescinded the profitable Anglo-Japanese alliance and accepted naval inequality with Great Britain and the United States. She did so again at the London Conference of 1930. In neither case, however, did this forced acceptance of naval inequality prove popular, a point exploited by those who promoted Japanese interests at any price. Nor did the Japanese government explain clearly to the populace why these treaties were in Japan's interests. This failure was particularly the case in 1921–1922 when Japan could not afford a naval shipbuilding race.

We know now that American and British diplomats could have been more sensitive to Japan's exaggerated fears and her search for equality, autonomy, and economic self-sufficiency. The failure to do so created strong adverse repercussions within the Japanese polity. As Akira Iriye indicates in his essay, however, Japan's desires were ignored by American makers of foreign policy in the same period. This American indifference inadvertently played into the hands of Japanese militarists and ultranationalists. American foreign and domestic policy unintentionally weakened those political elements in Japan that favored accommodation with the United States, cooperative membership in the League of Nations, and the peaceful resolution of international tensions.

What were some specific events between 1918 and 1931 that helped to create significant shifts in Japanese public opinion? In particular, the Anglo-American side did not fully appreciate the Japanese fear of communism, the humiliating naval restrictions imposed on Japan, the Japanese role in China, or the damage perpetrated by Western tariffs. The Japanese had always been suspicious of Russia. A communist Russia in nearby Eastern Siberia created a Japanese version of the later anticommunism of the McCarthy era in the United States. Feelings of anxiety, irrationality, and hostility among Japanese were exacerbated later in the 1930s as the Soviet Union accelerated the development and military buildup of the area. The Japanese army projected its rearmament plans on the basis of the Soviet Union as its number one enemy. By 1930 most Japanese came to look upon Manchuria as essential to the national security and economic self-sufficiency of Japan—an attitude that the Japanese army skillfully exploited in 1931–1932. The Japanese, however, failed to appreciate two things. First, Manchuria was, after all, Chinese soil that Chiang Kai-shek's nationalist government wanted to make a part of China devoid of extensive Japanese interests. In addition, the seizure of Manchuria could not be disguised; it was naked aggression that deserved the West's denunciation.

The rise of Chinese communism, especially after the mid-1930s, created the fear that unless Japan performed preemptory surgery there another neighbor would become communist. (Ironically, perhaps no factor was more important than the accelerated penetration of China by Japan for causing that country to accept the Chinese Communist party and communism.) Simultaneously, the rise of an increasingly militant Chinese nationalism during the 1920s and 1930s agitated for an immediate end to all foreign investments and concessions. That movement put Japan and China on a collision course. On all of these issues Japan expected sympathy and understanding. The American and British governments saw correctly, however, that much of the Japanese argument was mere casuistry to cloak Japanese territorial ambitions. Japanese sincerity seemed most insincere.

From the Japanese perspective the American attitude toward China was frustrating because of America's vacillating interpretation of the Open Door policy. More to the point, the Japanese resented it and the Americans' assumption that they could proclaim it in Japan's backyard. Although imperialism in China by the West and Japan had continued in the twentieth century, the United States had done nothing. Although the Root-Takahira (1908) and Lansing-Ishii (1917) agreements gave tacit U.S. recognition to the preeminent rights of Japan in China based on contiguity, the Americans insisted on a less generous interpretation of the meaning of the Open Door policy by the terms of the Nine-Power Treaty of 1921.

All of these Japanese irritations merged in 1930 and 1931 as a result of the London Naval Conference of 1930 and the deepening world depression. The Japanese government of Prime Minister Hamaguchi Osachi had pledged publicly to the Japanese navy that it would achieve a 10:7 ratio in capital warships in London. But the Americans and British forced them to accept a 10:6 ratio at a time when some U.S. naval strategists agreed that a 10:7 ratio was needed by Japan to defend its Western Pacific sphere. (To be sure, most American admirals agreed with the 10:6 arrangement.) Protests broke out immediately throughout Japan. Spokesmen for the Army and Navy accused the Hamaguchi cabinet of betraying Japan's "total national defense" requirements and of violating the "independence of command" guaranteed the military by the Japanese constitution. This situation, coupled with Hamaguchi's advocacy of Japan's acceptance of the gold standard, led to protests throughout Japan and the shooting of the prime minister by a right-wing patriot. The United States and Great Britain had won only a pyrrhic victory. Civilian governments in Japan never really recovered from the negative results of the London Conference. Those naval leaders willing to support the London agreement found themselves isolated from the more numerous hot-headed ones.

Although a severe economic depression did not hit the West until 1929, Japan had suffered from an economic recession throughout the decade. Her struggling economy was placed in a deeper economic crisis by reduced exports caused by Western economic nationalism. The Japanese people suffered deeply as production plummeted and Japanese farmers experienced a two-fifths drop in their income, largely the result of a disastrous curtailment of the silk market.

Against the advice of one thousand economists, President Herbert Hoover approved the Hawley-Smoot Tariff of 1930, the highest tariff in American history. Similar to European tariffs this clearly discriminated against Japan, a nation seriously lacking in strategic resources. These tariffs prevented Japan from selling products that would enable her to buy those scarce resources. International trade was a two-way street. If Japan could not sell, neither could she buy. Now the cry was raised by ultranationalists in Japan that, if Japan could not sell, she had to either abandon her drive to become a rich, powerful industrial nation or seize those resources on the continent. This compelling argument won many new converts; it increasingly neutralized the internationalists and peace advocates. Their opposition to the Kwantung army's seizure of Manchuria was feeble and ineffective.

The lesson that some Japanese thought they had learned from Germany's experience in World War I was that Japan must achieve autarky to merit real power status. Japan might be a member of the Big Five in the League of Nations, but to a sensitive and proud Japanese people the record seemed clear. They were taken for granted and regarded as inferior; their complaints against the status quo were not being heard. They believed there would be no change in that attitude by the West. Little by little the Japanese developed a sense of being surrounded by enemies. Paranoia increased. Increasingly the ultranationalists gained the upper hand in the government.

What the Japanese establishment failed to appreciate was that expansion on the mainland was not a long-range solution to Japan's plight, an assertion borne out by Japan's economic success after the mid-1950s. More patience and diplomacy were required. After all, the West was in the midst of the worst depression it had ever experienced. Japan's solution lay in diplomacy, not arms.

Nevertheless, these real economic conditions, fanned by the fear of the Soviet Union, led the middle-level officers of the Japanese Kwantung army, with the cooperation of the general staff and some officials in the War Ministry, to operate without authorization from the civilian government. It blew up a portion of the South Manchurian Railway at Mukden on September 18, 1931, as a pretext for seizing Manchuria, an action that proved popular in Japan. From Japan's perspective its soldiers had shed blood in the area in 1894–1895 and 1904–1905; the Japanese also believed that China's repeated inability to develop and control the area entitled Japan to take this action in what had become a dangerous power vacuum. When the League of Nations' Lytton Report and the Hoover-Stimson Doctrine of Non-Recognition criticized Japanese aggression, military thought became divided roughly between the Imperial Way and Control factions. The former became righteous, arrogant, and defensively aggressive; the latter element was no less committed to long-range internal and external objectives but was more moderate in regard to short-range timing and means. Both factions complained that Japan was denied the freedom to act to ensure her own survival. The Japanese withdrawal from the League of Nations to protest this alleged persecution also proved to be popular, a lesson not forgotten by the Japanese military and ultranationalists.

All of these grievances contributed to a dangerous shift in Japanese politics. From a position in which the military had been subordinate to the civilian elements favoring multilateral diplomacy and peaceful accommodation, the expansionists now attained equal power by allying with the entrenched bureaucracy and the right-wing nationalists. An indecisive Japanese public created an uneasy balance. This condition permitted an ominous drift in Japanese politics during the remainder of the 1930s.

For all intents and purposes Japan became a nation at war after 1931. The voice of reason became the voice of treason. Civilian opponents of Japan's new aggressive foreign policy were assassinated with increasing frequency. The actions of nationalistic Chinese to boycott Japanese goods and to eliminate Japanese concessions and investments led to increased tension between the two countries and the killing of one another's nationals. Japanese businessmen and ultranationalists repeated the same demands on their government: defend national honor; restore order in China; prevent the rise of Chinese communism; teach the ungrateful Chinese a lesson. Each Japanese attempt to do so fed Chinese nationalism, escalated Japan's corresponding military involvement, and consequently gave rise to anti-Japanese feeling in the United States. The failure of many in Japan to understand the relationship between cause—repeated brutality toward the Chinese and expansion in China—and effect—Anglo-American anxiety and opposition seems incomprehensible today. But war blinds the combatant to reason, as Americans discovered later during the Vietnam War.

Japanese-American relations deteriorated in the 1930s. Japan's bombing of the Mukden railway and its subsequent withdrawal from the League of Nations confirmed the Western belief that the Japanese were aggressive and insincere. Americans came to believe that the Japanese government seemed unalterably resolved to extend its empire regardless of the costs. Although the Japanese government initially had announced that it had no designs on all of Manchuria, by 1932 it had become a puppet state. Although Japanese diplomats would assure the Anglo-Americans that Japan had fulfilled her needs, the Japanese army would give the lie to those statements time after time in Manchuria and North China. Japan's successful annexation of Manchuria through armed aggression was a direct challenge to the rule of international law, the peace system, and the multilateral diplomacy established by the Anglo-American-dominated world in the post-Versailles era. The official American response was Secretary of State Stimson's weak Non-Recognition Doctrine of 1932. At a time when the Americans and Europeans should have acted decisively against the Japanese aggression with stiff economic sanctions and perhaps a show of force, the United States weakly protested that aggression would not be recognized. The failure of the Americans to do anything concrete in 1932 beyond sending the fleet to Shanghai, as a result of bitter fighting that broke out between the Japanese and Chinese in that city, led Japanese of samurai spirit to scorn and ridicule the "righteous" Americans who had no stomach for battle. The Japanese conquest of North China between 1935 and 1937 led only to more pious, moral Anglo-American criticism with no hint of naval action or economic sanctions. The overwhelming popularity of the Kwantung army's rapid conquest, first of Manchuria and then of North China, emboldened the militarists and ultranationalists. Japan in the 1930s seemed bent on gaining as much as she could. Her success contributed to the strength of the militarists' arguments. This climate ushered in a propensity to risk even more.

Despite the existence of isolationism and a seeming passivity regarding Japanese military actions, there was growing American indignation toward Japan. The Japanese government's signing of the Anti-Comintern Pact with Nazi Germany and Fascist Italy in 1936 seemed a clear signal to American policymakers that the militarists were in full control and that Japan was committed to an aggressive foreign policy. Accompanying these sentiments was one of strong sympathy for a hapless China. Japan's pursuit of all-out war in north, central, and south China from 1937 on, tried the patience of the U.S. State Department to the breaking point. The conviction grew among the American public that Japan's intransigent militarists would recognize American opposition only by economic sanctions, and, if need be, by force. The first step came on July 26, 1939, when the U.S. government notified Japan that in six months it was abrogating the commercial treaty of 1911.

The contest of wills had begun. Misperceptions, misunderstandings, and miscalculations increased in an emotionally charged atmosphere. Japan was determined "to achieve autonomy" and to solve the China question in her own way. The United States was just as determined to contain Japan, to uphold its historic Open Door policy in China, and to check the Japanese by economic actions in concert with its allies. War was imminent.

China became Japan's historical parallel to America's Vietnam.[5] Unwittingly the army and navy found themselves tied down in China despite the fact that their primary potential enemies were the Soviet Union and the United States, respectively. The more Japan struggled, however, the more she became mired in the vast expanses of Chinese quicksand. By 1940 Japan needed desperately to end the war in China, but Chiang Kai-shek, trading space for time, retreated one thousand miles into the interior. He sought—successfully—to tie the United States even more tightly to his sagging government. Although American assistance to China was severely limited and never became more than minimal, its psychological significance to the nationalist government was enormous. The Japanese government could not see that the way to end the war was to achieve a negotiated settlement with Chiang Kai-shek. Instead they reasoned that if the Americans would discontinue aid to the nationalist government the latter would be forced to negotiate a settlement. That may have been true, but the Japanese government was really counting on a situation in which the discontinuation of American support would force Chiang Kai-shek into a negotiated settlement that would recognize some type of Japanese territorial gains in China. All three parties understood the Japanese rationale clearly; the United States refused to cooperate with the Japanese plan. Each month that the Sino-Japanese War continued the Japanese military became more desperate. In the meantime, the Americans interpreted the Japanese signing of the Tripartite Pact of 1940 with Germany and Italy as directed toward the United States. The three nations appeared to have reached a decision to carve up the world among them. Japan's occupation of all of French Indochina seemed to confirm that suspicion.

The Japanese quest for economic self-sufficiency and empire was met by increased economic sanctions by the United States. The Japanese leadership developed a siege mentality that led to the argument that the only solution to the American, British, and Dutch oil blockade was war. They saw no other options. When Nazi Germany attacked their traditional foe, the Soviet Union, and seemed the inevitable victor in the late fall of 1941, Japan took the opportunity to eliminate U.S. interference in the Pacific.

But was the Pacific War inevitable? Was there no way out of these escalating antagonisms in the diplomacy of the last two or three years before the outbreak of the war? Did some Japanese leaders sincerely seek to avoid war? Did the United States and its Allies miss opportunities to heal the breach and assume incorrectly that the militarists were in such control that there was no way out of the impasse? Was there no way for the Americans to help the advocates of peace within the Japanese government? Had America become a prisoner of its Chinese ally's objectives? In short, despite the Japanese expansion into China, and later into French Indochina, could Japanese and American diplomats have extricated themselves from the impending tragedy? Could Americans have delayed the war six months and thereby have perhaps prevented it altogether? The following essays deal with these questions.

NOTES

A grateful acknowledgment for suggestions on style and content is extended to my former colleague at Illinois State University, Dr. Edward L. Schapsmeier, Distinguished Professor of American History.

1. Akira Iriye, "Imperialism in East Asia," in *Modern East Asia: Essays in Interpretation,* ed. James B. Crowley (New York: Harcourt, Brace & World, 1970), p. 138.

2. Marius B. Jansen, *Japan and China: from War to Peace 1894-1972* (Chicago: Rand McNally College Publishing Company, 1975), p. 74.

3. Ibid.

4. Hilary Conroy, "Meiji Imperialism: Mostly Ad Hoc," in *Japan Examined: Perspectives on Modern Japanese History,* ed. Harry Wray and Hilary Conroy (Honolulu: University of Hawaii Press, 1983), p. 140; Iriye, p. 137.

5. See Hilary Conroy, "Japan's War in China: Historical Parallel to Vietnam?" *Pacific Affairs* 43, no. 1 (Spring 1970): pp. 61-72; and David Lu, ed., *Perspectives on Japan's External Relations* (Lewisburg, Pa.: Bucknell University, 1982), pp. 15-25.

2. U.S. Policy toward Japan before World War II

AKIRA IRIYE

THERE are many ways to evaluate foreign policy. Since there can be no "foreign" policy without the existence of a society to which other societies are "foreign" or external, one must first examine if a particular policy satisfies the needs of that society. These needs range from social integration and political stability to economic development and cultural fulfillment. Does a country's foreign policy at a given moment respond to these needs? Does it promote or retard social change so as to maximize chances for the attainment of the society's goals? Society consists of groups, classes, and other units whose interests and aspirations are often in conflict. Whose aspirations does a particular policy represent, and whose interests does it advance? How do various groups make known their wishes to policymakers, and what are the mechanisms through which the latter can be penalized for acting against the desires of certain segments of the population?

These questions concern factors within a country. The same types of questions must be raised, however, with regard to all countries that are involved in diplomatic relations. Obviously, though, what is satisfactory from the perspective of one country is not necessarily acceptable to another. A policy that responds to and fulfills the needs of American farmers, for instance, might be an achievement for the U.S. government vis-a-vis its domestic constituents, but it could be a wrong choice from the standpoint of those in other countries. If it provoked fierce opposition in another government, it would have to be considered a good policy domestically but a disaster in terms of the relationship between the two countries. Efforts to reconcile the conflicting policies would then be made, but such efforts might alienate domestic groups, thereby bringing about undesirable internal developments and undermining political stability. If the risk became too great, the leaders would have to decide whether to further exacerbate relations with another country or to stabilize domestic conditions. Quite often policymakers operate in an area where marginal differences in their perceptions of possible changes domestically and externally affect decisions. Should they give priority to the maintenance of stable relations with another country or to satisfying the needs of the domestic social system? They do not always consciously ask such a question, but it should at least serve as a heuristic framework for evaluating specific foreign policy decisions.

This much background seems essential if we are to pose meaningful questions about American policy toward Japan before Pearl Harbor. Too often writers have been content with a superficial analysis, asking whether the United States was too moralistic and idealistic in its dealings with Japan, or what it might have done to prevent the Pearl Harbor catastrophe. Such questions ignore that the policymakers in Washington were first and foremost concerned with America's domestic tranquility and well-being. For them Japanese action in Asia and the Pacific was of no serious concern unless it caused significant segments of the American population to question official policy and created potentially destabilizing forces within the polity. Like the Spanish civil war of Nazi *revanchism*, Japanese aggression in China did not affect the daily life and thinking of more than a small minority of Americans. It is true that church organizations, college students, and some intellectual leaders early bestirred themselves to condemn Japan and call for support of China. They could do so without jeopardizing their own positions of power in society. But their political influence was not such as to generate a large-scale movement to press the government to more vigorous action against Japan. They were mostly talking to one another and did not seriously disturb the existing social and political order in America. American society, in other words, could continue to function without modifying its external relations vis-a-vis Japan or China.

This does not mean, of course, that American society could not have maintained equilibrium even if the government had undertaken new approaches in its Asian policy. The fact that Asia was not a major preoccupation of most Americans could have enabled the policymakers to experiment with some initiatives without fear of determined opposition at home. The second Roosevelt administration (1937–1941) did begin to act more boldly and assertively in Asia than in Europe because it assumed that the public would remain largely indifferent or passive. The abrogation of the treaty of commerce with Japan that was announced in July 1939, for instance, made relatively little impression on American public opinion. Little fear was expressed that such a step would lead to war with Japan. If there had been a serious large-scale movement in the United States against involvement in Asia, the government would have hesitated before undertaking such a bold step, or it might have taken drastic measures in a more secretive way so as not to shock the public. This was exactly what was done with Europe. The Roosevelt administration sent secret emissaries to London to exchange strategic information and made clandestine arrangements with France to supply the latter with aircraft. These arrangements were kept from the public for fear that their revelation would fuel the already formidable isolationist sentiment. Given a divided public opinion on the European question, the government had to tread cautiously lest its control over foreign policy become challenged and political order itself destabilized. In comparison, the U.S. internal social order did not appear to be seriously undermined by bolder decisions taken against Japan.

Here was a situation, then, where a relative lack of concern on the part of the American people provided the government with a certain degree of freedom of action; it could either do little or take bold initiatives without seriously disturbing the social order. To that extent it may be said that American policy was a success; it managed to prevent the fragmentation of public opinion and succeeded in maintaining domestic stability, a prerequisite if the nation was to be prepared for a major confrontation with another power.[1]

These factors were little related to considerations of Japanese-American relations as such. It is highly suggestive that the decision to abrogate the treaty of commerce was made without consulting Ambassador Joseph C. Grew, the one official who was keenly aware of Japanese politics, who was at that time in the United States. U.S. policymakers were generally not concerned with domestic conditions in Japan. The Japanese government, on its part, had to cope with the new situation as best it could. It too had to worry about the maintenance of national unity, although in Japan the control of the military was more essential than that of public opinion. Even so, compared with the situation in the United States, a larger segment of the Japanese population was concerned with trans-Pacific relations, and various groups and individuals could be expected to have strong views on the matter. For the Japanese polity to continue to function, therefore, national decisions must minimize disruptive influences generated at various social levels.[2] In 1939 this meant a prudent policy of equilibrium in Japanese-American relations because the momentum of the

Sino-Japanese War had been lost, and there was no widespread enthusiasm for another war against either the Soviet Union or the United States. To bring the Chinese war to an end without disturbing the balance of forces in Japan was the cardinal goal of Tokyo's leaders. Their failure to do so was creating a sense of malaise and unease, giving the impression of aimlessness and lack of leadership. It was to put an end to such drift that the cabinet of Hiranuma Kiichirō tried to negotiate a German alliance. The abrogation of the American commercial treaty could thus have served to give segments of Japanese society a renewed sense of purpose. This might have been accomplished if the Hiranuma government had been able to persuade the army, the navy, the political parties, the business community, the press, and other groups that the nation was at a crossroads and that it either would have to dedicate itself to the establishment of a new Asian order no longer controlled by the whims of American action, or reorient its foreign policy to minimize conflict with the United States. The latter alternative would have entailed a reaffirmation of the interdependence between the two countries.

This choice would have compelled various groups and individuals in Japan to think afresh about their nation's destiny and relationship with the outside world. It might have been extremely difficult to arrive at a generally accepted consensus; the country might have become hopelessly splintered into pro- and anti-Anglo-American forces. The result could have been either a further stalemate of Japanese politics or the emergence of a strong government with "national" plans. In this sense the bold action of July 1939 by Washington could have contributed to a new political arrangement in Japan. But these developments alone could not have ensured a better relationship between the two countries. Only if those in power in Japan had persuaded themselves that a pro-American orientation would not undermine their roles and positions could the Japanese have reacted to American action with an affirmative response. They might, on the contrary, have decided that either inaction or hostility toward the United States would be better calculated to guarantee social equilibrium. Nevertheless, the signing of the Nazi-Soviet non-aggression pact in August prevented the execution of these realignments in Japan solely on the basis of alternative approaches to the United States.

Such extraneous coincidences should not obscure the fact that in the summer of 1939 there were any number of possibilities in Japanese-American relations and that Japan's response depended more on the nature of internal social relations than on changes induced from the outside. At that time Japanese society was not organized on any principle of anti-Americanism. There was, to be sure, shrill rhetoric of pan-Asianism that stressed Japan's ties to Asia and the need to rid the nation of pernicious Anglo-American influences. Paradoxically, the intensity of such propaganda revealed the tenacity of Western influence and orientation in Japanese life. Under the circumstances, to deny the people the products of modern Western civilization—be they food, clothing, movies, or political thoughts—would have required an act of supreme national sacrifice, which in turn could have been demanded only in circumstances of war or near war. The vision of a new order in Asia held no alluring prospects except for those who had no stake in life at home. Just as the war in China had opened up new opportunities to those who had not found comfortable niches in society, the prospect of exploiting the rich resources of Southeast Asia attracted persons without strong ties to the status quo. By the same token, the ruling classes could not easily countenance a genuine movement for "going south" without considering its consequences for the domestic social order. Their reluctance to undertake southern expansion was nowhere more clearly revealed than in their failure to map out a strategy for occupying and administering Indochina, Malaya, the Dutch East Indies, and other areas.[3] Pan-Asianism was a harmless slogan to mouth, especially if it enhanced one's prestige and guaranteed one's job. It was quite another matter, however, to plan for a new order in Asia in earnest. Actually, many of those active in the movement for national transformation "from above" were primarily preoccupied with domestic reconstruction and had no time for an extensive design for the rest of Asia. Even the "new order" embracing China, Manchukuo, and Japan had gotten nowhere, and the Japanese leaders quarreled among themselves about the degree to which policy in China should be integrated into overall national planning.

Under the circumstances, it was far from certain that the Japanese would opt for a policy aimed against the United States. Like the American leaders, Japan's policymakers were concerned with domestic stability and national unity. There was little reason to think that these goals could be attained through an antagonistic stance against America. On the other hand, a policy of "understanding" with Washington could be plausible as long as it did not upset existing social arrangements. Japanese society during the 1930s had produced new political alignments and organizations after the turmoil of the world economic crisis. Predominant social relations were now defined in terms of general mobilization for the prosecution of the war in China, but they were also a response to the need to act upon the society's own transformation because of the changes in international trade and politics. These changes, especially after 1929, had forced rearrangements in Japanese society, but these had not been consolidated. Thus there persisted a sense of uncertainty about Japanese politics and a feeling of aimlessness about national goals. Old groups had not completely disappeared, and the new ruling elite was not yet completely entrenched.

It is in such a context that one may plausibly talk of the impact of American policy upon Japan and discuss the shortsightedness of Washington's decisions. These policies and decisions primarily affected domestic American forces. To the extent that they influenced Japanese behavior, they must be analyzed in the context of Japan's political and social history. Thus, it is meaningless to talk of American policy as being "realistic" or "unrealistic" without considering developments within both societies.

After 1939 significant changes took place in both the United States and Japan. The outbreak of war in Europe exacerbated the tension between the interventionists and anti-interventionists in America, not purely in ideological terms but essentially in terms of their respective positions in society. Most Americans wanted to preserve their way of life, but they were not sure whether the best way to do so would be by coming to the aid of Great Britain, as the interventionists advocated, or by avoiding involvement in Europe's fratricide, as the isolationists urged. The isolationists were unhappy about the growth of presidential power and about aspects of the New Deal policies. They felt that the country could not afford costly engagements overseas. The interventionists, on the other hand, associated national security and well-being with the survival of Great Britain and its allies. They believed that the German control of Europe would inevitably bring about an American-German confrontation in the western hemisphere, which could threaten the survival of American society. For this reason, they believed, the United States should be prepared to play a more active role in the balance of power in Europe. Also, the American-British entente could end the regionalist tendencies that had divided the world into closed economic blocs and spheres of influence. By actively cooperating with Great Britain against Germany, the United States not only would be ensuring its own security but also would be contributing to the reopening of global economic opportunities. This would be in the interest of those in America who were oriented toward foreign trade and investment, groups whose commitment to the political system was considered increasingly important to the Roosevelt administration.

The debate between the interventionists and their opponents was intense because opportunities for intervention in Europe were now greater and because both recognized the domestic implications of intervention. The administration tried to step up American aid to Britain without undermining domestic equilibrium. President Roosevelt was reluctant to push the nation further for fear of alienating significant segments of the population, in particular those who did not identify with the British cause and those whose priorities and commitments were not affected by the outcome of the struggle in Europe.

In such a situation, aid to China against Japan took on new significance. It was calculated to appeal both to the interventionists and the isolationists. The former needed no persuading, although some insisted on meeting the European crisis first rather than becoming involved in both Asia and Europe. However, even they were able to see the growing link between the two wars after the signing of the German-Japanese alliance in September 1940. The isolationists, on the other hand, might not object to a program designed to curb Japanese power and expansion in Asia and the Pacific; their main concern was Europe, and their self-perception allowed them little room to connect events in Asia with their own roles and stakes in society. Thus, the administration's offer of loans to China and the embargoing of export items to Japan met with little resistance. They were not seen as decisions by the ruling classes to continue to control power and opportunities in America.

These trends in American policy perpetuated the uncertainty in Japan. The Tokyo government had signed a treaty of alliance with Germany in 1940 in the hope that it would unify national opinion and clarify the course of the country's future. The Axis pact never succeeded in committing Japan irrevocably to "southern expansionism" or to an anti-American stand.[4] There were not strong enough constituencies in Japan for such action because business, academic, and political leaders with a pro-Anglo-American orientation were never silenced. They even affected military thinking so that early in 1941 the army became strongly interested in the idea of a compromise with the United States. Throughout the rest of the year a delicate balance persisted among these different groups. In the end, of course, the army and the navy, as well as those with a stake in a "national defense state," concluded that their power and status depended on ending the atmosphere of uncertainty and bringing about a sense of national purpose. This could be achieved only through war. Pan-Asian ideology served as a convenient unifier of Japanese thought and behavior *after* the attack on Pearl Harbor. Pro-American forces—some diplomats and military leaders, the court circles, economic and intellectual groups with ties to the West—had a colossal task during the summer and fall of 1941 to present the country with a completely different definition of national unity. They failed not so much because the idea was any less realistic than the pan-Asian conception but because they feared social chaos and even a revolution if they tried to impose their will upon Japanese society. They would go along with the anti-Americans and the pan-Asians to preserve societal unity, but a few years later they would maneuver to reorient Japanese policy among pro-American lines, again in the name of the preservation of national policy.

These observations raise intriguing questions about the impact of American decisions on Japan. It may be noted that U.S. policy was a success to the extent that it checked Japan's irrevocably pro-German stance. But the United States could perhaps have gone further and tried to do something to strengthen the pro-American forces in Japan. Such action would be taken toward the end of the war to encourage the emergence of "friendly Japanese" to put an end to the hostilities. But before 1941 a bold initiative to influence Japan's internal politics could have been implemented only if it had been reinforced by ideas and interests within the United States to which it could appeal. Ironically, it was only after the outbreak of the Japanese-American war that the relations between the two countries became sufficiently diverse so that they came to hinge on the interdependence among various groups across the Pacific.

NOTES

1. [The preceding paragraph is of great significance in terms of the questions of whether American foreign policy was too impetuous in the last year before the war broke out and whether the war could have been avoided. If we extrapolate from what Iriye has written, he seems to believe that the United States could have delayed the outbreak of the war by stalling and granting concessions. If such were the case, Professor Ikei's argument that the war could have been avoided by delaying its outbreak becomes more credible. The Japanese would have been more willing to make concessions after January 1942 because the Soviet Union had forced a German retreat from Moscow and Leningrad. See p. 50.—EDS.]

2. [It seems fair to say here that Iriye agrees with the view of other scholars in this volume who argue that a soft-line American approach would have been more productive in terms of internal Japanese politics.—EDS.]

3. [For a similar view, see the Murakami essay, particularly pp. 142–145.—EDS.]

4. [The Iriye interpretation that the Tripartite Pact was directed toward domestic public opinion places him among the group of scholars in this volume who maintain that policymakers in Washington, D.C., overreacted against it. See the essays by Hosoya, Tsunoda, and Ikei. This view is strongly opposed by Barnhart, Utley, Hata, and Fujiwara.—EDS.]

3. Franklin Delano Roosevelt, the New Deal, and Japan

GARY DEAN BEST

TODAY, more than forty years after Pearl Harbor, most diplomatic historians with a special interest in United States-Japanese relations feel that the war between the two countries should and could have been avoided. Most agree that the cause of peace could have been better served by those responsible for U.S. foreign policy during the years immediately before Pearl Harbor; some are inclined, in fact, to place most of the blame for the breakdown of peaceful relations between the two countries on the United States. Yet surveys of American historians consistently find them ranking Franklin Delano Roosevelt as a great President, including him among the top two or three in our history. Roosevelt has apparently emerged unscathed in the eyes of historians from the tragic results of his administration's foreign policies, with his subordinates being blamed for his diplomatic mistakes. In the case of U.S. relations with Japan, the principal target of criticism has been Secretary of State Cordell Hull.

When Roosevelt constructed his cabinet during the months before his inauguration he shunned the men of experience, expertise, and demonstrated ability in his party, and selected mediocrities. As one observer put it charitably, Roosevelt's cabinet members were for the most part "men who look forward, instead of backward, to fame."[1] By some accounts profoundly jealous of men of equal or greater stature than himself, Roosevelt surrounded himself with cabinet members and advisers who, with rare exceptions, would have been unlikely candidates for their posts under any other President. A useful comparison is that between Roosevelt's cabinet and that of President Warren G. Harding. Although the two men were very similar in many other ways, Harding consciously set out to obtain the best cabinet possible, even at the risk of alienating members of his own party. There seemed an even better reason for Roosevelt to follow the same course in 1933, if only to inspire confidence in his administration in the midst of the depression. But Roosevelt did not do so.

In such a cabinet it was not remarkable to find Cordell Hull as Secretary of State. When chief braintruster Raymond Moley warned Roosevelt in January 1933 that Hull knew nothing about foreign affairs, Roosevelt responded that he would "be glad to have some fine idealism in the State Department."[2] Although "idealism" was apparently qualification enough for the position in Roosevelt's eyes, most historians today would regard that quality in Hull as perhaps his most serious disqualification for the office. In other ways, however, Hull was ill-fitted not only for the responsibilities to which Roosevelt appointed him but even for service in the cabinet.[3] Although during his congressional career he embraced many of the programs of the progressive wing in the Democratic Party, Hull did not mesh well with the social worker and agrarian varieties of liberalism that dominated Roosevelt's New Deal. The closest to a traditional Democrat of any in Roosevelt's cabinet, Hull was the object of ridicule among the young liberals with whom Roosevelt surrounded himself. However, as Roosevelt's few "sound" advisers grew disenchanted with the New Deal policies and left the administration, Hull emerged more and more as a political asset. His stubborn advocacy of freer international trade, especially through reciprocal trade agreements, won support from many wavering Democrats when Roosevelt ran for reelection in 1936. Hull endured humiliations from the President and his young advisers, especially in the early New Deal years, and grew increasingly disenchanted with Roosevelt's domestic policies beginning in 1937. Nevertheless, he remained in office, probably because he hoped to be Roosevelt's successor in 1941.

The ability of those around Roosevelt to remain in his favor depended on how quickly and easily they could adjust to his views. It took some longer than others to realize that Roosevelt rarely took advice; he favored only the "advice" that agreed with his own disposition. The task therefore for those around him was to sense the President's mood and to advise and act in accordance with it. Those who guessed wrong frequently found the limb sawed out from under them if they went too far. Cordell Hull first endured that experience at the World Economic Conference in the summer of 1933. Fortunately for Hull, the direction of Roosevelt's disposition where American relations with East Asia were concerned was never in doubt. Nearly two months before his inauguration, Roosevelt publicly indicated his agreement with the hostile policies of Hoover's Secretary of State Henry L. Stimson toward Japan—policies about which Hoover himself had strong misgivings. In fact, Roosevelt told Stimson that he wished the Stimson hard line toward Japan had been adopted earlier. He had, Roosevelt said, a hereditary interest in China, since one of his ancestors had been involved in the China trade. It was not the last time the story would be told; because of that ancestral connection with China Roosevelt fancied himself an authority on East Asia and sympathized with the Chinese.[4]

Roosevelt's leading braintrusters Raymond Moley and Rexford Tugwell were appalled by Roosevelt's commitment to the Stimson policy of hostility toward Japan. In his diary entry for January 17, 1933, Tugwell noted that he had just experienced "the first real difference of opinion with F.D.R.," and wrote:

> I sympathize with the Chinese, too. But I firmly believe it is a commitment which may lead us to war with Japan. I said so and registered a vigorous dissent from any such position. . . . He has a strong personal sympathy with the Chinese; and this added to a sudden trust in Stimson has carried him over. *He admitted the possibility of war and said it might be better to have it now than later.* This horrified me and I said so. . . . Moley was present but did not support me. (italics mine)[5]

According to Moley's account of the conversation in *The First New Deal,* he had found Roosevelt's reasoning "so incredible" that he "lacked words to express my disagreement."[6] In a later addendum to his diary, Tugwell wrote:

> That the Stimson non-recognition doctrine was not the way to approach the Japanese question I was convinced. I also thought it dangerous doctrine at any time. For what reason did the President-elect choose this particular issue to establish a collaboration with the outgoing administration which he had refused in every other instance? This is a puzzle to me still. Was Stimson another elder for whom Roosevelt felt the same kind of uncritical loyalty that he had for [Louis] Brandeis? There is an argument here which could, and doubtless will, go on and on. Two whole administrations later, when the consequences of the doctrine were being consummated in war, he chose Stimson to be his Secretary of War.

When the Secretary of State—one distinctly on the defensive within the administration and therefore even more inclined to prove his loyalty and usefulness to the President—sought to adjust himself to the disposition of his President, he found the direction in which that adjustment must proceed clear from the beginning of the Roosevelt administration; indeed, it antedated it. It required sympathy for China and hostility toward Japan, without ruling out the possibility or even the necessity of war between the United States and Japan. Indeed, it would seem that Hull learned his lesson too well, perhaps having even surpassed Roosevelt in his devotion to the cause by 1941.

Roosevelt's foreign policies, like his domestic policies, proceeded less from theories than from prejudices. Nevertheless, Roosevelt's attitude toward Japan and, later toward Germany, meant the substantive adoption of a geopolitical concept of the world different from that of his predecessor in the White House. The extent of the change would not become apparent until later in the 1930s when Roosevelt's policies became clearer and the critics, including Hoover, grew more vociferous, but its direction was already revealed by the end of 1933 in Roosevelt's expression of willingness to go to war with Japan over China and in his decision later in the year to extend U.S. diplomatic recognition to the Soviet Union. In breaking with the policy of nonrecognition of the USSR followed by one Democratic and three Republican presidents before him, Roosevelt was motivated, in part at least, by a belief that the action would restrain Japan in East Asia. The geopolitical concept with which such attitudes and actions meshed was one that viewed Japan (and later Germany and Italy) as the principal threat to the status quo and the Soviet Union as a potential ally in defense of it. Proponents of this concept believed, wrongly, that the destruction of Nazi Germany and imperialist Japan would bring a return to the peaceful world of the 1920s. The opposing geopolitical concept regarded the Soviet Union and international communism as the major threats to the status quo, with Germany and Japan the principal obstacles to Soviet and communist expansion. Advocates of this point of view were certain, rightly as it turned out, that the destruction of these two nations would result in further expansion by the Soviet Union, the triumph of communism in China and elsewhere, and the eventual shouldering by the United States of the costly burden of containing Soviet communism that had previously been borne by Germany and Japan. They did not sympathize with German or Japanese expansion, but they refused to regard it as a threat to the United States.[7] Where East Asia was concerned, their view was well summarized in a 1935 State Department memorandum by John V. A. MacMurray who opposed war with Japan, arguing that:

the elimination of Japan . . . would be no blessing to the Far East or to the world. It would merely create a new set of stresses, and substitute for Japan the U.S.S.R. as the successor to Imperial Russia—as a contestant (and at least an equally unscrupulous and dangerous one) for the mastery of the East. Nobody except perhaps Russia would gain from our victory in such a war.[8]

Reflecting on MacMurray's memorandum as the United States fought against communist armies in Korea, George Kennan, the astute scholar-diplomat, wrote in his book *American Diplomacy, 1900–1950:*

These words need no other commentary than the situation we have before us today in Korea. It is an ironic fact that today our past objectives in Asia are ostensibly in large measure achieved. . . . The Japanese are finally out of China proper and out of Manchuria and Korea as well. The effects of their expulsion from those areas have been precisely what wise and realistic people warned us all along they would be. Today we have fallen heir to the problems and responsibilities the Japanese had faced and borne in the Korean-Manchurian area for nearly half a century, and there is a certain perverse justice in the pain we are suffering from a burden which, when it was borne by others, we held in such low esteem.[9]

Another factor affecting relations between the United States and Japan was the worldwide depression that already gripped both countries when Roosevelt was inaugurated in March 1933. The geographic and resultant economic differences between the two countries appeared to present options for the United States in dealing with the depression that were denied Japan. Japan's shortage of food and paucity of raw materials gave her no option other than to seek an international solution to her economic distress—through the peaceful expansion of trade if possible, but via forceful expansion if necessary. The relative self-sufficiency of the United States, in contrast, suggested to many that this country could seek relief from the depression either through international economic cooperation or through policies that looked to a narrow economic nationalism. The former course would have complemented Japan's needs; the latter choice would clearly have worked against the peaceful expansion of Japan's trade since the United States was then, as now, one of Japan's major trading partners.

Although elected on a platform that promised the lowering of barriers to foreign trade, Roosevelt's New Deal quickly embarked on a domestic program committed to raising prices through the Agricultural Adjustment Act, the National Industrial Recovery Act, and monetary devices. That these actions were incompatible with lowered tariffs on imports appears only gradually to have occurred to the president and his advisers. Clearly, however, any effort to maintain high prices in the United States would benefit only the workers and farmers of other nations if their cheaper products were allowed to compete for the American market.

Before President Hoover left office he had arranged for American participation in a World Economic Conference to be held in London in the summer of 1933. As the date of the conference neared, the Roosevelt administration faced a difficult choice. Roosevelt could repudiate the nationalistic course upon which he had already embarked and seek instead to achieve recovery through international economic cooperation, or he could continue with the New Deal's nationalistic experiments and monetary policies and turn his back on the effort to promote international economic cooperation at the World Economic Conference.[10] Secretary of State Hull embarked for London believing that Roosevelt was committed to international economic cooperation. His illusions, along with the conference itself, were soon shattered by Roosevelt's refusal to commit the United States to even the tentative agreements worked out there. Hull returned to the United States humiliated. Critics of Roosevelt's "sabotage" of the World Economic Conference wondered if the failure of international economic cooperation would not lead eventually to war.

In 1934 Roosevelt sought and obtained from Congress authority to negotiate reciprocal trade agreements. Thereafter Hull busied himself with negotiating bilateral trade pacts. None was signed with Japan. International economic cooperation of the scope envisioned before the World Economic Conference was not taken up again before Pearl Harbor. Ironically, however, in the Atlantic Charter of August 1941, signed by Roosevelt and British Prime Minister Churchill less than four months before the United States entered the war, the United States and Great Britain pledged to "endeavor, with due respect for their existing obligations, to further the enjoyment by all States, great or small, victor or vanquished, of access, on equal terms, to the trade and to the raw materials of the world which are needed for their economic prosperity." It is tragic that such a policy was championed by Roosevelt only when a large part of the world was already at war but was shunned by his administration in 1933 and subsequently when it might have been useful in preserving peace.

In the first eight years of his administration Roosevelt was busy with another war—waged against business and banking in the United States. Ignoring, or oblivious to, the fact that economic recovery from the depression could come only through the revival of business, Roosevelt's New Deal pursued what columnist Walter Lippmann called a policy of "terroristic attacks" on business. The worldwide recovery from the depression, which began in the summer of 1932, was therefore retarded in the United States, although recovery continued in other countries, including Japan. Although Roosevelt was able to induce artificial prosperity through deficit spending—most notably in his reelection year of 1936—the stagnation of the durable goods industries and the continued high level of unemployment even in 1936 (16.9 percent) showed that the New Deal's hostile attitude toward business had not resulted in a genuine economic recovery. The renewed collapse of 1937 and 1938—which sent unemployment back to 19 percent in the latter years—vividly demonstrated that Keynesian "pump-priming" could not work (as Keynes himself pointed out to Roosevelt) if the pump itself was simultaneously being dismantled by destructive New Deal policies. Thereafter the economy showed only slight improvement, with the unemployment rate falling only to 17.2 percent in 1939 and to 14.6 percent in 1940, despite the stimulus to the economy furnished by the outbreak of the war in Europe during the former year. By 1938 almost every industrialized nation in the world was well ahead of the United States in recovering from the depression, some of them having surpassed their pre-depression economic levels.

The failure of Roosevelt's domestic policies had its tragic aspects both domestically and externally. For the millions of Americans who remained unemployed and on relief due to the failure of the New Deal the tragedy was obvious, but perhaps that in foreign affairs was even greater. As early as 1938, columnist Walter Lippmann and others began to call Roosevelt's attention to the need for American economic recovery so that the United States would be able to influence the deteriorating world situation. Lippmann advised the President to end his war on business, to reverse his policies that eroded the confidence of business, and to cooperate, finally, with business to promote economic recovery so that the United States could deal with other

countries from a position of strength. Such advice went ignored by
Roosevelt until American involvement in the war was imminent. As
with his conversion to international economic cooperation in the
Atlantic Charter, Roosevelt's conversion to a cooperative, pro-recov-
ery emphasis in his domestic policies toward business came only when
it was too late to exert an influence for peace. The result was that
instead of American economic strength serving perhaps to discourage
aggression, American economic weakness encouraged the contempt
of potential aggressors. As Shōichi Saeki's essay in *Mutual Images,*
edited by Akira Iriye, documents, the Japanese image of the United
States by the late 1930s had become that "of America as gigantic yet
feeble, a huge but fragile country beset by fatal weaknesses."[11]

On December 4, 1941, three days before the attack on Pearl Harbor, Rexford Tugwell recorded in his diary:

> As I look back at seeing the President the other day he seems to have been
> a man with his mind made up, at peace with the issue before him. I think
> now it is war. And my mind goes back to his telling me even in 1933 that
> 'we may as well fight now as later.'

The events of December 7, 1941, resulted in part from the attitudes
and policies that began to direct the United States in 1933. A new
President launched the United States on mistaken foreign and
domestic policies that ended in the prolonging of the depression and
in war, rather than in recovery and peace. Of the latter aspect,
Tugwell added a note to his diary in the midst of the Korean War:

> I have often speculated on the course events might have taken if the pol-
> icy had been a different one. Suppose, for instance, we had set out delib-
> erately to assist Japan in finding resources and markets; suppose we had
> tried to encourage her liberal forces and discourage the militarists; sup-
> pose we had encouraged the development of relations with China which
> would have given her a privileged position such as we have in Central and
> South America.
>
> Such an alternative was reasonable in 1933. Perhaps the military had
> too much power to have been turned aside from their aggressions at any
> time after that. But nothing could be more ridiculous than the reversal of
> policy toward Japan after her defeat. Having destroyed the only effective
> check to Russian imperialism in the East, we have not only lost our posi-
> tion in China, for which the Japanese affair was undertaken, but have

been forced to meet a now-combined Chino-Russian force with force of our own. The Japanese might have prevented all this if our statesmanship had been different.

This was a choice of no one but the President.

And the President was Franklin Delano Roosevelt.

NOTES

1. *Magazine of Wall Street,* 4 March 1933.

2. Raymond Moley, *After Seven Years* (New York; London: Harper & Brothers, 1939), p. 114.

3. [Best's criticism of Hull as an idealist are in agreement with those of most historians. Only Utley in this volume views Hull as a realist. However, Utley agrees that Hull failed as a diplomat because of his "all or nothing" attitude.—EDS.]

4. [See Ikei's essay for the opposite view that a Stimson hard-line approach against Japan after the Mukden Incident would have stopped Japan at an early expansionist stage. See pp. 50–51.—EDS.]

5. This and the following Tugwell quotations are from the Rexford Tugwell Diary, Franklin D. Roosevelt Presidential Library, Hyde Park, New York.

6. Raymond Moley, *The First New Deal* (New York: Harcourt, Brace & World, 1966), pp. xii, 50–52.

7. [Although Best's essay should stimulate much rethinking regarding President Roosevelt's domestic and foreign policies, it should be noted that President Roosevelt was dealing with the tough contemporary facts delineated so well by Heinrichs. Nazi Germany, Fascist Italy, and Imperial Japan had committed aggression in the 1930s while the Soviet Union, with the exception of Poland, had been preoccupied with building 'socialism in one country' during the same time. Best, however, not only joins those who think that the U.S. could have avoided the Pacific War, but goes beyond them in arguing that the failure to do so created the conditions for Soviet expansion in Europe and Asia and the conquest of communism in China.—EDS.]

8. Quoted in George Kennan, *American Diplomacy, 1900–1950* (Chicago: The University of Chicago Press, 1951), pp. 51–52.

9. Ibid., p. 52.

10. [It should be recalled, however, that President Hoover's internationalism seemed compromised by his refusal to veto the Hawley-Smoot Tariff Act of 1931, the highest tariff in American history. One thousand economists had petitioned him to do so.—EDS.]

11. Shōichi Saeki, "Images of the United States as a hypothetical enemy," in *Mutual Images,* ed. Akira Iriye (Cambridge, Mass.: Harvard University Press, 1975), p. 113.

4. Principles Versus Realities: U.S. Prewar Foreign Policy toward Japan

JOHN K. EMMERSON[1]

JOSEPH C. GREW, American ambassador in Japan from 1932 to 1941, saw during those years a developing Japanese-American rift over "principles" and "realities." In 1900 Americans had proclaimed the Open Door policy in China, and in 1922 the Nine-Power Treaty had bound the United States to "respect" (but not "defend") the sovereignty, independence, and territorial and administrative integrity of China. We never committed ourselves to going to war in support of these principles. Henry L. Stimson, secretary of war in 1932, tried in vain to get British support to cite Japan as a violator of this treaty after the Manchurian "Incident" *(jiken)* of September 1931. After the more serious China "Affair" *(jihen)* broke out in July 1937, President Franklin D. Roosevelt proposed a "quarantine" of aggressors, principally Japan. The public outcry was deafening, with calls for impeachment of the president and organized campaigns to "Keep the U. S. out of war!" In Tokyo, Ambassador Grew exclaimed to the administrative officer who handed him the telegram summarizing the "quarantine" speech: "There goes everything I have tried to accomplish in my entire mission to Japan." Even Cordell Hull, secretary of state, thought "quarantine" too drastic a word, believing that Americans had to be led gradually out of their isolationist mood.

By 1939 war had spread in China, and anti-Japanese feeling was growing in the United States. Notice to terminate the American commercial treaty with Japan was greeted with public approval.[2] Grew, on home leave, was astonished at the strength of sentiment for a trade embargo and warned the State Department and his fellow citizens that a policy of sanctions could lead to war. Back in Japan, he tried to explain to the Japanese American feelings over the empire's "sacred" war in China. In his "horse's mouth" speech, delivered to the America-Japan Society in Tokyo on October 19, he admonished his listeners: "The American people . . . have good reason to believe that an effort is being made to establish control, in Japan's own inter-

37

est, of large areas on the continent of Asia and to impose upon those
areas a system of closed economy." Grew noted that Japanese leaders
paid attention to his speech and were sobered by it.

Widening divergences were developing between those in charge of
East Asian affairs at the State Department and Grew's embassy staff
in Tokyo. The ambassador's New England conscience supported
wholeheartedly the "principles" on which our policy stood, but he
also recognized the "realities" that guided Japan: strategic protection
against Soviet attack; economic security through control of raw materials in China; and eradication of anti-Japanese and communist
activities and propaganda in China. He saw two courses for American
policy. The first was "intransigence," the refusal to negotiate a new
treaty of commerce and the imposition of an embargo. The other,
which he recommended, was a willingness to discuss a new treaty and
to postpone an embargo. In the process the American side would of
course urge the observance of the Nine-Power Treaty and respect for
American rights in China. Grew believed that Japan's determination
to gain influence in China would not be deterred by the termination
of the treaty or by an embargo. On the contrary, the Japanese samurai
spirit of stoicism and determination would be hardened. War could
result but not renunciation of the nation's aims, which, from the
time of Meiji, had been "prosperity and military strength" (fukoku
kyōhei), to which had been added a "hegemonial position in East
Asia."[3]

Stanley K. Hornbeck, whose only experience in Asia had been a
teaching stint in China, was the senior adviser on Far Eastern matters
to Secretary of State Hull. He found Grew's arguments unpersuasive
and red-penciled his dispatches and diaries with bold dissents. Hornbeck's prescribed method was to "freeze out" the Japanese, to "put
the screws on." He visualized Grew and his staff as subjected to the
stultifying atmosphere of Tokyo in which well-meaning Japanese
"friends" told them what they wanted to hear.

The year 1940 brought an intensification of "spiritual mobilization," the abolition of political parties and their replacement by the
"New Structure" and the "Imperial Rule Assistance Association." In
September Japan joined Nazi Germany and Fascist Italy in the Tripartite Pact and in November glorified the national mythology by
lavishly celebrating the 2600th anniversary of the founding of the
country.

On September 12 Grew shifted his position and for the first time recommended the gradual, progressive application of countermeasures against Japan. He warned that a "drastic" embargo would likely encounter retaliation that might take the form of a "sudden stroke" by the military, and he therefore counseled Washington to face squarely the consequences of whatever action it might take.

Grew was crushed by Japan's adherence to the Axis on September 27. Admiral Yonai Mitsumasa, the previous prime minister, had assured him that this would not happen. He confided to his diary that a typhoon could hardly have more effectively demolished the foundation of Japanese-American relations. The Japanese recognized the seriousness of the step. In the Imperial Conference that made the decision, the president of the Privy Council pleaded only for time: "Even though a Japanese-American clash may be unavoidable in the end, I hope that sufficient care will be exercised to make sure that it will not come in the near future."

The mood of an historical period is not communicated in the dry documents of diplomacy. Those of us who lived in Tokyo in the prewar years constantly considered the possibility of war between Japan and the United States but clung to the belief that it could be prevented. We watched the efforts on the home front to sustain a war in China in which the imperial armies were becoming "bogged down." We disparaged the Japanese. Their overblown slogans seemed ridiculous: "Eight Corners of the Universe under One Roof," "the Holy War," "a Hundred Million People with One Heart," "the New Order in East Asia," and "the Co-Prosperity Sphere in East Asia." The evidence of food, fuel, and clothing shortages was all around us. Disintegrating "staple fiber" *(sufu)* supplanted cotton cloth. Necessities were rationed. When gasoline became unavailable for private automobiles, they were converted into wood-burners. Taxi drivers would stop their cars, go to the back, and stoke the fire in the compartment where the trunk had been. The Datsun automobile was regarded by most foreigners as a joke, as was Suntory whiskey. Air-raid drills *(bōkū-enshū)*, with frantic positioning of black curtains over windows at the sound of sirens, were pathetic gestures to protect flammable wooden houses. Early morning regimented calisthenics in the streets, to blaring radio instructions, looked like brave but ineffectual attempts to build the national physique. All the while, flag-waving sendoffs of sons and brothers to war were daily occurrences.

These observations confirmed, if confirmation was needed, the "realities" of Japan's vulnerability and total dependence on the outside world for essential raw materials. For Japan of the 1930s, military power was the accepted way to build economic power. Whereas to us, a Japanese war against the "invincible" United States appeared preposterous, the leaders of the empire, dedicated to policies established since the Meiji period, were ready, if faced with no other perceived alternative, to go to war.

On January 27, 1941, Grew sent a telegram, later to become famous, reporting a rumor from the Peruvian ambassador that the Japanese military had planned a mass attack on Pearl Harbor to be executed in case of "trouble" with the United States. We expected that the Japanese might make a grab in Southeast Asia. Grew worried that the United States would not fight to save Singapore, which he regarded as a vital point. In our minds, however, a direct assault on American territory was insane and therefore unthinkable. We now know that studies for the Pearl Harbor raid were under way at the time we sent our telegram and that the Naval General Staff had at first rejected the proposal. When in October I returned to the United States via Hawaii, I was informed that the Navy had stepped up its air reconnaissance of the islands on the basis of our message.

Ambassador Grew had an old-fashioned faith in the efficacy of diplomacy. He believed that, in the end, the Japanese were reasonable people and that "constructive conciliation" was possible. In May Hull asked him whether the Japanese would observe an agreement if one were reached with the United States. Grew recorded in his diary that his reply was "perhaps the most important telegram" he had sent from Tokyo, drafted "early in the morning after a night of most careful and prayerful thought." His answer was affirmative, that a bilateral undertaking, sanctioned by the army and navy and approved by the cabinet, the privy council, and the emperor, would be carried out in good faith. Hornbeck in Washington disagreed. He believed that certain Japanese were trying to pull the wool over Grew's eyes, that the country's leaders were bent on expansion, and that good faith could not be presumed.

The crisis of the summer of 1941 was the American freezing order. I wrote my wife: "On July 26 things happened. It was Saturday. The announcement of Japanese entry into French Indochina was made at noon and by 2 o'clock we heard that the United States government had frozen Japanese assets in the United States. There was much flurry in the *taishikan* [embassy] as you can imagine. That night the ambassador remarked that it was quite unusual to find the whole staff of secretaries in the office at 7:30 on a Saturday night!" The freezing order underscored the difficulties facing Japan and confirmed, in Japanese eyes, the fact of ABCD (American-British-Chinese-Dutch) encirclement.

From April top-secret conversations continued between Secretary of State Cordell Hull and Ambassador Nomura Kichisaburō in Washington and between Ambassador Grew and Prime Minister Konoe Fumimaro in Tokyo. No one in the embassy except the ambassador and counselor was supposed to know of the talks, but I managed to read the telegrams. Grew was encouraged when Konoe proposed in August that he meet President Roosevelt "somewhere in the Pacific." The drama of such an encounter appealed to FDR, who probably imagined a "Pacific Charter" to complement the Atlantic Charter that he had signed with Winston Churchill. The Lord Privy Seal, Marquis Kido Kōichi, had cautioned Konoe about the gravity of Japan's situation, emphasizing the disparity between strength and goals and advising an adjustment of relations with the United States.

Hornbeck and his associates in the State Department's Office of Far Eastern Affairs took a jaundiced view of a suggested Konoe-Roosevelt rendezvous, to be held on an American warship off Alaska. They insisted that a general agreement should be reached *before* the conference, to ensure its success. For the Japanese, this was impossible. Konoe could not, in advance, convince the military chiefs to support an accord that would inevitably have included some withdrawals of military forces from China and other minimum concessions. Konoe's only hope was to secure an on-the-spot agreement that, with the concurrence of the military officers accompanying him and with the emperor's sanction, could have been presented as a *fait accompli* in Tokyo, in the form of an imperial rescript. This would have been possible, of course, only if the U.S. government had been willing to ask for less than the complete withdrawal of Japanese troops from China.

From April 1941 Hull had insisted on his four principles: (1) respect for the territorial integrity and sovereignty of all nations; (2) non-interference in the internal affairs of other countries; (3) equality, including equality of commercial opportunity; and (4) non-disturbance of the status quo in the Pacific except as the status quo might be altered by peaceful means. Grew reported, after a secret meeting with Konoe on September 6, that the prime minister, and thus the Japanese government, had "conclusively and wholeheartedly" accepted Hull's principles. Konoe recorded that the principles were "splendid" *(kekkō)* and that he agreed with them "in principle," but that a meeting with President Roosevelt would be necessary to work out certain problems.

In any case, Hull's principles were confronted by Japan's realities: raw materials, China, military power. The Japanese were not used to moralizing or to accepting general concepts as guides for action. Their wartime slogans were not principles but symbols to clothe actions the government was already taking.

It is perhaps unproductive to speculate on what would have happened had a battleship meeting between Konoe and Roosevelt taken place. Probably no agreement would have been reached, given the toughness of Japan's military, the rigid attitude of the American government toward the observance of principles, and the preoccupation of the U.S. policymakers with China. Japan's military leaders might well have placed obstacles to any concessions that Konoe might have been prepared to make, although they were keenly conscious of the country's predicament and the need for a quick solution by peaceful means, if not by war. There was the ghost of a chance that the emperor's word might have prevailed; it did in August 1945, to end the war.[4]

The situation was tense in Tokyo in the fall of 1941. Dependents of government officials had been evacuated by the beginning of the year; the wives and children of private Americans and others without urgent business in Asia had been strongly advised by the U.S. government to leave the Far East. Our embassy community was one of enforced bachelors and single employees. Police surveillance of foreigners, especially Americans, was intensified. One's Japanese friends feared to come to the embassy, and it was not politic to seek them out. We sensed the danger of hostilities and were convinced that, if pushed, the Japanese would fight. War would probably erupt in Southeast Asia.

Three basic issues separated the two sides: Japan's adherence to the Axis pact, the principle of equal commercial opportunity, and Japanese troops in China. By the latter part of 1941 the Japanese were already disillusioned by their German ally. Joining the Axis had not been a profitable move; they had received no help from Hitler or Mussolini. To denounce the Axis publicly would have been difficult, but Japanese negotiators had assured their American counterparts that the Tripartite Pact would become a dead letter automatically if a

Japanese-American agreement was achieved. The problem of equal
commercial opportunity was not insolvable. The presence of Japanese
forces in China and Indochina was the problem. The army was over-
committed on the continent and had not succeeded in destroying the
nationalist government of China. Japan's leaders were ready to effect
partial withdrawals from both Indochina and mainland China. They
could not, however, accept the demand for a total evacuation from
both countries, probably including Manchuria, that was contained in
the note delivered to Ambassador Nomura on November 26 and that
they regarded as an ultimatum. A nation that, although mired in
fruitless combat, had not been defeated could not at once abandon
an enterprise into which so many years of sacrifice had been
expended. Americans were later in Vietnam to suffer at first hand the
excruciating experience of withdrawing from a prolonged war. In
1941 our obsession with China as a "Great Power" and an ally and
with the Chinese as "the good guys" made it impossible for us to, in
the phrase current in the corridors of the State Department, "sell
China down the river."[5]

Hornbeck believed that by turning the screws we could force the
Japanese into submission, that a tough attitude would cause them to
abandon their aims in Asia. I returned to Washington in late October
and, as was the custom, paid a courtesy call on Mr. Hornbeck, the
senior official in the department concerned with Asia. He asked me
rhetorically, since he had read the stream of telegrams and dispatches
we had sent from Tokyo, "What do you people in the Embassy think
about war with Japan?" I replied without hesitation: "We think
Japan wants to dominate East Asia and hopes to do so without war.
But if this looks impossible, Japan will go to war in desperation."
Hornbeck looked at me with derision, "Name me one country which
has ever gone to war in desperation." No apt example came to mind,
and the conversation ended quickly. As the record shows, a few days
after my interview with him, Hornbeck, on November 27, committed himself to a prediction: "In the opinion of the undersigned, the
Japanese government does not desire or intend or expect to have
forthwith armed conflict with the United States."[6]

We did not anticipate an attack on Pearl Harbor. Unfortunately, we
had forgotten the Peruvian ambassador's rumor. We thought in the
State Department on that weekend of December 6–7 that an armed
action might well take place in Southeast Asia, probably in Indochina, or to secure a foothold in the Netherlands East Indies. I do not

remember that we were so complacent as Hornbeck. In his defense, he later explained that his judgment of November 27 had been based on his "scrutiny of materials which emanated from 'intelligence' sources, some British and some American." These, of course, must have included the Japanese official cable traffic, decoded under the system known as MAGIC.

Both sides made mistaken judgments of each other. The Americans underestimated the Japanese strength and determination; the Japanese convinced themselves that the United States, after receiving a knockout blow at Pearl Harbor, would not pursue them to the far reaches of the western and southern Pacific. The popular attitude of American superiority, in which strains of racism were present, was illustrated by a cartoon current at the time, in which a diminutive Japanese soldier on the other side of the Pacific ocean sweats to blow up a tremendous balloon bearing painted, scowling, piano-keys teeth, horn-rimmed glasses, military cap, and tag: "Japanese Bluff." Uncle Sam stands confidently on his own shore, wearing jauntily a Navy cap, readying a sling shot behind him and smiling slyly, with satisfaction.

The basic conflict was still one between principles and realities. We insisted on Japan's commitment to support our principles, and Pearl Harbor forced us to go to war over them. By territorial and administrative integrity, we meant the integrity of China. Reduced to its simplest terms, a war with Japan would be a war about China, and also a war about Southeast Asia. We did not realize the extent of the "desperation" that would motivate the Japanese if they saw their national objectives—their security and their economic welfare—jeopardized. The Pearl Harbor attack manifested this desperation—an explosion that became a kind of national *seppuku* (suicide).

NOTES

1. [Because of Mr. Emmerson's illness and death while this volume was in preparation, he could not be asked to supply documentation for his essay. However, several of the quotations in his essay are from his own recollections as a foreign service officer at the U.S. Embassy in Tokyo and later in Washington in the pre-Pearl Harbor period under discussion. He is therefore a primary source on these matters, a participant in the events. As a participant, his judgments and/or biases, such as they were, should be considered in juxtaposition to the opinions and/or attitudes of others.—EDS.]

2. [Note Emmerson's implicit agreement with Iriye that by late 1939 and 1940 a strong foreign policy vis-à-vis Japan was popular. Iriye thought that was because it

brought together those who favored interventionist or isolationist policies in Europe. See pp. 18–19.—EDS.]

3. [Note here the agreement between Grew, Emmerson, and Hosoya on the impact of historic samurai thinking on Japanese foreign policy.—EDS.]

4. [Although Emmerson is not optimistic regarding the success of a Konoe-Roosevelt summit, it is clear that he agrees with the position of Ikei and Tsunoda that American policy failed in not having agreed to one. For an opposite view see the Barnhart essay.—EDS.]

5. [Emmerson clearly believed that war could have been avoided by a more flexible American foreign policy. His assessment of Hornbeck is consistent with that of the majority of the essayists in this volume. For different views on whether the war was avoidable and whether Hornbeck was mistaken, see the essays by Barnhart and Fujiwara. Barnhart insists that "Hornbeck was consistently correct in his assessments of Japan's aims in the Far East." Both men believe the war was unavoidable since the Japanese militarists could not be deviated from their expansionistic course.—EDS.]

6. [For a discussion of Hornbeck's statement of November 27 and his role in general, see James C. Thomson, Jr., "The Role of the Department of State," in *Pearl Harbor as History: Japanese-American Relations 1931-1941,* ed. Dorothy Borg and Shumpei Okamoto (New York: Columbia University Press, 1973), pp. 81–106, as well as subsequent essays in this volume, especially that of Michael Barnhart.—EDS.]

5. Examples of Mismanagement in U.S. Policy toward Japan before World War II

IKEI MASARU

IT is clear that American policy toward Japan before World War II was mismanaged and showed bias. For example, the United States did not recognize the seriousness of the Mukden Incident after its occurrence on September 18, 1931. This was so for a number of reasons. First, the United States misunderstood the political situation in Japan at that time, particularly by overestimating the strength of the forces favoring peace. American leaders believed that the cabinet form of government had been firmly established in Japan. The United States also believed that Japan's cooperation in the successful London (Naval Disarmament) Conference of 1930 symbolized the strength of those peaceful elements. In addition, Americans believed that Foreign Minister Shidehara's peaceful policy toward China had brought a turn away from the belligerent attitude represented by the military in Japan. Finally, the United States believed that the universal manhood suffrage law was as significant in Japanese history as the Magna Carta was in Western history.

Accordingly, therefore, Americans thought that the civilian government under Prime Minister Wakatsuki and Foreign Minister Shidehara would be able to control the Kwantung army. When these expectations were not realized there was a change in the American attitude. Specifically, five possible methods of bringing about a change in the Japanese policy came under consideration. One prospect was the convening of an international conference by the Nine Powers. This, however, seemed likely to undermine the policy of the League of Nations; moreover, it was opposed by Great Britain and France. A second possibility was the recall of the U.S. ambassador to Japan, but the U.S. State Department opposed this hard-line approach. A third prospect was an embargo of weapons and loans to Japan. However, many Americans argued that since the difficulty in Manchuria was between Japan and China, any restrictions on arms exports and loans should be against both countries. Thus, this approach, too, could not be carried out. Another possible course of action, the suspension of all trade between the United States and Japan was opposed by American business circles and the U.S. State Department. Finally, there was the option of using American military power to bring an end to the conflict in Manchuria. President Herbert Hoover, however, was totally opposed to any such action.

These five possible courses of action having been rejected, there was only one option left—to try to bring the force of public opinion against Japan by issuing a statement denouncing her actions in Manchuria. That statement, the Stimson Doctrine, had almost no effect on Japan, however, for several reasons. First, the Japanese concept of international law and morality was different from that which Stimson was trying to express. Moreover, the Stimson Doctrine failed to attract the broad support of European countries that Stimson had counted on. Finally, Stimson's voice in the American government was limited by a combination of pressure from President Hoover and indifference from Congress, both of whom were preoccupied with the depression in the United States. Therefore, Stimson's non-recognition doctrine had no impact on the Japanese, and the Japanese continued to believed that the United States could be easily handled.

The second example of mismanagement in American policy toward Japan before World War II is related to China. First, the Americans and the Japanese differed in their views of China and the Chinese. For the United States, China was a country whose modernization and independence were to be encouraged and in which the principles of the Open Door and the equality of economic opportunity should be applied. The Japanese attitude was that China should be either under Japanese control or at least under Japanese leadership. A second factor was the American attitude toward the Sino-Japanese War, which began in 1937. Stanley Hornbeck, chief of the Far East division of the U.S. State Department, believed that it was desirable to keep Japanese troops pinned down in China. Given Hornbeck's influence on foreign policy formulation, it might be said that the policy of the United States was one of quietly expecting, or even looking forward to, the continuation of the Sino-Japanese War. America's failure to take a strong position with regard to that war only led to the escalation of the Japanese invasion.

A third major problem in American policy toward Japan in this period was the American attitude toward the Axis alliance. The United States interpreted the Japanese alliance with Nazi Germany and Fascist Italy as demonstrating an intent by Japan to seek a division of the world by these three powers. Japan might in fact have harbored such an intention, but the purpose and motivation for entering the Axis alliance was to deter Great Britain and the United States in the Pacific.

When one compares American policy toward Japan with that toward Europe, it is eminently clear that issues related to Japan took a secondary place in American thinking. After war broke out between Germany and the Soviet Union the United States took a harder line toward Japan. From that emerged the American demand that Japan withdraw from the Axis alliance, an action that was unacceptable to the Japanese, who viewed the alliance primarily as a defensive measure against the United States.

Another major issue between Japan and the United States was the American attitude toward Japan's push to the south. The United States over-responded to the Japanese occupation of southern Indochina. Although the United States bitterly criticized Japan for this occupation, at the same time it signed a treaty with Denmark to establish a naval base in Greenland. On the day that Japan occupied southern Indochina, the United States signed a treaty with Iceland to establish a military presence there. Despite these American moves, paralleling those of Japan in French Indochina, the United States froze Japanese assets in the United States and moved to halt the flow of oil to Japan.

A fifth difficulty between the two nations was over America's attitude during the U.S.-Japanese negotiations on the eve of the outbreak of war. One can first point to the hard-line position of Secretary of State Cordell Hull. Hull turned down Japan's proposal for a summit meeting between Prime Minister Konoe and President Roosevelt. Then Hull presented the "Hull Note," which included a demand for immediate and unconditional withdrawal of all Japanese troops from China. This demand was light years removed from either of the proposed compromises put forward by Japan. A second problem was the communication gap between Washington and Tokyo. Although Ambassador Joseph Grew had a good grasp of the situation in Japan, his views were not seriously considered by Hull, Hornbeck, and other U.S. policymakers. Hornbeck, in particular, was well known as a pro-China hand. However, Hornbeck's hard-line policy toward Japan only served to push the Japanese further in their drive south and into conflict with the United States.

Having discussed these points, the following conclusions seem appropriate. Japanese foreign policy would probably not have been altered by a policy of continued American appeasement, but if the United States had taken a more cautious attitude toward Japan the outbreak of war between the United States and Japan probably would not have occurred as early as December 7, 1941. If the war had been delayed, what might have happened? For one thing, with greater time to prepare herself militarily, the United States might have been able to convince Japan that war would not be a sensible course of action. Second, given more time, Japan might have seen that Germany and Italy were destined to lose the war in Europe and would likely have been discouraged from going to war with the United States.

I do not entirely agree with the thesis of Professor Charles Beard in, *President Roosevelt and the Coming of the War, 1941: A Study of Appearances and Reality,* in which he argues that President Roosevelt invited the Japanese attack on Pearl Harbor.[1] I do believe, however, that if the United States had taken a different approach in dealing with Japan, the outbreak of war would at least have been delayed resulting perhaps in a change of Japanese policy away from war.

NOTE

1. [We were unable to obtain or arrange precise documentation for Professor Ikei's essay. However, his reference to Charles Beard should remind the reader of the "revisionist school" that, following Beard's lead, put heavy blame on President Roosevelt for "inviting" the Pearl Harbor disaster. The editors of Gordon Prange's monumental *At Dawn We Slept: The Untold Story of Pearl Harbor* were at pains to refute these in a special appendix entitled "Revisionists Revisited," pp. 839–850, and Alvin Coox in his essay in this volume "repulses" them even more. The Klein-Conroy essay seems to transfer at least some of the blame for FDR's problem onto Churchill. However, we have to ask whether Waldo Heinrich's essay might revive "revisionism" in another form.—EDS.]

6. Miscalculations in Deterrent Policy: U.S.-Japanese Relations, 1938–1941

Hosoya Chihiro

Hard-liners in the U.S. government such as Stanley Hornbeck, Cordell Hull, Henry Stimson, and Henry Morgenthau, who favored economic sanctions against Japan in the years immediately preceding the Japanese attack on Pearl Harbor, seriously miscalculated the impact of such a policy on Japan. Instead of deterring the Japanese from pursuing an expansionist policy, these economic sanctions exacerbated U.S.-Japanese relations, encouraged Japan's southward expansion, and provoked Japanese hard-liners to risk war with the United States. The advocates of the hard-line policy toward Japan misunderstood the psychology of the Japanese, particularly the middle levels of the military, the Japanese decision-making process, and Japanese economic realities. They also rode roughshod over the prudent proposals of the soft-liners in the U.S. State Department such as the director of the Far Eastern Division, Maxwell Hamilton, and Ambassador Joseph Grew in Japan.[1]

The demand of the hard-liners for economic sanctions against Japan played into the hands of the ultranationalists in the Japanese government. The latter argued that the imposition of economic sanctions by the United States necessitated risk and expansion by Japan. In such a climate Japanese moderates found it impossible to counsel caution and accommodation. Their counterparts in the U.S. government similarly learned that they were no match for those who foolishly believed that Japan would not dare attack the United States and that economic reprisals would so cripple Japan that she would acquiesce to American pressures.

After the Marco Polo Bridge Incident of July 7, 1937, Japan adopted an increasingly aggressive course in China. After the *Panay* incident on December 12, the Japanese occupation forces there increasingly interfered with U.S. economic interests. These actions stiffened the American attitude and led to diplomatic protests.

When these actions had limited effect on the Japanese military, hard-liners in the U.S. government favored an imposition of economic sanctions against Japan.[2] They believed that Japan's economic dependence on the United States gave them a decided advantage in restraining Japanese expansion. Hence they counseled strong, punitive economic actions against Japan such as prohibiting the importing and exporting of selected goods, suspending credit, restricting monetary exchange, and even imposing a total economic boycott. The legal obstacle confronting them was the 1911 U.S.-Japanese Treaty of Commerce and Navigation.

The first official to advocate the abrogation of this treaty was Hornbeck in a memorandum of July 19, 1938. Initially, he had few supporters. The mood in Washington, D.C., changed, however, when the Japanese government announced on November 3, 1938, a "New Order in East Asia" and Foreign Minister Arita Hachirō stated on November 18 that the large-scale involvement of Japan in China could not help violating U.S. economic interests and that pre-war standards and principles would need to be altered to fit the present and future conditions in Asia. These Japanese actions were taken to be a violation of the Nine-Power Treaty. They created a majority opinion within the State Department that was favorable to an abrogation of the U.S.-Japanese Treaty of Commerce and Navigation. In a curiously argued report issued on December 5, Francis Sayre, assistant secretary of state, maintained correctly that full-scale economic reprisals against Japan posed the serious danger of a military conflict and would create widespread domestic economic disturbances. Paradoxically, however, he went on to maintain that the commercial treaty should be abolished and that steps should be taken to end the granting of credits and loans.[3]

In rapid succession the U.S. government announced on January 14, 1939, a "moral embargo" on airplanes and parts and on February 7, 1939, a cessation of credit to Japan. However, soft-liners in the State Department, represented by Grew and Hamilton, argued that a moderate policy would lead to a revival of the moderate faction (Shidehara diplomacy) in Japan and would also blunt the efforts of the hard-liners who were advocating a strengthened coalition with Nazi Germany. These moderate arguments temporarily bore fruit. Further study by the State Department led to a decision to hand Japan an *aide memoire* proposing a new commercial treaty that would exclude articles five and fourteen in the existing treaty. Such a move would be a less severe shock to Japan but would still make it possible to impose embargoes and discriminatory duties.[4]

Unfortunately, on April 27, before the *aide memoire* could be submitted to Japan, the chairman of the Foreign Relations Committee, Key Pitman, submitted a resolution to the Senate that scuttled the State Department's plans. This resolution gave the president the "power to effect an embargo and limit credits against a country which infringes the Nine-Power Treaty and injures American lives and interests." Hamilton feared that the planned revision of the commercial treaty would appear to be connected to the Senate bill and would produce too strong an impression concerning U.S. policy toward Japan. As a result the State Department decided in May to postpone the *aide memoire*.[5]

The hard-line faction in the State Department, led by Hornbeck, could not prevail in 1938 and 1939 because the moderates were supported at that time by the military.[6] The military leaders did not feel the country was sufficiently ready for a conflict with Japan. A Hornbeck memorandum to Sayre on December 29, 1938, argued a position that would be repeated incessantly until the Pearl Harbor attack, namely that a strong U.S. stand of "comprehensive and thoroughgoing program of measures of material pressure" could prevent military conflict and lead to a revision in Japanese policy.[7] Hornbeck's view was echoed in the Senate and by the general populace. A Gallup poll survey showed 66 percent in favor of a boycott on Japanese goods and 78 percent in favor of an embargo on weapons and munitions to Japan. When Japan blockaded the Tientsin settlement in June over Britain's refusal to return four accused Chinese to the Japanese and news circulated of Japan's intention to remove English interests from China, an aroused American public opinion strengthened the hard-line faction's stand on Japanese policy. On July 26, 1939, President Roosevelt announced that the treaty of commerce would be void after January 26, 1940. Hull and Sayre believed that the U.S. ability to impose economic sanctions thereafter would have a "sobering effect" on Japan because of her economic dependence on America.[8]

In Japan Foreign Minister Arita was more optimistic about the American announcement than were those from the anxious economic circles engaged in trade with the United States or the pro-Anglo-American groups. Arita assessed the American move as largely political, "first in order to settle the question of its rights and interests in China, and second as a gesture in connection with the coming elections this fall."[9] Although he thought a solution could be found, a document developed by the foreign office, which reflected the more hard-line approach of its middle-level officials, opposed a passive "wait and see policy." Instead, the document demanded that Japan should "denounce the unfriendly attitude of the U.S. Government" and appeal to the American public and isolationist faction there.[10]

The hard-liners in Japan suffered a temporary setback when the Nazis signed a non-aggression pact with the Soviet Union. The Hiranuma cabinet fell in late August, and the new Prime Minister, Abe Nobuyuki, by his own volition as well as orders from the emperor sought to improve U.S.-Japanese relations. Documents developed on October 4 and October 20 by, respectively, the foreign office (based on an army plan) and the Japanese navy argued for bettering U.S.-Japanese relations through the favorable treatment of U.S. interests in China and U.S. citizens residing there. The navy document also advocated holding a U.S.-Japanese conference in Tokyo to conclude a new commercial treaty or at least to obtain a "generalized, temporary agreement even if it fails to affirm specifically the principle of non-discriminatory treatment." It called for avoiding discussion of the Nine-Power Treaty, opening the Yangtze and Canton rivers, compensating U.S. interests in China, and moderating restrictions on U.S. cultural work.[11] Here was an opportunity for the U.S. government to improve U.S.-Japanese relations, but the Japanese conciliatory attitude did not bear fruit because of miscalculations by the hard-liners in the U.S. government.

On the surface, it appeared that these conciliatory Japanese decisions confirmed the thesis of the U.S. hard-liners that a tough approach against Japan would be effective. But two points mitigate against acceptance of this view. First, the German-Soviet non-aggression pact had frightened many Japanese. Second, the same navy document mentioned above also incorporated a hard-line policy. It warned that non-diplomatic measures might have to be adopted against the United States to counter U.S. pressure. The argument was that if Japan were to advance southward or to make more rapid war preparations, Japan would have to enter into arrangements with other countries to obtain necessary raw materials. Furthermore, the document claimed that the alleged tendency of U.S. foreign policy to change rapidly forced Japan to accelerate her war preparations to meet all contingencies.

As a result of the Abe government's effort to improve relations with the United States, Japanese concessions were made at the Tokyo conference in meetings of November 4 and December 18, 1939. The Japanese promised that talks about concessions to U.S. citizens for losses sustained in China through Japanese bombings, settlement problems, and taxes and currency problems would prove satisfactory to the United States and that the Yangtze and Canton rivers would be opened in two months. In return the Japanese wanted mutual concessions and negotiations for the concluding of a new commercial treaty of *modus vivendi*. On December 22 the Japanese ambassador to the United States, Horinouchi Kensuke, presented the details of the *modus vivendi* to Hull. It called for: (1) the principle of the most-favored-nation treatment for commerce, navigation, and tariffs; (2) freedom of entry, travel, and residence where the purpose was that of trade; (3) the handling of taxes, duties, and commissions, direct or indirect, on the basis of non-discrimination or the most-favored-nation principle.

Diametrically opposite reactions to Abe's efforts to improve U.S.-Japanese relations occurred within the U.S. government. Ambassador Grew consistently called for a conciliatory policy. In support of the *modus vivendi* proposed by Japan he said the following in a strongly worded telegram to Washington on December 18, 1939:

> The simple fact is that we are here dealing not with a unified Japan but with a Japanese Government which is endeavoring courageously, even with only gradual success, to fight against a recalcitrant Japanese Army, a battle which happens to be our own battle. . . . If we now rebuff the Government we shall not be serving to discredit the Japanese Army but rather to furnish the Army with powerful arguments to be used in its own support. I am convinced that we are in a position either to direct American-Japanese relations into a progressively healthy channel or to accelerate their movement straight down hill.[12]

The strong reaction of the hard-liners to the *modus vivendi* was demonstrated repeatedly over the next two years. In a memorandum issued the next day Hornbeck argued:

> In my opinion adoption as a major premise of the thought that the 'civilian' element in the Japanese nation, may gain an ascendancy over the 'military' element and, having done so, would alter the objectives of Japanese policy can lead to nothing but confusion and error in reasoning. . . . Practically the whole of the Japanese population believes in and is

enthusiastic over the policy of expansion and aggrandisement of the Japanese empire.[13]

He urged policymakers to believe that the Japanese were insincere; within them "there is a change neither of attitude nor of heart." He and Grew were far apart in their assessments. Grew, however, had been on the Japanese scene for almost a decade; Hornbeck did not know Japan and was strongly pro-Chinese.[14]

Secretary Hull became increasingly sympathetic to Hornbeck's view. Although he did not support the hard-line faction's argument (stated in a December 11, 1939, memorandum to Roosevelt) to impose duties on Japanese commerce upon the termination of the commerce treaty, he refused to heed Grew's advice to implement a new treaty or a *modus vivendi* (December 20).[15] The consequent failure of the Tokyo conference was the final straw that brought about the collapse of the Abe cabinet. The new cabinet headed by Admiral Yonai Mitsumasa and Foreign Minister Arita submitted the same proposal with no new approaches. That effort failed, and the Treaty of Commerce and Navigation lapsed on January 26, 1940.

Despite the Japanese awareness that a lapse of the treaty did not mean an automatic levy of discriminatory tariffs or restrictions on Japanese products, the psychological impact was profound. Immediately, the foreign office concluded that they "must end as quickly as possible the present high level of economic dependence on the U.S. and press on for a policy to establish an economic system which would not be endangered by the U.S. attitude."[16] When the Nazi Blitzkrieg defeated Norway, the Netherlands, Belgium, Luxemburg, and France between April and June, 1940, many Japanese feared that Japan "might miss the bus." They saw an opportunity by a quick southward movement to obtain oil and other materials from the Dutch East Indies and to prevent the transport of war supplies to Chiang Kaishek from French Indochina.

All factions in the U.S. government were opposed to a Japanese southern advance and an alliance with Germany, but they differed on how to prevent these possibilities. Grew wanted the United States to break the deadlock with Japan by discussing a new commercial treaty and by extending credit to Japan for non-military supplies. At a meeting of Hull, Hamilton, and Hornbeck on May 24, the latter feared that American concessions would be perceived as a sign of weakness and would encourage new Japanese aggression. He opposed any new moves.[17] In May and June, however, Hull seemed to have adopted a more conciliatory attitude. He even allowed the opening of conferences by Grew with Foreign Minister Arita to discuss the promotion of trade and the strengthening of relations between the two countries. These talks failed because Grew had to assert that the *sine qua non* for improved U.S.-Japanese relations was non-interference in U.S. interests and the halting of the use of force in effecting national policy. Foreign Minister Arita was just as adamant that the obstacle to that goal was the lack of a commercial treaty. Grew, at least, sought to initiate talks in support of a *modus vivendi* from Washington, but by July Hull was no longer interested. He may have been interested in these talks in May and June only because of the altered condition in Europe and Hornbeck's advice that such talks might stall the feared Japanese advance southward.

The failure of the Grew-Arita talks contributed to the fall of the Yonai cabinet and to the creation of a more aggressive cabinet led by Konoe Fumimaro with Matsuoka Yōsuke as foreign minister. It was recognized that such a cabinet would be more favorable to both a southern advance and a coalition with Italy and Germany. When Japan closed the Burma Road, Hornbeck advocated either immediate export restrictions on aviation gasoline or the implementation of a full-scale embargo on exports. The rationale was that these actions would "retard or prevent new adventuring."[18]

In the meantime the U.S. government took a number of steps beyond diplomatic action. It ordered the continued stationing of the fleet in Hawaii on May 4 to deter a Japanese attack on the Dutch Indies and also passed the National Defense Act, which gave the president power to license the export of arms, munitions, raw materials, airplane parts, optical instruments, and other items. Scrap iron and petroleum were omitted because, as Hamilton put it, "such restrictions or prohibition would tend to impel Japan towards moving into the Dutch East Indies. . . ."[19]

The appointment of Henry Stimson as secretary of war also hardened the U.S. position. Stimson had been advocating a strong policy of economic sanctions against Japan since the Manchurian Incident of 1931. He was very close to the Secretary of the Treasury Morgenthau and to Hornbeck and other hand-liners. From hindsight we can see that he and Hornbeck suffered from the same two misconceptions: (1) that Japan would never dare wage war against the United States despite American actions against her, and (2) that Japan's southern advance would prove unlikely because of her deeper involvement in the Chinese quicksand. Stimson argued to prohibit the export of munitions and war materials to Japan as well as imports from Japan. At a dinner party at the British embassy on July 18 he said, "The only way to treat Japan is not to give in to her on anything."[20]

The soft-liners fought an ever-losing battle. A conference requested by President Roosevelt to discuss Morgenthau's proposed moratorium on petroleum was held in late July. It included Morgenthau, the secretaries of the army and navy, and Acting Secretary of State Sumner Welles. Although Welles argued vigorously for Hull against Morgenthau regarding a proposed export licensing system for products including petroleum and scrap iron, he was able to achieve only a small compromise on July 26. The compromise on petroleum limited export restrictions to aviation motor fuel and lubricants; scrap iron restrictions were limited to Number 1 heavy melting iron and steel scrap. Stimson was elated and wrote in his diary: "We have won at a long battle, which we have been waging against Japan for about four years."[21] In fact, however, given developments in Japan, they had not won at all.

The severe economic sanctions deeply shocked citizens in every quarter of Japan. The army's general staff argued strongly on August 2 for strengthening the southern expansion policy. The first section of the navy's general staff on August 1 drew up "A Study Relating to Policy Towards French Indo-China" that echoed the army's response to the economic sanctions imposed by the United States. The conviction of the Japanese military that a "U.S. imposition of complete embargo" would make the "use of military forces toward the south . . . a matter of life and death" was confirmed by the navy's general staff toward the end of August. Such a policy also received unanimous support at a round-table conference of the middle-echelon officers of the army and navy.[22] Although the minister for naval affairs, Yoshida Zengo, opposed the use of force in the event of a complete embargo, the middle-echelon officers of the Japanese army and navy did not.

Needless to say, the ideal southern policy for Japan was one in which Japan could establish control over Indochina and the Dutch Indies so as to ensure the obtaining of essential products without resorting to the use of force and with minimal U.S. opposition. With this in mind, Foreign Minister Matsuoka began negotiations with the French ambassador to Japan, Charles Arsene-Henry, on August 1.

Matsuoka demanded economic concessions and asked for permission for Japanese troops to pass through the Tonkin region and to use airport facilities in Indochina. In addition, Kobayashi Ichizō was appointed special ambassador to the Dutch Indies on August 27 to conduct negotiations there to ensure the availability of petroleum imports of more than three million tons a year for a five-year period. The faltering of these negotiations on practical details delayed the entry of the Japanese army. Thereupon, the army and navy authorities demanded that the Japanese cabinet set a definite time limit on the negotiations, in the interest of peace.

Although the argument that an impasse in the negotiations should be met by a military advance gradually gained strength, that policy was still opposed in August at the highest level of the navy. The officers feared that a "forceful advance" might produce an "intensification of American export restrictions." On September 9, however, the middle-echelon officers in the army and navy took a firm stand in response to U.S. economic pressures. They maintained that a delay in Japan's advance would make it appear as if Japan had submitted to U.S. pressure. Finally, on September 10, with the assent of the Minister of the Navy, the army and navy agreed to issue an ultimatum. Regardless of the result of the negotiations they would advance into Indochina after September 22. This plan received final approval at the four ministers' conference of September 13.[23]

The enforcement of U.S. economic sanctions had stiffened the attitude of the middle-echelon officers and provoked them to execute the plan for a southern advance. Their action, however, escalated things further. Far from learning anything from the results of their hard-line action, the American proponents of this approach now demanded more economic sanctions to halt Japanese aggression.

Successive pieces of information regarding Japan's new demands toward Indochina and the Dutch Indies reached the U.S. government in the first two weeks of August. On August 15 Morgenthau again stressed to Hornbeck the need for a full embargo on oil to Japan. Both were convinced that such an embargo would prevent Japan from any resolute action such as occupying the Dutch East Indies. On the next day, Hornbeck told representatives of the Dutch East Indies oil companies not to submit to Japanese pressure, especially to the demand for a large quantity of aviation gasoline.

On September 6, when the Japanese troops caused an incident on the Indochina border, the U.S. cabinet witnessed a sharp exchange of words between Morgenthau and Stimson on the one hand and Hull on the other concerning the question of an embargo on petroleum.[24] Hornbeck on September 11 stressed to Stimson the need for a more active policy of restraining Japanese actions and promoting friendly relations with the Soviet Union. On September 19, after hearing about the latest Japanese ultimatum regarding Indochina, the American cabinet met again to examine the question of a complete embargo on aviation gasoline. Although Hull feared that an oil embargo would incite Japan to attack the Dutch East Indies, Stimson and Morgenthau demanded a complete embargo on oil. State Department opposition limited economic sanctions to a prohibition on the export of all grades of scrap iron.[25]

On October 5, Foreign Minister Matsuoka expressed his displeasure to Ambassador Grew at this U.S. action. He stated that "such embargoes would intensely anger the Japanese people."[26] On October 8, Ambassador Horinouchi, in a hand-delivered note to Hull, heatedly protested restrictions that he claimed constituted a "virtual embargo" and an "unfriendly act" that "may cause future relations between the United States and Japan to become 'unpredictable.' "[27]

In Japan the hard-liners now made their own miscalculations. On September 27 the Tripartite Pact between Japan, Germany, and Italy was signed. Matsuoka expected that the strengthening of the Axis would enhance Japan's position. He believed the pact would frustrate the U.S. intention to intervene in a Japanese southern advance and would lessen the possibility of the outbreak of war with the United States.

The U.S. reaction was completely contrary to what Matsuoka had divined. According to a U.S. public opinion survey of late September, the attitude toward Japan had worsened. The number of Americans favoring strong action against Japan had greatly increased. A cabinet meeting on October 4 led to the consensus that the United States would not yield one inch to Japanese intimidation. A navy squadron was proposed for sailing to the Dutch East Indies or Singapore. Furthermore, Roosevelt stated on October 12 that the United States would not be intimidated. The Tripartite Pact had failed dismally to produce the impact the Japanese hard-liners had predicted. Instead, it had exacerbated relations with the United States. Middle-echelon army officers intensified their cry for an acceleration of southern expansion. Even before the enactment of the Tripartite Pact, Japan had demanded permission to move troops into southern Indochina and did so on July 28.[28]

The Japanese pressures on Indochina led the U.S. government on July 25 to freeze Japanese assets in the United States and to impose an embargo against Japan. The lines were drawn. Hull wrote: "Nothing will stop them except force. . . . The point is how long we can maneuver the situation until the military matter in Europe is brought to a conclusion."[29] From hindsight it is curious why Hull stated such an objective but pursued policies that played into the hands of Japanese hard-liners and contributed to their escalated aggression.

Middle-echelon officers in the Japanese navy were resolved to go to war because of the oil embargo. They were anxious about the existing supply of oil turning the Japanese navy into a "scarecrow navy." A secret war diary of the army general staff noted on August 1 that the "atmosphere of the inevitability of war with England and the U.S. had gradually deepened" and on August 2 "the Military Affairs Section of the Ministry of War proposed an Imperial Conference to determine to go to war with England and the United States."[30] Simultaneously, Ambassador Grew was in a state of despair as a result of the oil embargo. He wrote, "The vicious circle of reprisals and counter reprisals is on. The obvious conclusion is eventual war."[31]

Thus, the American hard-liners' policy of first proposing and then imposing economic sanctions to deter a Japanese southern advance and war failed badly. To understand how it produced the opposite effect it is necessary to consider two miscalculations about the Japanese made by the hard-line faction of the U.S. government. One was that Japan would seek to avoid war with the United States at all costs. The other assumption followed from the first, namely that Japan would inevitably submit to unbending American resolution. However, economic pressure did not restrain Japan from a southern advance. Instead it accelerated a Japanese southern policy even at the risk of possible war with the United States.

Why had the hard-liners miscalculated? First, their predictions of Japan's reactions were based on an analysis of Japan's upper-level policymakers. They lacked an understanding of the important role played by the middle-echelon military officers in the making of Japanese foreign policy. This middle-echelon group was more adventurous, more contemptous of compromise, and more militaristic.

Second, the hard-liners were prone to making false analogies from the past. For example, Hornbeck argued that the exaggerated gestures of men such as Matsuoka in the past actually reflected a lack of Japanese resolve to wage war. Similarly, Stimson drafted an "historical memorandum as to Japan's relations with the U.S. which may

have a bearing upon the present situation." In a cabinet meeting of
October 4 he tried to apply that document's analysis of an event in
U.S.-Japanese relations at the time of the Siberian expedition. Stimson said that "in the autumn of 1919 President Wilson got his dan-
der up and put an embargo on all cotton going to Japan and a boycott on her silk, with the result that she crawled down within two
months and brought all of her troops out from Siberia like whipped
puppies."[32] This account was related to the Japanese increase of expe-
ditionary forces in Siberia in 1918 in violation of an agreement
between the two countries. Stimson either overlooked or ignored the
fact that Japanese domestic conditions in 1918 were very different
from those in 1940 in regard to both the power relationship between
the civilian leaders and the military leaders and the leadership within
the military.[33]

Third, the hard-line faction concluded that, in light of the disparity in strength between Japan and the United States, Japanese decision makers could not rationally decide on war. In this regard they
made the mistake of applying to the Japanese in unaltered form the
western model of decision making based upon rational behavior. Lack
of knowledge about the psychology of the Japanese people and especially of the middle-echelon military officers in the period immediately preceding the war led the hard-line faction to miscalculate Japanese psychology. That psychology was marked by a predisposition to
making crucial decisions in the face of extremely great, even illogical,
risks—as was expressed in Tōjō Hideki's often quoted statement that
"sometimes a man has to jump with his eyes closed, from the temple
of Kiyomizu into the ravine below." This predisposition was also
characterized by an absolute abhorrence of submission. They would
choose "death rather than humiliation." Grew understood that mentality. He wrote, "Japan is a nation of hard warriors, still inculcated
with the samurai do-or-die spirit which had by tradition and inherit-
ance become ingrained in the race.[34] He was correct in warning the
decision makers at home not to miscalculate the peculiarities in the
Japanese mode of action. Had his advice been followed the Pacific
War might very well have been avoided. Grew was prudent. The
same thing could not be said for the hard-liners.

NOTES

Reprinted from "Miscalculations in Deterrent Policy: Japanese-U.S. Relations, 1938–1941" by Hosoya Chihiro from *Journal of Peace Research,* no. 2, 1968, by permission of Norwegian University Press, Oslo. With the permission of the author, the original article has been extensively edited and adapted for presentation here.

1. Paul W. Schroeder, *The Axis Alliance and Japanese-American Relations, 1941,* (Ithaca, NY: Cornell University Press, 1958) pp. 202–204.

2. Dorothy Borg, "The United States and the Far Eastern Crisis of 1933–1938," Files of the State Department, File 771, 942/627, National Archives.

3. U.S. Department of State, *Papers Relating to the Foreign Relations of the United States,* 1938, vol. III (Washington, D.C.: 1955) pp. 535–537 (hereafter cited as *Foreign Relations Papers*).

4. Files of the State Department, File 711, 94/1396, National Archives; *Foreign Relations Papers,* 1937, vol. III, pp. 603–604.

5. *Foreign Relations Papers,* 1939, vol. III, pp. 535–537.

6. Willian Langer and S. Everett Gleason, *The Challenge to Isolation, 1937–1940,* (New York: Harper & Row, 1952), p. 150.

7. *Foreign Relations Papers,* 1938, vol. III, pp. 425–427.

8. Cordell Hull, *The Memoirs of Cordell Hull,* vol. I (New York: Macmillan, 1948), pp. 636–639; *Foreign Relations Papers,* 1938, vol. III, pp. 406–409.

9. *Foreign Relations Papers,* 1938, vol. III, pp. 406–409; Morishima Matsumoto, *Shinjuwan, Lisbon, Tokyo,* 1950, p. 1.

10. Konoe Shiryō (Konoe Documents); Nihon Kokusaiseiji Gakkai, Taiheiyō Sensō Gen-In Kenkyūbu, *Taiheiyō-sensō e no michi,* (The Road to the Pacific War), 5, 1963, pp. 161–163 (hereafter cited as *Taiheiyō-sensō e no michi).*

11. Konoe Documents, *op.cit.*

12. *Foreign Relations Papers,* 1939, vol. III, pp. 620–622.

13. Files of the State Department, File 711, 942/454, National Archives.

14. [Note that almost every author is in agreement that Hornbeck was both a hard-liner and very pro-Chinese. See Emmerson, pp. 38, 41–43, Ikei, pp. 48–49. For a recent, similar judgment by a contemporary working in the State Department, see: Edwin O. Reischauer, *My Life Between Japan and the United States,* pp. 86–87. But also note that Barnhart maintains vigorously that Hronbeck's hard-line approach was "correct."—EDS.]

15. Files of the State Department, File 711, 741/1302, National Archives; *Foreign Relations Papers,* 1939, vol. III, pp. 547–549.

16. *Taiheiyō-sensō e no michi,* 1963, vol. VII, p. 43.

17. *Foreign Relations Papers,* 1941, vol. IV, pp. 342–344. [Hull's more flexible attitude above gives some support to Professor Utley's argument that Hull was not a hard-liner, only a realist. For opposite views emphasizing Hull as an inflexible idealist see: Best, p. 30, Emmerson, p. 42, Graebner, pp. 114–116.—EDS.]

18. *Foreign Relations Papers,* 1941, vol. IV, pp. 586–587. [For an expression of this widespread view, see Emmerson, pp. 43–44.—EDS.]

19. *Foreign Relations Papers,* 1941, vol. IV, p. 588.

20. Langer and Gleason, *Challenge,* p. 721.

21. *Stimson Diary,* entry for August 1, 1940.

22. Morishima, *Shinjuwan*, p. 28; Gendai shi shiryō (Documents on contemporary history), Misuzu Shobō, Ni Chu Sensō, 30, 1965, pp. 369–371, 497–501, 504–507.

23. Ibid., pp. 386–387; *Taiheiyō-sensō e no michi*, vol. VI, pp. 216–217.

24. Herbert Feis, *The Road to Pearl Harbor: The Coming of the War between the United States and Japan* (Princeton: Princeton University Press, 1950), p. 92.

25. *Stimson Diary*, entries for September 11, 1940, and September 19, 1940.

26. Joseph C. Grew, *Ten Years in Japan* (New York: Simon and Schuster, 1944), p. 345.

27. *Foreign Relations Papers*, 1940, vol. IV, p. 608.

28. [The precise meaning of the Tripartite Pact and how it should be interpreted is a problem that the student of Japanese-American relations prior to the outbreak of the war must consider. Note the varied interpretations by Ikei, Emmerson, Hata, Graebner, and Iriye. The problem is compounded by the passage of time and the changed interpretations by successive Japanese cabinets.—EDS.]

29. Feis, *Road*, pp. 248–249.

30. Sanbō honbu (Army general staff), Sugiyama memo, n.d.

31. Feis, *Road*, pp. 248–249.

32. *Stimson Diary*, entries for October 2, 1940, and October 4, 1940.

33. Hosoya Chihiro, "Shiberia Shuppei wo Meguru Nichibei Kankei" (Japanese-American Relations and the Siberian Expedition), *Kokusai Seiji*, 1961, pp. 73–90.

34. *Foreign Relations Papers*, 1939, vol. III, pp. 606–607.

7. Hornbeck Was Right:
The Realist Approach to
American Policy toward Japan

MICHAEL BARNHART

STANLEY HORNBECK, chief of the State Department's Far Eastern Division and, after 1938, political adviser for East Asian affairs, has often been the object of criticism, even derision, for his role in America's relations with Japan before Pearl Harbor. Historians are fond of citing his prediction, eleven days before the surprise attack on the American fleet, that the odds were five to one against any war by December 15. Hornbeck, the story goes, invariably underestimated both the willingness of the Japanese Empire to risk war with the United States and that empire's ability to wage such a war. As a result, he consistently recommended hard-line policies that made a peaceful solution of the two countries' differences difficult, and perhaps impossible.

These arguments are wide of the mark. Nearly alone among the top American policymakers, Hornbeck had a clear sense of what America's interests were in East Asia, what power the United States could wield in that corner of the world, and what policies could best use that power to achieve those interests. Moreover, Hornbeck was consistently correct in his assessments of Japan's aims in the Far East.

Hornbeck believed that his country's interests were best expressed by the Open Door policy. For Hornbeck, the chief principle of that policy was respect for the territorial and administrative integrity of all nations. This was no high-sounding altruism. As long as no nation achieved hegemony over East Asia, the fundamental security of the United States would not be endangered.

Hornbeck realized that the United States was not likely to use military force to uphold this tenet. The nation's direct stake in Asia, unless hegemony actually threatened, was too small. Hornbeck maintained, however, that any effort to influence Japan or China had to be backed by a strong military. Hornbeck did not approve of bluffs. The United States, he argued throughout the decade before Pearl

Harbor, ought to make clear its positions and be prepared to support them. Military force was the ultimate, but not the only, instrument of support. Hornbeck recognized that the enviable economic strength of America—and the economic vulnerability of Japan—gave another weapon of great potency to the government he served.

Consideration of this weapon first came with the Manchurian Incident of September 1931. Soon thereafter cables from the American embassy in Tokyo were cautioning against a firm stand lest Japanese moderates opposed to territorial expansion lose ground to hotheads in a fever of Oriental patriotism. Hornbeck saw matters differently. The military had risen to power not out of some dark conspiracy or temporary aberration but because all Japanese political leaders, including civilians, agreed with the military's aims of territorial expansion abroad and reform at home.[1] The West, then, must either take concrete actions to block Japan's program or reconcile itself to an aggressive Japan in Asia. In Hornbeck's own words, it had to "put up or shut up."[2] Hornbeck believed that the brutal occupation of Manchuria called for economic pressure on Japan and held that Japan would be "reasonable" if such pressure were begun. When President Herbert Hoover dissented and Secretary of State Henry Stimson settled for American nonrecognition of Japan's conquest, Hornbeck was displeased, terming his country's response "flabby and impotent," which indeed it was.[3] Stimson's subsequent open letter to Senator William Borah, threatening an American naval buildup, was more to Hornbeck's taste.

For the next five years Hornbeck counseled silence. When Amau Eiji of the Japanese foreign office declared in April 1934 that Tokyo would oppose the efforts of all other nations to extend economic or military assistance to China, Hornbeck argued that the United States should make no strong protest. Hornbeck disagreed strongly with the thrust of the so-called Amau Doctrine, but he felt that economic or military force was not appropriate and that harsh words would only strain relations further and accomplish nothing. When pro-Japanese "autonomous regimes" were created in northern Chinese provinces around Peking, Hornbeck advised passivity on the grounds that protest would be futile. In both cases, the administration of Franklin Roosevelt agreed.

This cautious stance predictably changed after Japan dramatically escalated her drive for Asian dominion with the onset of full-scale fighting against China after the Marco Polo Bridge Incident of July

1937. The United States, Hornbeck argued, now had to choose between "peace with security" and "disapproval of aggression." The former, he warned, would be temporary if the expansionist plans of aggressive nations continued unchecked. On the other hand, an outright alliance with China was beyond America's interests. Rather coldly, Hornbeck conceded that although a decisive defeat for China had to be avoided, the continuation of the Sino-Japanese War made it unlikely that Tokyo would risk war against the British or Americans as well. The best course, therefore, was to aid China while avoiding direct involvement.

Within a year, Hornbeck's watchful concern grew to alarm. After literally scores of new laws, including the powerful National General Mobilization Law, were passed by the Japanese Diet, Hornbeck rightly concluded that the military and expansionist elements were using the patriotism generated by the war in China to revolutionize the Japanese economy and place it firmly under martial control. He feared that the result would be a militaristic Japan that would devote all its energies to aggression. This in turn would compel the United States to enlarge its own naval forces in self-defense. Hornbeck fully realized the expense that would be involved and was all the more appalled that the Japanese buildup was fueled largely by exports of American scrap iron, machine tools, and petroleum products to Japan. It made no sense, Hornbeck argued, to engage in "any economic transaction with those nations which can in any sense be construed as facilitating their armaments and therefore their potential danger to peaceful nations."[4] He therefore supported, from 1938 to 1941, efforts to impose economic pressure on Japan by denying the shipments of strategic American materials.

Until 1940 he labored largely in vain. After Japan used American-made equipment in the bombings of Chinese civilians, public pressure compelled the Roosevelt administration to call for a "moral embargo" on exports of aircraft, air munitions, and aeronautical equipment to Tokyo. The embargo did not, however, have the force of law and did not include the materials the Japanese used to construct bombers and bombs. In the meantime, representatives of special purchasing missions sponsored by the Japanese military visited the United States to secure large quantities of the most crucial commodities. Hornbeck railed against the moral embargo. It simply prodded Japan to buy goods in anticipation of further cutoffs—thus rendering these cutoffs less effective when they were applied. What was needed was "a calculated program of positive pressure" to inhibit the buildup of war materials in Japan.

The pressures adopted in Washington were anything but calculated. Hornbeck's colleagues in the State Department did not want to give the appearance of antagonizing Japan by adopting measures designed directly against her. Consequently, they allowed cutoffs of exports in the spring and summer of 1940—but only when justified by the need to conserve materials for America's own growing armament needs. The effect was to embargo shipments of aviation gasoline and high-quality scrap iron in July—not out of any consideration about how the embargo might affect relations with Tokyo but because the bureaucrats in charge of the defense effort certified that these materials were necessary in America.

To be sure, the State Department remained involved in deciding which materials were to be embargoed. As its officials became increasingly convinced (long after Hornbeck had been) that Japan did endanger American security interests, they allowed more goods to be banned. Shipments of all types of scrap iron and an array of exotic alloy metals were stopped after Japan allied with Nazi Germany and Fascist Italy in September. Embargoes on machine tools and industrial equipment shortly followed.

Embargoes on oil, however, did not. As 1941 dawned the United States was still selling all grades of petroleum products except the very highest quality aviation gasoline. Hornbeck shook his head. The United States, he wrote in January, not only was supplying crude oil that could easily be refined into aviation gasoline for Japanese warplanes, but also was supplying Tokyo with oil tanks and drums to allow Japan to build up her reserves of all petroleum products. Moreover, the Japanese were rapidly increasing their purchases of these products in early 1941.

Japan's occupation of southern French Indochina in late July, a step that directly endangered British and Dutch possessions in Asia just as London was fighting alone against the Nazis in Europe, finally compelled Roosevelt to consider an oil embargo. Even then, many in the State Department opposed a complete cutoff, arguing that Japan would be provoked into an attack on British Malaya and the oil-rich Dutch East Indies. Hornbeck dismissed these fears. The United States could not allow the possibility of war with Japan to deter it from taking steps advantageous to its own interests. These interests, now more than ever, Hornbeck went on, clearly dictated checking Japan's efforts to stockpile additional oil. The Japanese either would or would not attack on the basis of their own considerations, and they would not attack the British and Dutch if they knew that this meant an unwinnable war against America.

The oil embargo was implemented by freezing all Japanese assets in the United States, effectively depriving Japan of the means to purchase any American goods, petroleum included. Rather belatedly, the Japanese cabinet led by Prince Konoe Fumimaro realized the price they were to pay for seizing French Indochina. Konoe appealed to Roosevelt for a summit conference to resolve Japanese-American differences. Hornbeck was wary of any meeting. The Chinese, the British, and the American people would see it as a Far Eastern Munich. Hornbeck's main objection was, however, even more apt: could Konoe truly commit the Japanese army and navy to any agreements he might make? Roosevelt declined to meet the Japanese leader.

Informal negotiations, going on since April, still offered some hope for avoiding armed conflict. These reached their end in the final offer, called Proposal B, from Japan in late November. The Japanese asked for a restoration of U.S.-Japanese trade relations before the asset freeze of July (meaning a resumption of American oil shipments), American help to enable Japan to procure materials, including oil, from the Dutch East Indies, and an American promise not to "hinder" peace efforts between Japan and China (meaning an end of American aid to the Chinese). In exchange, the Japanese offered to withdraw their troops from the southern half of Indochina.

Hornbeck opposed acceptance. Japan's final offer would make an immediate attack on British and Dutch holdings unlikely. But what would happen in the spring of 1942 when, for all the military experts could tell, Britain or Russia or both might be knocked out of the war? For that matter, Proposal B, if agreed to, promised the virtual defeat of China while the United States provided Japan with additional stockpiles of oil! The United States government rejected Proposal B.

The result was the unforeseen attack on Pearl Harbor and the equally unforeseen Japanese victories of the spring of 1942. Nevertheless, historians should not allow perfect hindsight to cloud their judgments of the past. We know now that Britain, Russia, and China survived into 1942 and beyond. We know now that everyone in the West badly underestimated the prowess of the Japanese military—at least over the short term. Yet with this hindsight, with our far deeper

and surer knowledge of the inner workings of the Japanese government and the state of the Japanese economy, present-day scholars
ought to conclude that Hornbeck's judgments were correct ones.

First, the United States would have been better off by following
Hornbeck's advice more consistently than it did. Hornbeck has been
identified, and properly so, with the advocacy of economic pressure
against Japan. The invasion of Manchuria in 1931 was begun by a
group of junior officers, with the tacit but reluctant support of their
superiors in Tokyo. Those superiors had advised delay, fearing adverse
international reaction. If the United States had announced its determination to shut off exports, Japan would have been in an impossible
position. The Imperial Army of 1931 had virtually no stockpiles of oil
or other strategic materials. The Imperial Navy's storage program had
barely left the ground. This same realization six years later, after the
start of the war against China, was voiced by top economic officers in
the army. These men openly conceded that an embargo on American
oil, scrap iron, machine tools, or a host of other goods would have
been catastrophic. They were clearly relieved when their special
purchasing missions to the United States had all their orders filled.

It is not likely that even severe American economic pressure would
have deflected Japan from its basic goal of domination once the war
against China was well underway. Too much came to be invested in
that conflict for the Japanese. Hornbeck's call for a program of calculated pressures was designed as much to weaken Japan in any coming
clash with the United States as to cripple her attempts to subjugate
China. Had the United States, for example, limited its exports of
scrap iron and oil from 1938 to 1941 to "normal, peacetime"
amounts, as Hornbeck advocated, Japan would have found it impossible to support two massive campaigns in China—one against Nanking, one against Wuhan—while simultaneously constructing the
navy that would deal such sharp defeats to the West in 1941–1942.

Second, Hornbeck's policies, when they were followed, served
America's national interests well. Frequently the argument is raised
that the United States ought to have pursued a less hard-line policy so
to have encouraged the resurgence of Japanese "moderates." These
moderates, it continues, then would have redirected Japanese policy
back toward a closer alignment with the West or, at the least, have
agreed to some sort of *modus vivendi* that would have averted war.[5]

This reasoning does not stand scrutiny. Hornbeck maintained
Washington's silence in the face of the irritating Amau Doctrine and

the provocative creation of pro-Japanese regimes in northern China. Why did not the Japanese moderates emerge then? The sad fact is that there were no Japanese moderates with the will or ability to deflect their country from the course chosen for it by the military and the aggressive civilian leaders like Konoe. When Konoe—who had presided over the start of the war with China, who had promoted the mobilization law, and who had supported the seizure of Indochina— comprehended that his policies were leading to a collision with America, he tried to step back. As Hornbeck correctly understood, however, by the autumn of 1941 even a prime minister could not stop what had become an indelible policy that directly threatened American interests.

Proposal B could have been accepted, buying the United States time—perhaps as much as six or nine months—to build more planes and ships and to train more soldiers. Again, however, Hornbeck held the wider view. Buying more time might have been good for the United States, but it held great danger for the allies: Britain, the Soviet Union, and, most of all, China. The survival of these allies was, as the experience of the war that came showed, of greater interest to the United States.[6]

Reflecting on his government's rejection of Proposal B, Hornbeck wrote the memo giving 5–1 odds against war with Japan by December 15. The historians who chide Hornbeck for this errant forecast should read his memo's conclusions:

> There is no warrant for any feeling on our part that the situation in the Pacific has been made worse, as regards the interests of the United States by refusal on the part of the American Government to make a deal with Japan in terms of "concessions" by us in return for "pledges" (qualified and hedged around pledges) by Japan to keep the peace while continuing to make war and to prepare for more war. Japan has been at *war* in eastern Asia and the western Pacific for several years past. Japan has threatened to make war on each and every one of her near neighbors and even on the United States. No price that we might have paid to Japan would buy or produce peace in the Pacific or security for the United States (and/or Great Britain and/or China and/or Russia) in the Pacific.
>
> The question of more war or less war in the Pacific rests at this moment in the control of minds and hearts in Tokyo, not in the control of minds and hearts in Washington.[7]

Hornbeck was right.[8]

NOTES

1. [Fewer historians today, compared to thirty years ago, would disagree with the view that "all Japanese political leaders, including civilians, agreed with the military aims" of territorial expansion in Manchuria, but they would qualify that greatly by adding a key element of timing.—EDS.]

2. Memorandum, 5 December 1931, Box 453, Stanley K. Hornbeck Papers (Stanford, Calif.: Hoover Institution).

3. [No historians in this volume and few outside of it would disagree with Professor Barnhart that Hornbeck was correct in this instance.—EDS.]

4. Memorandum, 14 February 1938, Box 457, Stanley K. Hornbeck Papers (Stanford, Calif.: Hoover Institution).

5. [We can see here that Barnhart flatly denies Hosoya's thesis (and to a lesser extent the views of Utley, Ikei, Emmerson, and Tsunoda) that a soft-line policy would have aided Japanese moderates. He even denies that there were any Japanese moderates with that kind of will or ability. The answer to these questions may lie less in the area of diplomatic history than in a greater knowledge of domestic Japanese politics in the 1930s. For this reason Iriye's essay seems significant in his belief that Japanese politics were more volatile and fragile. Tsunoda's interpretation of moderate Foreign Minister Togo's reaction to the Hull ultimatum is a dramatic contradiction of Barnhart's view. For a limited discussion of who the moderates were see the Hosoya and Conroy essays.—EDS.]

6. [Here Barnhart, like Best and Ikei, is speculating about the impact of a delay in the outbreak of the war. Professor Ikei cannot prove that the delay of the war for six months would have prevented war, but Barnhart offers no evidence to support his interesting view that a delay would have been harmful to America's allies. Were Britain and China in such imminent danger of falling that another six months' delay would have proved catastrophic? Did the Soviet Union's success in forcing a German retreat three weeks after Pearl Harbor have any relationship to the otubreak of the Pacific War? For a directly opposite view, see Ikei.—EDS.]

7. U.S. Department of State, *Papers Relating to the Foreign Relations of the United States, 1941,* vol. 4 (Washington, D.C., 1941).

8. [Contrast Barnhart's conclusion with Best's judgment that those who wanted war with Japan were wrong in terms of long-range American interests.—EDS.]

8. The Road to the Pacific War

HATA IKUHIKO[1]

WAS the Pacific War inevitable? Historians, both American and Japanese, have advanced various theories on the subject of who was responsible for starting the war. So far, they have not reached a conclusion. The Japanese government sought justification for the war in the Hull Note, which demanded that Japan retreat to her position of pre-Manchurian Incident days. However, on the very day the Hull Note was received, a Japanese task force left its secret base in the Kurile Islands for its surprise attack on Pearl Harbor. Inasmuch as most wars are the culmination of a gradually deteriorating crisis situation, it is not appropriate to try to find the turning point between war and peace a few days before the outbreak of the war.[2] In this writer's opinion, the point of no return on the road to the Pacific War was the formation of the Tripartite (Axis) alliance in the fall of 1940.[3]

Foreign Minister Matsuoka Yōsuke, who promoted the idea of the Tripartite Pact, had a grand illusion of global strategy. It was to add the USSR to the alliance. By doing so, he reasoned, the balance of power could be restored as a dichotomy between the Eurasian and the American continents. However, the realization of his illusion went no further than the signing of a neutrality pact between Japan and the USSR.

By "shaking hands with the Satan" of Nazism through the formation of the Axis alliance, Japan became unequivocally an enemy of the United States. China, which was at the brink of disintegration, sensed this and resolved to continue her fight against Japan. The USSR was driven into the American camp by Germany's incomprehensible attack on Soviet Russia. The confrontation between the Axis powers and the anti-Axis powers turned into that of the have nations and the have-not nations. For a war in which material wealth and

Translated by Taeko Wellington

73

technology were to become deciding factors, the outcome was self-evident from the beginning.

When he made his decision to plunge into the war, Prime Minister Tōjō was in a desperate state of mind; to justify his policies he quoted the Japanese, saying that it is sometimes necessary to "jump from the high terrace of Kiyomizu temple *(Kiyomizu no butai kara tobioriru)*."[4] He was given the unfortunate role of reaping the harvest of the seeds of mistrust that Japan had sowed during the ten years since the Manchurian Incident. Unless he was willing to abandon everything Japan had gained to that point—which was almost an impossibility—he could not expect any kind of concession from the United States, whose determination to strike down Japan was forged on the day the Tripartite Alliance was formed.

NOTES

1. [For a more detailed analysis, see Hata's essay entitled "From Mukden to Pearl Harbor" in Harry Wray and Hilary Conroy, eds., *Japan Examined: Perspectives on Modern Japanese History* (Honolulu: University of Hawaii Press, 1983). This is included in a section entitled "Japan's Foreign Policy in the 1930's: Search for Autonomy or Naked Aggression?" In June 1987, at the Pacific Coast regional conference of the Association for Asian Studies, Professor Hata presented a paper entitled "The Marco Polo Bridge Incident and Chiang Kai-shek's Decision to Fight."—EDS.]

2. [Contrast Hata's pessimistic view with the more optimistic views of Conroy, Klein, Tsunoda, Emmerson, Ikei, Hosoya, and Graebner that the potential to avoid war existed through November 1941.—EDS.]

3. [We see here the interpretation that the Tripartite Pact created a point of no return in Japanese-American relations. On this point, our essayists do not divide along nationalist lines. Hosoya, Iriye, Ikei, and Tsunoda do not agree. They interpret the alliance as either a defensive strategy or an action taken for domestic political considerations. In addition, Murakami interprets the Pact as intended to prevent Roosevelt from interfering in European and Asian affairs and to provide the opportunity for Japan to expand into Southeast Asia. She agrees, however, that the hard-liners in the Roosevelt administration seized upon it as proof of Japan's intention to cooperate with Germany and Italy to divide the world among them.—EDS.]

4. [Once again we see an irrational element attributed to Japanese foreign policy. For a related view see Mark C. Michelson's essay, "Fogbound in Tokyo: Domestic Politics in Japan's Foreign Policymaking," in Wray and Conroy's, *Japan Examined*. In their essays, Murakami and Fujiwara strongly disagree that the army's actions reflected irrational behavior. On the contrary, they argue that those actions were deliberate and well-planned.—EDS.]

9. Cordell Hull and the Diplomacy of Inflexibility

Jonathan G. Utley

Diplomacy ended on November 26, 1941. A tired and defeated Secretary of State Cordell Hull handed two Japanese envoys a statement of the extreme American position, brushed aside their protests, and washed his hands of the whole affair; it was now in the hands of the army and navy. Within two weeks the United States and Japan would be in a war Hull had labored to avoid. Since the outbreak of the Sino-Japanese War in July 1937, the secretary had spent more time and energy on the Japanese problem than on any other issue. He had refused to give in to the storm-cellar isolationists who favored pulling out of Asia, and he blocked the hard-liners who would have waged economic warfare against Japan. Tough, resolute, and doggedly singleminded, Cordell Hull framed a pragmatic policy that served the nation well during the first two years of the Sino-Japanese War. Unfortunately, by 1940 Hull was perpetuating a policy that no longer suited the changing situation in Asia. His inability to adapt to a changing world order pushed Japanese-American relations so far toward war that by the fall of 1941 neither nation could avoid the final plunge.

It is easy to dismiss Hull's inflexibility as idealism run rampant, as the short-sighted policies of a man who could only mumble about the principles of right conduct and the sanctity of treaties. Hull did believe in certain principles, not the least of which was the sanctity of treaties. However, a closer examination of his diplomatic actions reveals that this former judge who had ridden circuit in the hills of Tennessee during the late nineteenth century and had expanded his influence within the Democratic party over two decades in Congress understood how to use power. His failure should be attributed not to idealism or weakness but to his determination that Japanese-American differences be resolved rather than papered over.[1]

Hull despised Japanese aggression in China. He grieved over the loss of life, was concerned about the expulsion of American cultural and commercial interests, and was angered by Japan's blatant disregard of treaties and its use of force in China. The secretary worried that Japan's actions might convince people around the world that aggression was a perfectly acceptable way to resolve differences between nations. So Hull drafted a statement of what he considered to be the right conduct of nations (avoidance of war, respect for treaties, free trade, etc.). He labeled it the "Eight Pillars of Peace" and circulated it to the nations of the world. In August 1937, with great fanfare, he published the responses. As Hull publicly endorsed the principles of right conduct, however he also accepted the realities of Japanese conquests and even went so far as to urge China to negotiate with Japan to keep the war from spreading into Shanghai.[2] In these first few months of the war, Hull, like almost everyone in Washington, assumed that Japan would defeat the Chinese armies, extend control over five northern provinces of China, and force that beleaguered country to accept the new order. Although he disapproved of this the secretary realized that the United States lacked the military power to stop Japan and, more important, that U.S. interests in China were too small to warrant confronting Japan with either military or economic sanctions. The realities of power and self-interest underlay Hull's policy of not provoking Japan (not even name calling) while also refusing to assent to Japanese gains. He would wait until the war was over and then determine if any American interests might be salvaged.

During the first six months of the war the battle ran true to form. Japanese armies won victory after victory, occupying more and more Chinese territory. But Japan could not compel China to surrender. Chinese armies fell back and continued to fight, while guerilla activities behind Japanese lines expanded. Japan was trapped in a war it could not win. By early 1938, this reality began to sink into the minds of American foreign policy managers, and it fit nicely with Hull's established policy of waiting. Now, however, Hull was not waiting for Japan to win but for Japan to wear itself out and come to its senses.

Many people within the Roosevelt administration and across the country believed that Hull's cautious policy was too weak and urged stronger action, particularly economic pressure. In response to this pressure, in July 1938 the State Department proclaimed a "moral embargo" on the sale of aircraft to nations that were bombing civilians from the air. Although no nation was mentioned by name, Japan was the only one currently in that category. In December of the same year, the United States loaned China $25 million. Then in July 1939, Hull notified Japan that, after the obligatory six-month waiting period, the Japanese-American trade treaty would be abrogated. After January 1940, the United States could embargo any exports to Japan, including the oil Japan required to survive.

On the surface, such actions might appear to be a program of economic warfare against Japan. In reality, however, they were only annoyances that carefully avoided any serious pressure.[3] The moral embargo quieted a public that was angry over Japanese aerial attacks of Chinese civilians, but it did not stop Japan from buying parts, aviation gasoline, and scrap iron for its air war. Similarly, abrogation of the trade treaty silenced members of Congress who were contemplating a mandatory embargo on exports to Japan, and when the treaty ended, Hull took great care to see that the fire-eaters in the government did not impose economic sanctions.[4]

From 1937, Hull demonstrated in these and many other ways that Japan could do nothing in China to provoke a war with the United States because there was no vital national interest at stake in China. To Hull it seemed a safe policy. He would not risk war with Japan. He would wait for Japan to abandon the path of forceful aggression in favor of peaceful commercial expansion. It may not have been very assertive, but Hull thought it prudent.[5]

The American ambassador, Joseph C. Grew, disagreed. It was unrealistic to expect the Sino-Japanese War, no matter how long it dragged on, to topple the Japanese military. Eventually, Grew believed, hawks in the United States would succeed in imposing economic sanctions against Japan that would prompt Japan to retaliate, perhaps militarily. To break this spiral toward war, in the fall of 1939 Grew bluntly warned Japanese leaders that if they continued expelling American interests from China, Japan and the United States would eventually go to war. He urged Japanese moderates in the government to make a conciliatory offer to the United States. What he received was a promise to open part of the Yangtze River to commercial traffic at some unspecified date. In return, Japan wanted to negotiate a trade treaty to replace the one that was about to expire. Less than what Grew hoped for, it was better than nothing, and he urgently requested Hull to respond to the Japanese offer with an equally conciliatory action.

At this point, Cordell Hull made his first major tactical error; he refused to make a concession to Japan. His reasons were quite logical.

He assumed that Japan's rather small offering reflected a change of tactics, not a change of policy. If he opened negotiations for a new trade treaty now, it would send the wrong signals to the Japanese and raise hopes that ultimately must be dashed. A concession might bring a momentary easing of tension, but Hull was not interested in a momentary respite. He sought a lasting peace in Asia that could come only when Japanese moderates regained control of their country. Until then he would keep pressure on Japan, but always short of the economic sanctions that could provoke a war.[6]

In retrospect, by refusing to respond in kind to the Japanese offer, Hull weakened the already precarious position of the moderates in Japan. Ambassador Grew had already raised hopes of a settlement; Hull's intransigence crushed these hopes in January 1940 and undercut what little influence the moderates still had in Tokyo. It is questionable whether, at this late date, anything Hull could have done would have strengthened the moderates enough to allow them to break the military's control over Japanese foreign policy. But the secretary's insistence upon a total resolution of differences rather than a partial easing of tension sent Japanese-American relations, as Joe Grew warned, "downhill toward war."[7]

Hull's all-or-nothing diplomacy might have been defensible had not German armies overrun the Netherlands, conquered France, and placed Britain in jeopardy of invasion. Those events broke British power in East Asia, left the French colony of Indochina vulnerable to Japan, and raised the specter of Japanese control over the oil-rich Dutch East Indies. To the United States, Japan in Southeast Asia was quite a different matter from Japan in China. Strategically, Southeast Asia was linked to Europe. If Germany seized the Suez Canal and Japan dominated Southeast Asia, the two powers would be linked through the Indian Ocean, and Germany would gain access to rubber, tin, oil, and a host of other raw materials of Southeast Asia. Britain would be cut off from the resources and manpower of British India, Australia, and New Zealand. If that happened, it might be impossible to break the Japanese-German Axis.

In addition to the strategic importance of Southeast Asia, there were strong, long-term economic reasons to keep that region out of Japanese hands. Roosevelt, Hull, and most American national leaders looked upon the world as an economic unit. Progress and prosperity came only if there was freedom to trade: a system of liberal commercialism. Japan and Germany espoused an autarkic system in which a nation carved out a sphere of influence for its exclusive use. The loss of China to such autarkic control was not important enough for the United States to fight Japan. But if Japan should extend its autarkic control over Southeast Asia as well, the impact on the world's economy would be intolerable.[8]

Thus, both for short-term strategic and long-term economic reasons, Hull could live with Japan in China but would not tolerate Japan's expansion into Southeast Asia. Notable by their absence from this analysis are the idealistic issues of morality and sanctity of treaties. Hull still believed in such principles and never missed an opportunity to support them with words. However, where words sufficed in defense of fundamental principles, action was required in defense of areas strategically and economically vital to the United States.

As German armies smashed through France in the spring of 1940, Japan began to edge toward the vulnerable East Indies. Hull responded with a sharp warning to Japan. His words were supported by the transfer of the U.S. fleet from its base in southern California to the Hawaiian Islands, two thousand miles closer to Japan. But Japan was not deterred. In September it occupied the northern half of French Indochina, and another sharp warning came from Washington, this time in the form of an embargo on the export of scrap metal to Japan.

By the spring of 1941, there was little reason for optimism. Japan appeared determined to expand into an area the United States considered vital. At some point, Hull was not sure just where the United States would draw the line and confront Japan. In the midst of these deteriorating relations, Hull met with Japanese Ambassador Nomura Kichisaburō in a series of one-on-one conversations to see if Japanese-American differences could be peacefully resolved. In these talks Hull took a very hard line. He refused to accept private assurances that Japan would remain neutral in the event of a U.S.-German war and insisted that Japan publicly renounce its military alliance with Germany (the Tripartite Pact). The secretary refused to consider anything less than total Japanese withdrawal from China and Southeast Asia (although Hull did not include Manchuria, by name, in these demands). Not unexpectedly, Japan rejected such sweeping demands, and the talks deadlocked.[9]

Hull's intransigence in these discussions sprang from his assessment of Japanese intentions. He believed that war would come if Japan continued its expansion into Southeast Asia. Since Japanese militarists were committed to that expansion, war could be avoided only if moderates replaced the militarists in the Japanese government. The concessions Hull demanded of Japan were designed to break the power of the militarists. For example, because extremists in Japan favored the alliance with Germany, Hull pressed for a public renunciation of the alliance rather than private assurances. Hull also insisted on a total and humiliating Japanese withdrawal from China that he hoped would discredit the military.[10] A limited face-saving withdrawal from China would only extricate the army from an embarrassing war it could not win, perpetuate the militarists in power, and enable Japan to redirect men and material toward Southeast Asia.[11]

Hull's analysis was correct. Only a debacle could break the power of the military in Japan, but that debacle did not come during the four years of the Sino-Japanese War. It came after nearly four additional years of fighting across the Pacific, the fire bombing of Japanese cities, the atomic bombing of two of those cities, and a military occupation by the United States. To expect Japan to undergo such a regeneration in 1941 because of the war in China was to wish for the moon. If Hull was to avoid the slide toward war he would have to seek limited, small agreements designed to deal with immediate tensions. But Hull thought such agreements useless, even counterproductive, in the search for a lasting peace in Asia. This was his second major tactical error. The kind of settlement Hull envisioned was probably beyond the realm of possibility. It was certainly wishful thinking to believe it could be achieved in just a few weeks of negotiations. Nonetheless, he made the effort—an effort that was doomed to failure.

While diplomacy was stalled, Japan continued its military expansion by occupying the southern half of French Indochina in July 1941. The United States responded by freezing Japanese assets, which ended all trade with Japan. Unable to get oil to fuel its war machine, Japan was forced to choose between acceding to American demands or pushing south to take the oil in the Dutch East Indies.

By August 1941, Cordell Hull found himself in a diplomatic predicament from which he did not know how to escape. Japanese Premier Konoe Fumimaro thought that one way out was a personal meeting with Roosevelt to cut through the diplomatic haggling and find a common ground for a Japanese-American agreement. Hull strongly objected and talked his chief out of the idea. If Japan was ready to abandon its aggression in Asia, Hull argued, no meeting was necessary; if it was not prepared to do so, a summit would be worse than useless. Hull worried that a Roosevelt-Konoe meeting and the vaguely worded statement that would inevitably emerge at the end of such a meeting would demoralize China and lead to the collapse of Chinese resistance. Continued Chinese military resistance to Japan was an essential part of American strategic plans. The War Department was rapidly building up defenses in the Philippine Islands. Army tacticians were confident that if the diplomats could avoid a war until the spring of 1942 the Philippines would be invulnerable to any Japanese assault. This conclusion was based on the premise that Chinese resistance would continue to tie down a million Japanese soldiers in China. Hull's problem was that if he negotiated an agreement that bought the time the Army tacticians demanded, China might feel betrayed and give up on the war. If he did not make some concession to Japan, Japan would probably launch an attack against the Philippines before their defenses were completed. To find a way out of this dilemma required flexibility, energy, and confidence.[12] Hull had never demonstrated flexibility; he was running out of energy and confidence.

November 1941 was Cordell Hull's low point. He had gone over the items dividing Japan and the United States so many times that he had nothing new to offer. Attempts to reach a permanent settlement had failed, and Hull could not bring himself to draft a *modus vivendi,* a temporary diplomatic agreement, that would resolve nothing but postpone a war. Seeing diplomacy dead in the water, a few lower-echelon officers in the State Department proposed a far-reaching Japanese-American agreement that would guarantee Japan access to the markets and raw materials it was trying to take by force. Such a proposal went too far for the men who controlled American foreign policy. Hull showed no interest in it, and foreign policy managers in the State, War, and Navy departments vetoed any significant concessions to Japan. By November 22 the original proposal had been transformed into a cautious *modus vivendi* in which the United States would sell Japan limited amounts of oil unsuitable for making aviation gasoline if Japan withdrew its troops from southern Indochina and limited troops in northern Indochina to 25,000.[13]

Before making the offer to Japan, Hull talked with the British, Australian, Dutch, and Chinese representatives in Washington. The British were unenthusiastic, and the Chinese were adamantly opposed. The Chinese ambassador warned that it would appear as a betrayal and might mean the collapse of Chinese resistance. Worn down by nearly eight months of diplomatic negotiation, Hull was physically exhausted and emotionally drained. The tremendous burden he had been carrying had taken its toll. When the Chinese and British objected to his plan, the secretary felt betrayed and gave up.[14]

It was Hull's decision to "kick the whole thing over" (Hull's words) and give up on diplomacy. But his decision of November 26 had little bearing on the course of Japanese-American relations. Both nations had moved too far toward war to avoid slipping over the edge. As the primary architect of U.S. policy toward Asia during 1937–1941, Hull must accept a major share of the responsibility for the failure of diplomacy. If we are going to blame him, however, we should do it for the right reasons.

Hull was not motivated by an impulse to defend to the death the ideal of sanctity of treaties whenever and wherever it was challenged. Nor was he prepared to fight Japan to save the Chinese or the Open Door policy in China. Instead, Hull's view of vital national interests rested on a deeply held belief that the American way of life depended on the preservation of a world economic system that allowed free access to resources and markets.[15] Japan was the enemy not because it violated treaties and waged a horrendous war against the Chinese people (although Hull certainly hated these actions) but because it sought to bring all of East and Southeast Asia into its autarkic sphere to the detriment of the United States, Asia, and (Hull believed) ultimately Japan as well. Hull's views in this regard were shared by virtually every policy manager in Washington; that thinking had been at the center of American foreign policy for generations. To the extent to which this ideology was responsible for the coming of the war, we cannot single out Cordell Hull for any special responsibility.

If we are going to criticize Hull at all, it should be for his tactics. For years he waited and hoped that the war in China would prove so burdensome that the Japanese people would rebel, cast off their militaristic rulers, and turn toward peaceful commercial expansionism.[16] When Japanophobes urged strong action, Hull said we will wait. When voices more sensitive to the needs of Japan, Ambassador Grew's for example, urged conciliation, Hull said we will wait. It was not until 1941, when Japanese-American relations were fast deteriorating toward war, that Hull actively sought an agreement with Japan. Then he would settle for nothing less than Japan's total regeneration. The resolution of complex diplomatic problems is not, however, achieved through such sudden transformations. Unable to resolve fundamental differences with Japan, Hull should have sought a way for Japan and the United States to peacefully coexist with their differences. But that was not Hull's style. His was the diplomacy of all or nothing. He fell short of all and ended up with nothing.

NOTES

1. [Contrast this new interpretation of Hull's ideological orientation and diplomatic approach with the more traditional view of Hull in the essays by Emmerson, Hosoya, Tsunoda, Graebner, and Conroy.—EDS.]

2. Jonathan G. Utley, *Going to War with Japan, 1937-1941* (Knoxville: University of Tennessee Press, 1985), pp. 4–8.

3. [Readers should note the strikingly different interpretation of the impact that economic sanctions had on the Japanese in the essays by Emmerson and Hosoya. Is the reason for the differences that Utley is a student of American diplomatic history and Emmerson and Hosoya are reflecting a greater sensitivity to internal Japanese politics because of their residence in Japan, specializations, or other factors?—EDS.]

4. Utley, *Going to War,* pp. 35–37, 44–50, 64–81.

5. [Note the agreement between Barnhart and Utley in their interpretations of the actions of Hull and Hornbeck during this period. They differ, however, on the question of whether American policy could have assisted Japanese moderates to create a more accommodating foreign policy.—EDS.]

6. Utley, *Going to War,* pp. 71–72.

7. Grew to Hull, telegram, 18 December 1939, U.S. Department of State, *Papers Relating to the Foreign Relations of the United States, 1939* (Washington, D.C.: 1955), p. 622; Waldo H. Heinrichs, Jr., *American Ambassador: Joseph C. Grew and the Development of the United States Diplomatic Tradition* (Boston: Little Brown, 1966), pp. 297–310.

8. Utley, *Going to War,* pp. 67–69, 85–87, 90–91. [Contrast Utley's views on the importance of Southeast Asia in Japan's eyes with the view expressed in other essays, particularly those of Murakami, Graebner, and Fujiwara. The latter strongly deny the importance of Southeast Asia. They emphasize that region's importance only to the much higher stakes in China. See Barnhart's essay here and also in Harry Wray and Hilary Conroy, *Japan Examined* (Honolulu: University of Hawaii Press, 1983), for a view close to Utley's on the issues of autarky, economic sanctions, and 'realism' in American foreign policy for this period.—EDS.]

9. U.S. Department of State, *Foreign Relations, Japan 1931-41,* vol. 2 (Washington, D.C.: 1943), pp. 429–477.

10. [Hull's assessment of what would happen to the position of the military if a demand for Japan's total withdrawal from China occurred was diametrically opposed to that of Grew, a man who had been in Japan almost ten years. The question can be validly raised of what good it is to place an ambassador in a country if his, and his

staff's, assessment of domestic events and psychology is not only ignored but given an opposite conclusion in making policy.—EDS.]

11. Utley, *Going to War,* pp. 145–149.

12. Ibid., pp. 158–165.

13. Ibid., pp. 165–172.

14. Ibid., pp. 173–175. [On these points there is agreement with the Klein-Conroy and Graebner essays.—EDS.]

15. [Best's essay emphasizes Roosevelt and his foreign economic policy as nationalistic, but Utley's interpretation is the more traditional one of being internationalist in motivation.—EDS.]

16. [Contrast Hull's view that such a rebellion would lead Japan to a peaceful accommodation with the United States with that of Fujiwara. Fujiwara's assessment of both military and civilian officials' fears is that the Japanese public would demand a more bellicose, intransigent foreign policy. Hull's attitude may reflect the American view that the general public is inherently democratic and anti-war—a view that is open to serious question.—EDS.]

President Roosevelt signs the conscription law, 16
September 1940. Witnesses, from left: Secretary of War
Henry L. Stimson, Representative Andrew J. May
(chairman of the House Military Affairs Commission),
General George C. Marshall (army chief of staff),
Senator Morris Sheppard (Senate Military Affairs Com-
mission). Photograph from Mainichi Shinbunsha.

Joseph C. Grew, U.S. ambassador
to Japan, 1933–1941. Photograph
from Mainichi Shinbunsha.

From left: Army Minister Tōjō, Italian Ambassador Indelli, German Special Ambassador Heinrich Stahmer, Premier Konoe Fumimaro, Foreign Minister Matsuoka Yōsuke, German Ambassador Eugene Ott. Photograph from Mainichi Shinbunsha.

From left: Nomura Kichisaburō, Cordell Hull, Kurusu Saburō. 1941. Photograph from Mainichi Shinbunsha.

Matsuoka Yosuke, 22 April 1941. Photograph from Mainichi Shinbunsha.

From old to new premier, 20 October 1941. Left, Konoe Fumimaro; right, Tōjō Hideki. Photograph from Mainichi Shinbunsha.

Stanley K. Hornbeck. Photograph
from Mainichi Shinbunsha.

Tōjō cabinet ministers, 77th Diet emergency meeting, November 1941. Photograph
from Mainichi Shinbunsha.

10. On the So-Called Hull-Nomura Negotiations

TSUNODA JUN

FOREIGN Minister Tōgō Shigenori was the recipient of the so-called Hull Note on November 27, 1941. He had been removed as ambassador to Germany in 1938 because of his anti-Nazi position. Transferred to Moscow he again fell victim two years later to the so-called "Matsuoka cyclone" that removed all ambassadors considered to be friendly to the United States and Great Britain. After his return to Tokyo, Tōgō refused to submit his resignation as a gesture of protest against what he considered to be an inappropriate action by Foreign Minister Matsuoka.

Tōgō's most recent experiences showed clearly that he was still anti-Germany and pro-United States. In October 1941, when General Tōjō asked him to join his cabinet, Tōgō was impressed by Tōjō's pledge that he would adopt a foreign policy that could lead to either war or peace, but that in the meantime in deference to the emperor's wish he would establish national policy so as to place priority on the pursuit of peace. Encouraged by this statement, Tōgō agreed to join as foreign minister.

After reading the pertinent documents relating to the recent talks between the United States and Japan, Tōgō concluded that the United States might choose to go to war with Japan. He immediately determined that Japan had to make substantial concessions, a conclusion representing his own view rather than that of the government he represented.[1]

However, even for someone like Tōgō, Hull's note was disappointing. Tōgō suspected that Hull might deliberately have presented the issues in a form that was unacceptable to Japan. As a result he lost his justification to fight for peace in the face of the pro-war sentiment of the high command, which was even further incited by Hull's note.[2] No matter how Tōgō tried, he could not swallow the contents of the note, which provided no support for the stand he was taking against war.

In the meantime, the army's high command had been concerned

that Japan's Plan B, which was approved by the Imperial Conference on November 5, might be acceptable to the United States, in which event there would be no war. In fearing such an acceptance by the United States (November 13), the high command also secretly hoped that the negotiations with the United States would be broken off (November 23). It thus greeted the Hull note rejecting Plan B as "a message from heaven," making it easier for Japan to follow through on its decision for war. As the members of the high command congratulated themselves, Tōgō could easily discern their relief.

For his part, Hull responded to a telephone inquiry from Secretary of War Stimson on November 27, by saying: "I have washed my hands of it, and it is in the hands of you and Knox—the Army and the Navy." In later days, Hull also testified that he was aware that Japan would not accept his *modus vivendi* unless it was similar to their Plan B. He did not seriously consider that the Japanese would accept his note. Seen through the reactions of those in both countries who were hoping for war, one may safely state that the Hull Note was the most direct cause of Japan's steps toward the war.[3]

Around 9:30 a.m. on November 26, after talking to Hull on the telephone, Secretary Stimson called President Roosevelt to inform him that about 50,000 Japanese troops had been sighted south of Taiwan. Roosevelt was furious and was reported to have said that it was proof of Japan's treachery and that it changed everything. This might have entered into Hull's decision to present a note that was calculated to provoke the Japanese. Yet the troops in question were only being moved to Hainan Island. The troop concentration was merely a contingency plan. This movement in itself did not mean that Japan had already decided upon war. In the event the Imperial Conference decided against war, the troops would remain on Hainan Island; they could never engage in war without explicit Imperial sanction. The action was similar to the dispatch of heavy bombers to the Philippines by the United States. Thus there was clear one-sidedness and self-righteousness in Roosevelt's view equating the concentration of troops on Hainan Island with a Japanese decision for war. In the final analysis, however, Roosevelt's conclusion may have resulted also from a general climate of opinion in the United States that increasingly viewed many things as "proof of treachery"—a climate of illogical hostility.[4]

A close study of the documents makes it clear that the Hull note represented the harshest conditions presented by the United States to

Japan during the entire eight months of talks between the two countries. Matsuoka Yōsuke, who as foreign minister participated in the first half of the U.S.-Japanese negotiations, once confided to his close associate Ōhashi Chūichi: "I have never experienced negotiations like these, in which the longer one talks to the other party the harsher the conditions become."[5] Hull's note torpedoed any prospects of success.

Looking at these events that brought disaster, this writer, along with other historians, is inclined to succumb to the seduction of a mysterious maiden called "If." "If Cleopatra's nose had been a little shorter. . . ." "If the U.S.-Japanese talks of 1941 had not been initiated at all. . . ." Of course, from a larger perspective, one would have to admit that there were some irreconcilable differences between Japan and the United States. Japan's policy of expansion on the Asian continent went counter to the Open Door policy of the United States. Japan's Axis-oriented policy went counter to the American policy of aiding Great Britain in any action short of war. Thus, from 1937 the two countries were at loggerheads with regard to their policies toward both the Chinese mainland and Southeast Asia. Still, the United States never officially appeared to be an enemy of Japan, militarily. The conflicts between the two countries were confined to economic matters or were only indirect (e.g., the U.S. economic aid to China, participation in the Sino-Japanese War by U.S. volunteer airmen on the side of China, U.S. purchase of Southeast Asian resources, U.S. economic sanctions against Japan).

Even as late as the beginning of 1941, developments in China and Southeast Asia gave no indication of creating a major issue, and there was no significant issue that would have made a war between Japan and the United States inevitable. The Roosevelt administration was primarily interested in destroying Nazi Germany and maintaining a Europe-first strategy. There also remained a strong domestic desire for American neutrality in foreign countries, which could not be ignored by politicians.

Given these conditions, it is hardly conceivable that the United States would have suddenly presented the Hull Note without the circuitous developments that preceded it. I am not suggesting that the United States planned it that way, but one can suspect that it was the 1941 talks between the United States and Japan, discussed hereafter, that provided the stage for the presentation of the Hull Note. If there had been no talks between the United States and Japan, would there have been any other opportunity for that note to be presented?

On the question of the causes of the Pacific War, I wish to refer the reader to the eight volumes of the *Taiheiyō no sensō e no michi* (The Road to the Pacific War), which I edited. Here I simply wish to present three major points. First, the 1941 talks between the two countries were initiated by amateurs who lacked any training in diplomacy (Ikawa for Japan, and Drought, Walsh, and Walker for the United States). They failed to represent faithfully the basic international positions of their respective governments, and they acted as if those positions did not exist. They capriciously and freely attempted to solve the many outstanding issues between the two countries in this illusory manner. Second, these amateur diplomats mistakenly thought that they were in close contact with the leaders of their respective governments. Ikawa believed that the statements made by Drought, Walsh, and Walker represented the wishes of Roosevelt. At the same time, Drought, Walsh, and Walker assumed that Ikawa represented Prime Minister Konoe. Both parties passed along their erroneous interpretations to their own governments, with the result that their respective governments were misled. Finally, the Japanese government mistakenly regarded the "proposal for understanding" drafted by Ikawa and Drought to be an official proposal of the U.S. government. Secretary Hull believed the same document to be an official proposal of the Japanese government. When Matsuoka presented his counterproposal to this "U.S. proposal," the U.S. government regarded this sudden change as treachery. When Hull, in turn, presented his counterproposal to Matsuoka, it was Japan's turn to be dumbfounded and incensed by what seemed to be a major retreat from the earlier terms of the "U.S. proposal." The greatest byproduct of the "proposal for understanding" was misunderstanding between the two countries, which only reinforced their mutual suspicions about one another.

Telecommunication in those days was not well developed. Summit conferences were exceptions rather than the rule, and cablegrams served as the main means of communication between nations. Under such circumstances, suspicion once created was difficult to eradicate. An appropriate example can be found in America's deciphering of the Japanese code. Even the Tokyo military tribunal after the war did not deny the terrible American mistranslations of the Japanese originals. In the business of deciphering coded messages, inference was often used when things were not clear. In an atmosphere of mutual suspicion, it is not surprising that such American inferences found malicious Japanese intents where, in fact, none existed. Thus, a feeling of treachery in another party created misunderstanding, and misunderstanding further accentuated the feeling of treachery. The vicious circle continued.

As for a summit conference, Premier Konoe's intent was to use a U.S.-Japanese summit to resolve the dangerous issues between the two countries. Of the misunderstanding that had been plaguing the two countries since the inception of the talks, he cabled to Ambassador Nomura on August 7, 1941: "It is no longer possible to allow matters to take their course. The present condition of U.S.-Japan relations is exceptionally tense due to the misunderstanding between the two countries as well as maneuvering by third countries. This is happening in spite of the determined efforts of Japan." Based on this correct assessment of the problem, Konoe made the proposal to Roosevelt for a summit conference.

In this same spirit he issued the so-called Konoe message on August 26, and two days later Foreign Minister Toyoda also cabled Nomura: "It is essential to find some points where we can reach a compromise in the spirit of yielding to one another. That is to come through the exchange of opinions to clarify our respective views (through the summit conference)." Furthermore, to have them share the responsibility of reaching "compromise" solutions through "mutual yielding," Konoe planned to have a high-ranking general and admiral accompany him to the summit conference. The ship that was to carry the Japanese delegation, the *Nitta Maru,* was equipped with powerful communications equipment.

Toyoda later recalled that "if we had gone we would have wanted it to succeed absolutely. We wanted to solve the question of withdrawal of troops (from China) at the conference and beg Imperial sanction directly (through wireless)."[6] The emperor encouraged Konoe on the matter of the summit[7] conference on August 7. Konoe was confident that the emperor would approve the compromise solution he expected to reach at the summit, but he also had a foreboding that he would be assassinated upon his return. His feelings accurately portrayed the conditions existing in those days.

In the meantime, the army's high command on August 19 concluded that once a summit conference was convened "the negotiations would not be broken off, and, through temporary compromise and adjustment, would be successful." In more concrete terms, it foresaw the following scenario. Once the conference was convened,

Konoe would wire home reporting that he could not hold the Japanese position any further. The army would oppose any compromise,
but Konoe would then beg the emperor for permission to compromise; the emperor would order that Konoe's wire be accepted and
give an Imperial rescript to the army to that effect. The army would
be left with no alternative but total acceptance. The army regarded
the prospects for success of such negotiations at about 70 percent.[8]

Since the Japanese military lamented that they would be powerless
if the emperor supported Konoe's initiatives, it can be seen in view of
this that Hull's successful effort to cool Roosevelt's enthusiasm for
such a meeting was unfortunate. At first, Roosevelt spoke to Ambassador Nomura on August 17 suggesting Juneau, Alaska, as a possible
site for the summit, asking Nomura the number of days required to
travel from Japan to Juneau, and commenting on the weather conditions existing there in mid-October. On August 28, Roosevelt com-
plimented Nomura, saying that Konoe's message was a step forward,
giving the impression that he was looking forward to a conference
with Prince Konoe, and renewed his suggestion that Juneau be
chosen as the conference site.

Hull told Sumner Welles on August 9 that he had already indicated to Nomura that he had neither read nor given priority to considering or even reading documents received from Japan. His attitude
continued to be one of distrust of the Japanese. From this perspective
Hull insisted that the summit conference, if held at all, "should
. . . have as its purpose the ratification of essential points already
agreed to in principle." He never wavered in his opposition to
Konoe's statesmanlike approach that had as its purpose the dissolution of the very serious misunderstandings and feelings of treachery
of each side.

Was the United States so distrustful of Japan that it was not even
willing to hear the desperate plea of Konoe—a plea that was backed
by his willingness to risk assassination after his return? That was the
price he would have to pay for begging the emperor to restrain the
military. Yet, Konoe believed it was the necessary step to avoid war
with the United States once and for all.[9]

NOTES

1. Tōgō Shigenori, *Jidai no ichimen* (An aspect of the times) (Tokyo: Hara Shobō, 1952), p. 199.

2. Ibid., pp. 238, 249.

3. [Although their premises are different, Utley and Tsunoda agree that Hull's "all or nothing" attitude prevented diplomacy leading toward a reconciliation of differences. Heinrichs maintains that Roosevelt's concern over the Soviet Union did not allow any bargaining room for the United States by the fall of 1941.—EDS.]

4. [Pre-Pearl Harbor Japanese diplomacy is often seen as being based on irrational thinking, but we see here that Tsunoda accuses American policymakers of a similar mentality. The essays by Utley, Emmerson, and Ikei, in particular, and to a lesser extent those by Graebner and Conroy, make the same charge.—EDS.]

5. Ōhashi to Tsunoda, 1961.

6. Justice Department Documents.

7. U.S. Department of State, *Papers Relating to the Foreign Relations of the United States: Japan, 1931-41,* vol. 2 (Washington, D.C.: 1943), pp. 604-606; Joseph Grew, *Turbulent Era: A Diplomatic Record of Forty Years, 1904-45,* Walter Johnson, ed. (Boston: Houghton Mifflin, 1952), vol. 2, p. 1329.

8. Memorandum by a staff member, army high command.

9. [We see in Tsunoda's essay a passionate defense of the sincerity of Konoe and a belief that he could have successfully overridden the military elements by the strategy Tsunoda has described. Perhaps Barnhart, Hata, and Fujiwara are correct in maintaining that it was already too late to reverse Japanese policy. Still, one might wish in retrospect that the American side had tried the summit. Fujiwara's essay flatly rejects Tsunoda's view that Konoe planned anything beyond cosmetic concessions on the important issue of troop withdrawal from China. Conversely, Heinrichs denies that Roosevelt was ever interested in such a summit.—EDS.]

11. Ambassador Nomura and His "John Doe Associates": Pre-Pearl Harbor Diplomacy Revisited

HILARY CONROY

IN his fine study of what he calls the "Japanese-American War" published in 1981 Akira Iriye argues that the United States had a "Wilsonian" or "neo-Wilsonian" approach to Japan in the late 1930s, that is, an international system dominated by the Anglo-Saxon powers, primarily Great Britain and the United States, with Japan as a cooperating member.[1] By 1940 most Japanese leaders were unwilling to accept this kind of international arrangement, whereby, as was said of the Washington Conference's 5-5-3 structure, there were two Rolls Royces (Britain and the United States) and one Ford (Japan) in the race.

Instead, Japan embarked on a "Greater East Asia" project and in September 1940 formally entered into an alliance with Nazi Germany and Fascist Italy with the proclaimed objective of bringing about a new order of power in the world. This was heady stuff for Japan and fascist-minded Prince Konoe Fumimaro, three times premier between 1937 and 1941. He and his militaristic supporters bravely launched military expeditions into China, into the borderlands of Manchuria and Mongolia where they probed Soviet defenses, and into French Indochina after the fall of France.[2] War Minister Tōjō Hideki, who was to be premier at the time of Pearl Harbor, was following the logistics of these expansionist moves carefully, determined that Japan should not be vulnerable to cutoffs of resources and supplies.[3]

Although Tōjō, other army commanders, and the militant followers of Prince Konoe were sure of their course, there remained a weakened, but still influential, leadership group of Anglo-American-philes. These included civilian diplomats of the old school, like Shidehara Kijurō, and younger copies with future prospects like Yoshida Shigeru, naval officers with world experience who realized

97

that the Japanese navy usually lost its Pacific war-game simulations against the American navy, men like Admiral Nomura Kichisaburō, intellectuals like Minobe Tatsukichi and Yanaihara Tadao, ousted Tokyo University professors who had for the time being been silenced in their fight for freedom of thought and expression, and finally, Prince-Premier Konoe himself, who in his saner moments realized that war with the United States might turn out badly for Japan.

In fact, Konoe had been schooled to be a "Wilsonian" by his early mentor Prince Saionji, last of the Meiji elder statesmen, who had him in the Japanese entourage at the Versailles Conference of 1919. But Konoe, who was also a patron of the Black Dragon Society *(Koku-ryūkai)*, a role inherited from his father, opted for fascism in the 1930s and established a totalitarian political system in Japan with the single-party Imperial Rule Assistance Association *(Taisei yokusankai)* in September 1940. This was the same month that the Tripartite Pact was signed in Berlin by his vitriolic foreign minister Matsuoka Yōsuke.[4]

Although these events definitely put Konoe's second cabinet (22 July 1940–16 July 1941) on the road to confrontation with the United States, the versatile Prince, or the latent Saionji-inspired side of him, sought a way to have his cake and eat it also—that is, on one hand, to have the Axis alliance Matsuoka had brought him, with its German guarantees of freedom of Japanese action in the Pacific, and, on the other hand, to have peace, or at least détente, with the United States. That, it seems, is the explanation for the appointment as ambassador of then-retired Admiral Nomura, a "friend" of President Roosevelt from associations begun during the Wilson administration, while Matsuoka was wrapping up the Axis alliance with Germany and Italy.[5]

The purpose of this essay is to argue that there was a chance for peace in the Nomura mission to Washington.[6] The odds were not excellent, as the ambivalence of the Prince-Premier indicates, but they were decent, partly because Konoe's inclination tended more and more toward Nomura and away from Matsuoka. The prospects for peace also seemed good because Nomura was both persistent and, in a peculiar way, skillful in his diplomacy. To say this is to dispute some rather heavy scholarship on the subject. Akira Iriye's aforementioned study sees Japan and America beginning to move toward peace with a "redefining" of war aims on both sides, a process that began as early as the winter of 1942–1943 and gradually developed toward a "Japanese-American rapprochement" as the war drew to a close. But he sees no particular hope for the pre-Pearl Harbor diplomacy as long as Japan sought (by force) her "New Order" in East Asia, in defiance of American "neo-Wilsonian." Indeed, Admiral-Ambassador Nomura receives only the briefest mention in Iriye's study. Ishii Itarō, Japan's ambassador to Brazil, receives more attention as the die-hard advocate of an Anglo-American orientation for Japan.[7]

Whereas Iriye is negative on Nomura's peace effort by omission, Robert J. C. Butow, in his intensive study of the unofficial "John Doe" diplomacy of which Nomura was the center, condemns Nomura as positively harmful to pre-Pearl Harbor diplomatic efforts to avert a war between Japan and the United States. Butow argues, in his well researched, book-length study of pre-Pearl Harbor diplomacy, that Nomura was misled by four self-appointed peace advocates, whom he calls "The John Doe Associates." These were two American Catholic priests—Father James M. Drought and Bishop James E. Walsh—and two Japanese—a banker, Ikawa Tadao, and an army officer, Col. Iwakurō Hideo. The term "John Doe Associates" was ascribed to them by Stanley K. Hornbeck, the chief U.S. State Department adviser on Far Eastern affairs. These four had formed a peace-making, or at least peace-seeking, group in Tokyo about the time Ambassador Nomura was preparing to depart for the United States, late in 1940. Through Ikawa they had the ear of Premier Konoe but, as Butow shows through careful research into his personal background, it was Father Drought who played the leading role in the peace effort. "Impatience, imagination, and zeal made Drought a prodigious worker who was totally unsparing of himself."[8]

He not only initiated ideas, he sometimes invented them. Thus, Father Drought wrote speeches and memoranda that he wanted the Japanese foreign office and/or the U.S. State Department to use. He even "corrected" translations of dispatches that Ambassador Nomura received from Tokyo to portray Tokyo's position as more concessive than it actually was. He arranged private meetings for Nomura and the Japanese "John Doe" associates with Secretary Hull, so as to bypass "anti-Japanese" State Department officials such as Stanley Hornbeck. He was especially anxious to arrange a Pacific "summit meeting" between President Roosevelt and Premier Konoe. In fact, Father Drought at one point talked Nomura into making public a Japanese expression of semi-willingness to have such a summit to bring pressure on Hull and Roosevelt to arrange it. It should be noted that Drought, who was politically much more conservative than Roosevelt and felt that the latter needed a great deal of advice and assistance, had access to the Roosevelt administration through Postmaster General Frank Walker.[9]

Butow shows that Ambassador Nomura was especially vulnerable to such machinations because he was not an experienced diplomat. Chihiro Hosoya, who was the first to analyze Nomura's role and its vagaries, observed that although Nomura might have been a "good negotiator" he was a "bad communicator."[10] It is certainly true that the lines of communication between Tokyo's Gaimushō, where Foreign Minister Matsuoka was in charge, and the State Department of Cordell Hull were in a most curious state of disarray during the spring and summer of 1941. This grew out of a "draft proposal" for peace that Hull thought was being submitted to him by the Japanese but that Tokyo thought was a proposal *from* Hull. The seven-point proposal reached Hull on April 9. It accepted the "independence of China" and the "resumption of the Open Door," but stated that "the withdrawal of Japanese troops from Chinese territory" would be "in accordance with an agreement to be reached between China and Japan." By that agreement there would be a coalescence of the governments of Chiang Kai-shek (Chungking) and Wang Ching-wei (Nanking), acceptance of the "independence" of Manchukuo (Manchuria), and "joint defense against communistic activities."[11]

Actually Drought and the other "John Does" had drawn up the proposal as a good compromise. Nomura was agreeable, although he (and the John Does) had good reason to believe that it would not be acceptable to Matsuoka. Father Drought hinted at this in discussing the matter with Joseph Ballantine, the State Department interpreter assigned to work with (monitor?) the negotiations of the John Does with Nomura. However, Drought urged prompt action (acceptance) by the State Department on the grounds that this would present Matsuoka with a *fait accompli,* which he would have to accept or else resign. He also assumed that any problems or misunderstandings could be settled by Konoe and Roosevelt in a "summit" meeting, possibly in Honolulu.

Hull was willing to receive the draft but not to accept it. Indeed, he said that in reviewing it with State Department advisers, "our disappointment was keen." Although Nomura pressed Hull to begin negotiations on the proposal, Hull would say only that Nomura was "at the fullest liberty" to submit the document to his government "but [that] of course this does not imply any commitment whatever on the part of this Government with respect to the provisions of the document. . . ." Nomura cabled the draft proposal to Tokyo, recommending its full acceptance and implying that Hull had no objections."[12]

Certainly this is "bad communicating," if not outright deceit. In the weeks to come, as Foreign Minister Matsuoka came into the issue with his Axis alliance mentality, the words and the action from Tokyo were negative, to say the least. On May 14 Matsuoka had a stormy session with U.S. Ambassador Joseph Grew, in which he praised Hitler's "patience and generosity," qualities that he found lacking in the American leadership. His remarks were interpreted as being "bellicose both in tone and substance" by the American side.[13] Small wonder then, that when Nomura tried to soften the tone of Matsuoka's blusterings, whether with or without Drought's tampering with the translations, Hull concluded that the Japanese were very devious indeed and certainly not to be trusted. He became so angry at Nomura that during most of the summer he refused even to talk to him.

What Hull did not realize was that the confused communicating that so annoyed him was Ambassador Nomura's way of finding a way to a peace settlement, or at least a *modus vivendi,* in Japanese-American relations to which his boss, Foreign Minister Matsuoka, was opposed. Hull assumed that Matsuoka's bellicosity was the real Tokyo position and that Nomura's softer words were window dressing, or simply lies. Of course, if we read the situation in a straight line from Matsuoka negotiating the Axis alliance, relations with the United States worsening, Japanese entering Southeast Asia, the United States freezing Japanese assets and embargoing trade, Tōjō taking command, and the Japanese attacking Pearl Harbor, there would seem to be no reason to take Nomura's efforts seriously. However, to look at it that way fails to take into account two matters of importance. First, Nomura did not accept his appointment as ambassador without terms from Konoe and Matsuoka, and second, Matsuoka, not Nomura, was ousted when the tension between them created a confrontation in June–July 1941.

The two points are interconnected. Nomura, as a retired admiral, had his support base in the navy. When he took up the ambassadorship he received assurances all around, and especially from navy leaders, that his mission was to achieve peace with the United States. When he found that Matsuoka did not really want that and gave the Axis alliance a higher priority, he broke with Matsuoka, complained about him to Tokyo, and threatened to resign. Nomura saw his efforts rewarded with the ouster of Matsuoka from the Konoe cabinet on July 12 and the appointment of his friend and supporter Admiral Toyoda Teijirō as foreign minister in Matsuoka's place. Toyoda, like Nomura, was opposed to the Axis alliance and in favor of rapprochement with the United States.[14]

Here was the moment for bold diplomacy by Hull. He could have deescalated the tension in U.S.-Japanese relations by picking up Nomura's draft proposal in whichever version. (There seems to have been in addition to the main one drafted by Drought other drafts by Walsh, Ikawa, and Iwakuro, any of which alone or in combination was all right with Nomura.) Or, he could have agreed to the proposed Konoe-Roosevelt summit meeting to discuss matters. Hull did neither. Instead he took a haughty attitude of disdain for these amateurish efforts seasoned with Hornbeck's conviction that the Japanese had been bent on aggression since 1894 and that no amount of diplomacy could stop them.

While, as Butow says so charmingly, "Nomura remained what he had always been—a naval officer who was completely out of his element trying to navigate across the dry land he had to traverse as a diplomat,"[15] it should have been possible for Hull and the other professional diplomats involved to have assisted Nomura's good intentions. They could have abetted the progress he was making in turning Tokyo away from the Axis alliance and toward peace with the United States, rather than boxing him in. Instead, the professional diplomats entered into a caustic and disparaging legalistic analysis of his duplicity. Even this might have been considered more kindly as "double talk." Finally, on the big question of whether the rather pathetic efforts of Nomura and his John Doe associates might have moved Japan off her course of aggression, the answer must be that they alone could not. There is, however, the possibility that, properly and skillfully utilized, they might have provided (indeed almost did) the opportunity whereby the Tokyo government, many of whose leading members, including Premier Konoe himself, could change course toward a resumption of more friendly relations with the United States and Britain.[16] Konoe has been called a chameleon who changed his colors a number of times. He was certainly fascist-minded, if not a fascist, in the 1930s, but by 1941 he was hedging his bets. Nomura's appointment to Washington is partial testimony to that. It is clear from Japanese records that he was willing (anxious?) to meet Roosevelt in the Pacific,[17] even in Honolulu. Japanese navy leaders knew that in their simulated war games with the United States Japan usually lost. Even Gen. Tōjō Hideki, army minister in Konoe's cabinet, was turned off by the audacity of Matsuoka and helped bring about his ouster. The significance of Matsuoka's ouster from the Konoe cabinet was not capitalized upon by the American side.

Thus, we may conclude, there was a chance for a deescalation of tension and avoidance of the Pacific War as late as the time of the third Konoe Cabinet, July 18–October 16, 1941.[18]

NOTES

1. Akira Iriye, *Power and Culture: The Japanese-American War* (Cambridge, Mass.: Harvard University Press, 1981), pp. 18, 20. Britisher Christopher Thorne insists on calling it the "Far Eastern War." See his *The Issue of War* (New York: Oxford University Press, 1985).

2. See Oka Yoshitake, and Shumpei Okamoto and Patricia Murray, trans., *Konoe Fumimaro: A Political Biography* (Tokyo: University of Tokyo Press, 1983). Oka indicates (pp. 132–135) that Konoe went so far as to support the military chiefs in their demand for the Japanese occupation of southern French Indochina in late June–July 1941, although he was by then beginning to seek less belligerence toward the United States and the USSR. Oka's study was originally published in Japanese as *Konoe Fumimaro "unmei" no seijika.*

For more on Japan's border penetration of the USSR, see Alvin D. Coox, *Nomonhan: Japan against Russia, 1939,* vol. II (Stanford: Stanford University Press, 1985), pp. 986, 1164. Coox notes that Konoe decided to replace Tōgō Shigenori as ambassador to Moscow with Lt. Gen. Tatekawa Yoshitsugu "of Manchurian Incident fame" because Tōgō had "gone Western" and "had lost touch with the Japanese point of view." For more on Indochina, see Robert Butow, *Tōjō and the Coming of the War* (Princeton: Princeton University Press, 1961), pp. 192–196, 209–231; David J. Lu, *From the Marco Polo Bridge to Pearl Harbor* (Washington, D.C.: Public Affairs Press, 1961), pp. 141–148. For details, see Sachiko Murakami "Japan's Thrust into French Indochina" (Ph.D. diss., New York University, 1981).

3. Robert J. C. Butow makes this clear in his standard study of *Tōjō and the Coming of the War* (Princeton: Princeton University Press, 1961), pp. 224–225.

4. Retired Adm. Nomura Kichisaburō, before proceeding to the United States in November 1940 to become ambassador of Japan, sought assurances that peace with the United States was desired and warned Premier Konoe that war with the United States could come to "no good end." See Nomura Kichisaburō, *Beikoku ni Tsu-*

kaishite (Mission to the United States) (Tokyo: Iwanami Shoten, 1946), pp. 12–17; see also Oka, *Konoe Fumimaro*, pp. 139–141. On Shidehara, see Toru Takemoto, *Failure of Liberalism in Japan: Shidehara Kijūrō's Encounter with the Nonliberals* (Washington, D.C.: University Press of America, 1978). See also Nobuya Bamba and John F. Howes, ed., *Pacifism in Japan: The Christian and Socialist Tradition* (Vancouver: University of British Columbia Press, 1978), especially chapter 8; Ienaga Saburō, and Frank Baldwin, trans., *The Pacific War: World War II and the Japanese, 1931–1945* (New York: Pantheon Books, 1977); Yale Maxon, *Control of Japanese Foreign Policy: A Study of Civil-Military Rivalry, 1930–1945* (Berkeley: University of California Press, 1957) and Michael A. Barnhart, *Japan Prepares for Total War: The Search for Economic Security, 1919–1941* (Ithaca, N.Y.: Cornell University Press, 1987), for further details on these background matters.

5. See the author's article entitled "The Strange Diplomacy of Admiral Nomura," in *Proceedings of the American Philosophical Society* 114 (June 1970): pp. 205–216, for a preliminary discussion of Nomura's mission, including an extensive bibliography.

6. [Conroy's view that peace was still possible through October 1941 collides with the more pessimistic views of Hata, Barnhart, and Heinrichs.—EDS.]

7. Akita Iriye, *Power and Culture: The Japanese-American War* (Cambridge: Harvard University Press, 1981).

8. Robert J. C. Butow, *The John Doe Associates: Backdoor Diplomacy for Peace, 1941* (Stanford: Stanford University Press, 1974), p. 55. Konoe acknowledges the negotiating roles of Bishop Walsh and Father Drought by name and in that order in his diary *Konoe nikki* (Tokyo: Kyōdō shinsha, 1968), pp. 186–187.

9. Butow, *John Doe*, chapters 14–16.

10. Chihiro Hosoya, "Japan's Decision for War in 1941," *Peace Research in Japan* 1 (1967): pp. 41–51.

11. Nomura, *Beikoku ni*, pp. 2–9; Nobutaka Ike, *Japan's Decision for War: Records of the 1941 Policy Conferences* (Stanford: Stanford University Press, 1967), appendix A; U.S. Department of State, *Papers Relating to the Foreign Relations of the United States: Japan, 1931–41*, vol. II (Washington, D.C.: 1943), pp. 398–402 (hereafter cited as *Foreign Relations Papers*).

12. Hilary Conroy, "The Strange Diplomacy of Admiral Nomura," *Proceedings of the American Philosophical Society* 114, no. 3 (June 1970): pp. 210–211. Butow, *John Doe*, chaps. 10–14, discusses the "draft proposal" in great detail.

13. Grew to Secretary of State, 14 May 1941, *Foreign Relations Papers*, pp. 145–148; memorandum by Secretary of State, 14 May 1941; ibid., p. 426.

14. Conroy, *Strange Diplomacy*, pp. 211–214; Butow, *John Doe*, chaps. 17–18; Nomura, *Beikoku ni*, pp. 181–186; Marquis Kido Kōichi, *Kido nikki* (Kido diary), 15 July 1941 (Tokyo: Tokyo University Press, 1966), partial translation, International Military Tribunal for the Far East, IPS Doc., 1632, Library of Congress Microfilm.

15. Butow uses the metaphor of Nomura as a sailor out of his element on dry land repeatedly in his *The John Doe Associates*, pp. 8, 97, 206, 227, 307. According to Butow, Nomura himself had observed that "a sailor on land is quite helpless." Nomura also referred to himself as "the bones of a dead horse" at a time when the diplomacy seemed to be going nowhere. Butow, *John Doe*, p. 286.

16. [Once again we see here the view that American concessions could have had a

stronger influence on Japanese domestic politics and foreign policy than Hull, Hornbeck, and other hard-liners would concede.—EDS.]

17. David J. Lu in *From the Marco Polo Bridge to Pearl Harbor* (Washington, D.C.: Public Affairs Press, 1961), pp. 192–195, gives a good discussion of the summit meeting idea from Japanese documents. See also Oka Yoshitake, *Konoe Fumimaro*, pp. 139–143. On Konoe in general and his relationship with Nomura see *Konoe nikki*, pp. 207–221; Nomura, *Beikoku ni*, pp. 12–17; Oka, *Konoe Fumimaro*, pp. 134–139. Konoe considered himself a victim of "fate" (Oka, *Konoe Fumimaro*, pp. vii–viii) whose ruin came from too little individualism (ibid., p. 198).

18. In his original article on this general subject published in 1970 the author concluded by suggesting that "the old idea of warlike nations versus peace-loving nations is giving way to war-minded versus peace-minded elements *within each nation.*" See "The Strange Diplomacy of Admiral Nomura," p. 215. Since then, various studies have uncovered evidence of such in prewar Japan, some, intentially at least, influential. For example, see Nobuya Bamba and John F. Howes, ed., *Pacifism in Japan: The Christian and Socialist Tradition* (Vancouver: University of British Columbia Press, 1978); Alvin D. Coox annd Hilary Conroy, ed., *China and Japan: Search for Balance* (Santa Barbara, Calif.: ABC-CLIO Press, 1978); and Michael A. Barnhart, *Japan Prepares for Total War: The Search for Economic Security, 1919–1941* (Ithaca, New York: Cornell University Press, 1987). The personalities range from Tokyo University Professor Yanaihara Tadao to General of the Army Ishiwara Kanji. Also, Oka's biography of Konoe indicates that Konoe consulted the much-castigated peace advocate, ex-Foreign Minister Shidehara Kijūrō, at least once in the summer of 1941 (Oka, *Konoe Fumimaro,* pp. 135–136).

12. Nomura in Washington: Conversations in Lieu of Diplomacy

NORMAN A. GRAEBNER

NOMURA KICHISABURŌ, an admiral little versed in the art of diplomacy, arrived in Washington in mid-February 1941 to conduct Japan's final effort to reach an accommodation with the Roosevelt administration. At issue was peace in the Orient. Nomura had long regarded war between the two Pacific powers as an unwarranted tragedy. He had accepted the mission to Washington only because of the assurance that the Japanese government desired a rapprochement with the United States. He had repeatedly denounced the anti-American attitudes and behavior of Japanese officials; in Washington he would attempt to explain away their belligerence. Upon his arrival Nomura told reporters that there was "no question outstanding which cannot be settled . . . through a timely display of statesmanship by the responsible people on both sides." President Roosevelt received Nomura on Febuary 14. "I said," the ambassador recalled, "I believed deeply there must be no such thing as a fight between Japan and America and I am convinced that the day is coming when our two countries will cooperate to maintain the peace of the world. The President expressed the same sentiments. . . ."[1] Roosevelt reminded Nomura that the American people were troubled by Japanese aggression in the Far East. He suggested that Nomura sit down with Secretary of State Cordell Hull and other Washington officials to review the issues the clouded the relations between the two countries.[2]

Nomura's Japan faced an uncompromising China supported by an equally uncompromising United States. Official Washington assumed that China had a legal right to possess and govern its own territory; that assumption was sufficient to sustain a mutual American-Chinese interest in opposing Japanese expansionism. "We have considered it right and to our advantage," explained Stanley Hornbeck, Hull's special adviser for Far Eastern affairs, "that independent states remain independent."[3] With Japan engaged in open aggression, any settlement between Japan and China, Hornbeck argued, would serve the interests of Japan far more than those of the United States. Only by refusing to appease Japan would the United States terminate the perennial resistance of Japan's predatory elements to its peace conditions. "Maintenance of a firm front . . . vis-a-vis Japan," predicted Hornbeck in January 1941, "will hasten the arrival of the day when, those conditions having been met, peace and security in the Far East will be possible."[4] Hornbeck warned the administration that the United States dare not permit Japan's aggressions on the Asian mainland to continue beyond a settlement of the European war. Having disposed of Hitler, neither Britain nor the United States, he feared, would care to venture militarily into the Far East, where their interests were less apparent, to settle matters with an expanded Japanese empire.

Until 1940 U.S. policy in the Pacific was concerned less with the defense of China than with the perpetuation of the post-Versailles treaty structure. Unpunished aggression, however limited its impact on the global balance of power, would presumably encourage other aggressors and thereby undermine the legal foundations of world security and endanger the peace everywhere. Whereas the notion of indivisible peace demanded an effort to counter and hopefully terminate Japanese aggression, it did not establish any concern for China that might justify war in the Pacific. Only in the sense that Japanese expansion violated the treaty structure and thereby threatened international stability did it challenge American complacency. By 1941, however, the administration's concern for the credibility of the world's peace structure faced the added challenge of what appeared to be a single German-Italian-Japanese assault on the entire Versailles system. The Tripartite Pact of September 1940 merely confirmed that conviction. Thereafter Washington viewed China as a potential ally in the burgeoning struggle against the totalitarian powers. Aid to China replaced trade with Japan as the administration expanded its program of anti-Japanese sanctions. China would no longer suffer the consequences of American appeasement.[5]

Washington's inflexible support of Chinese integrity gave Japanese officials the unfortunate choice of fighting an endless and enervating war on the Asian mainland or of ending that war on Chinese terms. What troubled the Japanese most was the fact that the treaty system to which the United States paid homage favored the status quo and thus served the interests of the contented powers. For them the

Wilsonian principle of peaceful change was no more legitimate than the tradition that recognized the roles of efficiency and power in international life. Convinced that what was good for their country would benefit China as well, Tokyo officials asked that the United States refrain from opposing Japan and grant it a free hand to negotiate a settlement with Chinese leaders. To achieve that end Nomura hoped to frame an approach that would simultaneously protect Japan's quest for a new order in East Asia and gain some modification of the American commitment to principle. Successful Japanese diplomacy would tolerate no less.[6] Tokyo officials as well as the Japanese citizenry favored the expansion of Japanese power and influence in the western Pacific. Even as Nomura prepared for his Washington venture, Japan's foreign minister, Matsuoka Yōsuke, warned: "As long as the United States regards China instead of the East Pacific as its first line of defense, just so long will friendly relations remain an idle dream."[7] From the beginning Nomura's prospects for success were almost nonexistent.

Nomura discovered a promising formula in the treaty draft prepared by James E. Walsh and James M. Drought, two Maryknoll Catholic priests, with the help of two Japanese citizens—Ikawa Tadao, a banker, and Iwakuro Hideo, a confidant of several high-ranking Japanese officials. This proposed agreement, completed in January 1941, included a restatement of the Open Door policy, a guarantee of Chinese independence, and a negotiated withdrawal of Japanese forces unless the Japanese government promised in advance to abandon its policy of military conquest and "adopt the principles which this Government has been proclaiming and practicing as embodying the foundation on which all relations between nations should properly rest."[8] On April 16 Hull presented Nomura the four-point demands that became the final stand of the U.S. government: "(1) respect for the territorial integrity and the sovereignty of each and all nations; (2) support of the principle of non-interference in the internal affairs of other countries; (3) support of the principle of equality, including equality of commercial opportunity; (4) non-disturbance of the *status quo* in the Pacific except as the *status quo* may be altered by peaceful means."[9] There could be no negotiation, Hull declared, until Japan agreed to these four principles. Nomura, determined to continue the Washington conversations, failed to convey to Tokyo the uncompromising nature of Hull's demands.

Japan's reply of May 12 comprised a total rejection of Hull's principles. The Japanese denied that their pact with the Axis powers was other than defensive in intent. More important, they asked the U.S. government to help them establish peace in China by requesting Chiang Kai-shek to negotiate under the threat of the discontinuation of American aid to China should he refuse. What Tokyo required as a minimum condition was the freedom to negotiate an end to the Sino-Japanese War on the basis of Japan's superior power and efficiency. Hull rejected the Japanese formula because it failed again to state precisely what terms Japan intended to impose. The Japanese propositions, Hull complained in a statement to Nomura on June 6, veered "away from clear-cut commitments in regard to policies of peace and non-discriminatory treatment which are the fundamentals of a sound basis for peace in the Pacific area." Subsequent Japanese proposals varied in phraseology but not in substance. Hull, in response, explained the principles to which the United States was committed and to which he hoped the Tokyo government would eventually commit itself.

Unable to reach agreement with either the United States or China, the Japanese government, at its Imperial Conference of July 2, decided to establish its Greater East Asia Co-Prosperity Sphere and achieve a settlement of the China incident with a full invasion of Indochina. Whereas the new Konoe Fumimaro government in Tokyo still hoped to avoid war with the United States, it was now determined to choke off further Chinese resistance before the United States crippled Japan with economic sanctions. In mid-July General George C. Marshall informed Roosevelt that a decoded Japanese message contained an ultimatum to France for the Japanese occupation of naval and air bases in Indochina. On July 23 Nomura admitted to Undersecretary Sumner Welles that the Japanese government had concluded an agreement with the French Vichy regime for the occupation of southern Indochina. Nothing less, he explained, would guarantee the flow of rice to Japan and terminate the overland movement of supplies to China. Roosevelt received Nomura on July 24 and warned him that any Japanese move against the Dutch East Indies would provoke Dutch-British resistance and bring a general war to the Far East. Then he offered a proposal. If Japan refrained from occupying Indochina, he would "do everything within his power to obtain from the Governments of China, Great Britain, the Netherlands, and, of course, the United States itself a binding and solemn declaration, provided Japan would undertake the same commitment, to regard Indochina as a neutralized country."[10]

Finally on July 26 Roosevelt, having received no response from Tokyo, issued an executive order freezing Japanese assets in the United States and thus effectively terminating all U.S. commercial and financial relations with Japan. Much of Washington was delighted. For weeks, Hornbeck had argued that only a firm and uncompromising stand would dissuade Tokyo from challenging the United States directly. Much of the nation regarded some drastic retaliation appropriate both to punish Japan and to protect the country against war. Interior Secretary Harold Ickes admitted that further delay would have produced his resignation and a statement "raising hell generally with the State Department and its policy of appeasement."[11] *The Washington Post* lauded Roosevelt's decision. The only way to prevent a clash in the Pacific, ran its judgment, was for the American people "to back up the president in his wise foreign policy. He has the facts." *The New Republic* predicted that the embargo would strangle Japanese industry and advance the nation's moment of collapse.[12] Similarly, isolationist Burton Wheeler of Montana approved the freezing order to slow up the Japanese economy and "call their bluff so they will not start anything."[13] Roosevelt accepted this almost universal prophecy that Japan would not fight the United States.[14] This was tragic. In his confidence he failed to attach any objectives, achievable through diplomacy, to his embargo. Thus the economic sanctions would force Japan into a capitulation or an expanded war. With only a year's supply of oil on hand, the Japanese accelerated their move into Southeast Asia. The final crisis in U.S.-Japanese relations was only a matter of time.

In Tokyo Prince Konoe carried the burden of peace or war with the United States. On August 8 he requested a top-level conference with Roosevelt. Konoe invited the President to name the site. Konoe was no more prepared than Japanese leaders generally to negotiate away Japan's special interest in East Asia. Nevertheless, Ambassador Joseph C. Grew advised the administration to accept the Konoe proposal. The premier's political future, Grew argued, required some arrangement that would halt the drift toward war. Throughout the year Grew had placed his hopes for peace in the Hull-Nomura conversations; Washington seldom acknowledged his pleas for accommodation. It seemed clear to Grew that the Japanese government could not renounce its expansionist program and its Tripartite Pact or withdraw its troops from China. For that reason he warned the administration that Tokyo would choose war before it would desist from its course of aggression under foreign pressure. What troubled Grew in the autumn of 1941 was Washington's persistent refusal to consider the possibility that its inflexible resistance to Japanese demands might result in war rather than peace. The ambassador reminded the administration on November 3 that "action by Japan which might render unavoidable an armed conflict with the United States may come with dangerous and dramatic suddenness." Such appeals for caution could not penetrate Washington's pro-Chinese environment.[15]

Hull and Hornbeck viewed Konoe's proposal with suspicion. Hornbeck recalled later that the United States could not have made the concessions demanded without "abandoning principles in which the people of this country had consistently believed, which we had long advocated, and to which we were by treaty provisions expressly committed."[16] If Prince Konoe were prepared to fulfill the promises of his proposal, there would be no need for an agreement; any practical manifestation that Japan was proceeding in accordance with that assurance would automatically relieve the tension in the Far East. Hornbeck doubted that the two national leaders could agree on terms that would alter the course of the conflict in Asia. He reported on August 12 that Japanese-American relations had disintegrated so completely that the time had passed when a "little promptness and a little boldness can be regarded synonymous with . . . rashness."[17] Like Grew, Hornbeck understood the uncompromising nature of Japanese policy; unlike Grew, he recognized no danger of war in Japanese ambition. Hornbeck stood in the vanguard of the Washington hard-liners who believed that American hopes for peace in the Orient required the absolute rejection of compromise with Japan. With other American officials he placed the status quo of the Far East on the altar of diplomatic inflexibility. He assumed that Japan would capitulate rather than confront the United States with force. During the discussions over the decision to freeze Japanese assets in the United States, Hornbeck wrote: "I submit that under existing circumstances it is altogether impossible that Japan would deliberately take action in response to any action which the United States is likely to take in the Pacific, which act, if taken by Japan, would mean war between that country and this country."[18] Again in response to

Konoe's appeal Hornbeck assured the White House that a settlement with Japan was not an urgent matter. "We are not in great danger vis-a-vis Japan," he declared, "and Japan . . . does not possess military capacity sufficient to warrant an attack by her upon the United States. . . ."[19]

With Hull's formal rejection of a summit conference on October 2 Konoe as well as many senior officers in the Japanese navy were still reluctant to make a decision for war. The question of continued negotiations split the Japanese cabinet, however, and forced Konoe's resignation on October 16. War Minister Tōjō Hideki assumed the premiership. U.S.-Japanese relations had reached an impasse, not because Tokyo's demands had become greater, but because the Roosevelt administration had again made it clear that Tokyo could anticipate no compromise. Indeed, the Japanese, under intense economic pressure, would have accepted less after September than before. Japan had few alternatives remaining. Rejecting both costly concessions and immediate hostilities, Tokyo adopted a dual policy of continuing diplomatic efforts while completing operational preparations for war if diplomacy failed. To conduct the final negotiations with Hull, Tōjō dispatched Kurusu Saburō, an experienced Japanese diplomat, to Washington. The Imperial Conference of November 5 approved Tōjō's policies and gave Kurusu until November 25 to achieve an agreement. Thereafter the issue of war would go before the emperor.

Shortly after his arrival in Washington Kurusu conferred with Roosevelt and Hull at the White House. Hull demanded that Japan renounce the Tripartite Pact; Kurusu assured the secretary that Germany did not control Japanese policy. Kurusu accepted the principle that any Japanese treaty with China be based on a recognition of Chinese sovereignty, equality, and territorial integrity; what troubled him was Hull's persistent reminder that the Chinese and British must approve any Far Eastern settlement. This, Kurusu complained, rendered the United States hostage to the will of lesser powers. Hull admitted that the United States really had no diplomatic freedom when he insisted that Japan find its own way out of its self-imposed dilemma in China. The secretary came away from his first meeting with Kurusu convinced that the Japanese position was fixed.

Finally, on November 20 Kurusu submitted a formal proposal that included an immediate Japanese withdrawal from southern Indochina and an eventual withdrawal from all of Indochina in exchange for the reestablishment of normal trade relations, including the purchase of oil, as well as an American hands-off policy toward China. Kurusu virtually repudiated the Tripartite Pact. Hull hesitated to accept the Japanese formula but was fearful that an open rejection might mean war, for which the United States was ill prepared. During subsequent days the State Department prepared a *modus vivendi* similar to the Japanese proposal, designed to provide a breathing spell of three months. Meanwhile officials discussed an American response with ambassadors of countries with major interests in the Far East. Chinese spokesmen deluged Washington with pleas to uphold American principles of peaceful change. Churchill wondered what effect compromise would have on China. Eventually on November 25 objections to the *modus vivendi* compelled the administration to reconsider. "Mr. Hull," recalled Hornbeck, "was unhappy about those reactions, especially the emphatic objections, arguments and pleas of the Chinese; and he was especially impressed by the reported comment and query of Mr. Churchill."[20] American officals agreed that afternoon that the submission of the *modus vivendi* would be inadvisable; they prepared a reply based on Washington's long-established position. That evening Roosevelt and Hull agreed to the ten-point program that the secretary delivered to Kurusu and Nomura on November 26. The new proposal demanded that Japan, for a removal of the embargo and a new trade agreement, would withdraw all Japanese forces from both China and Indochina and recognize no Chinese government except that of Chiang Kai-shek. Hull reminded the Japanese diplomats that their country would profit far more from a policy of friendly relations with its neighbors in the Far East than from hazardous and costly policies of expansion. However limited the American interests in China, the Roosevelt administration in November 1941 preferred war with Japan to a confrontation with Chiang and his supporters in the United States.[21] Hull's note terminated the year's conversations. For Kurusu China's control of U.S. policy was beyond comprehension.

Throughout the crisis Hu Shih, the Chinese ambassador in Washington, attemped to bind the United States to China in the name of the Open Door policy and Wilsonian principles of peaceful change. Those principles, if effective, would ultimately assure the Chinese a successful escape from their long and unsatisfactory war without the need of military victory or compromise. Unfortunately, Western interests in China were secondary, whereas Japan's were primary. Consequently, China's efforts to create a coalition of powers capable of guaranteeing the Far Eastern treaty structure were doomed to failure. Thus, in pursuing the illusion of collective security, Chinese officials never faced the Japanese challenge directly; they made no effort to come to terms with Japanese military and economic superiority. Assuming the ultimate support of the United States, they demanded nothing less than total victory for their cause. Hu Shih perceived correctly that the United States would, in the long run, support the anti-Japanese policies of his government with military power. He worked hard and effectively to prevent a compromise during the November crisis. The support Hu Shih sought in Washington came easily enough. Whether China's uncompromising opposition to America's retreat from principle served the interests of China was doubtful.[22] However successful Chinese diplomacy was in Washington, it ended in disaster because it failed to recognize the intrinsic military and political weakness of the Chinese government and the limited Western interest in sustaining the purposes and even the existence of that government.

Washington would scarcely have presented the ten-point proposal to any country that it took seriously. The administration understood clearly that no Japanese government would accept it. But Hornbeck and others assured Roosevelt to the end that Japan would avoid war with the United States, especially if the nation remained resolute. Hornbeck developed the thesis that Japan always went to war suddenly and with a minimum of warning. Japan's open belligerence, he concluded, was evidence that Tokyo was engaged in a campaign of bluff. In mid-November John K. Emmerson, a young foreign service officer recently returned from Tokyo, informed Hornbeck under questioning that the embassy staff in Tokyo feared that Japan, from sheer desperation, might launch an attack on the United States to protect its position in East Asia. "Name me," replied the incredulous Hornbeck, "one country in history which ever went to war in desperation!"[23] On November 27 Hornbeck prepared a memorandum that he urgently called to Hull's attention. He declared that in his opinion "the Japanese Government does not desire or intend or expect to have forthwith armed conflict with the United States. The Japanese Government, while launching new offensive operations at some point or points in the Far East, will endeavor to avoid attacking or being attacked by the United States."[24] Armed with such assurances, Roosevelt refused throughout a critical year to alter the ends of U.S.

policy—the complete unraveling of the Japanese empire. He moved cautiously but unerringly toward a policy of escalation anchored to economic sanctions and a limited show of force.

With each major increment of pressure the nation's dominant foreign policy spokesmen, backed by the American press, anticipated a Japanese capitulation. As late as December 7, 1941, Edward T. Folliard observed in *The Washington Post:* "To the average American it seemed fantastic that Japan, which in four years hasn't been able to beat China, should now risk a war with the United States, unquestionably her master on the seas and in the air. Not only that, but the United States would have allies—Great Britain, the Netherlands Indies, China, and perhaps Russia." The assumption that the United States could guarantee the peace of the Pacific in direct proportion to its diplomatic inflexibility proved to be tragically wrong. Even as Hornbeck assured the administration in late November that the Japanese would avoid war with the United States at all costs, Tokyo dispatched its task force to Pearl Harbor. In his *Memoirs* Hull admitted that he could have reached an agreement with the Japanese government at any time by accepting a compromise. However, he continued, "We should have negated principles on which we had built our foreign policy and without which the world could not live in peace."[25] Somehow Hull could never understand that his policies had not served the cause of peace; neither had they guaranteed the triumph of his principles.

NOTES

1. Nomura quoted in Hilary Conroy, "Nomura Kichisaburō: The Diplomacy of Drama and Desperation," in *Diplomats in Crisis: United States-Chinese-Japanese Relations, 1919-1941,* ed. Richard Dean Burns and Edward M. Bennett (Santa Barbara, Calif.: ABC-CLIO Press, 1974), p. 301.

2. [The following agreement on Nomura exists among those essayists touching upon him: (1) he was a bumbling diplomat, (2) his appointment and continued tenure as ambassador reflected a serious intent in Japan to improve relations with the United States, (3) Hull did not accommodate himself adequately to Nomura's well-meant intentions and initiatives.—EDS.]

3. Hornbeck to Dorothy Borg, Box 34, Dorothy Borg File, Stanley K. Hornbeck Papers (Stanford, Calif.: Hoover Institution).

4. "Reflections on diplomacy with Japan," 31 Janauary 1941, Box 462, Folder January 1941, Stanley K. Hornbeck Papers.

5. [None of our essayists really denies that the Tripartite Pact had significance. The

differences among them are how it should be interpreted and to what extent it closed the door on peace.—EDS.]

6. [Note Graebner's greater emphasis on the Japanese objectives vis-a-vis China in Nomura's ambassadorial role to the United States. How much did those objectives predetermine his failure given the pro-Chinese attitudes in the Roosevelt administration? In their essay Klein and Conroy note that misguided British diplomacy made China the central issue at exactly the same time that Hull and Roosevelt were trying to reach a *modus vivendi* with Japan by pushing the China issue off center.—EDS.]

7. *Time,* 3 February 1941, p. 19.

8. U.S. Department of State, *Foreign Relations of the United States: Diplomatic Papers, 1941,* vol. IV, The Far East (Washington, D.C.: 1956), p. 54.

9. Memorandum of conversations between Hull and Nomura, 16 April 1941, Box 13, Secretary's File: Diplomatic Correspondence, Japan, Franklin D. Roosevelt Presidential Library, Hyde Park, New York. Nomura's report of this conversation was so limited that not until September did the Japanese government recognize the full significance of Hull's four principles. See Robert J. C. Butow, "The Hull-Nomura Conversations: A Fundamental Misconception," *American Historical Review* 65 (July 1960): pp. 822–836.

10. Quoted in Herbert Feis, *The Road to Pearl Harbor* (New York: Atheneum, 1963), pp. 215–16, 238.

11. Harold Ickes, *The Secret Diary of Harold Ickes* (New York: Simon and Schuster, 1954), p. 655.

12. Editorial, *The Washington Post,* 26 July 1941; *The New Republic,* 8 September 1941, pp. 295–96.

13. Wheeler quoted in Wayne S. Cole, *America First: The Battle Against Intervention, 1940-1941* (Madison: University of Wisconsin Press, 1953), pp. 189–90.

14. Note the unanimity of agreement between Emmerson and Graebner on the overconfident view in the United States that Japan would not dare attack the United States. These views show a Roosevelt administration that was less willing to provoke Japan deliberately into war, as Best implies, but that was rather more inclined to make the false assumption that a hard-line American foreign policy would not lead Japan into war. The results of either course may be similar, but the American psychology and motivation ascribed by Emmerson and Graebner are sufficiently different from Best's view that they merit the readers' attention.—EDS.]

15. [The question must be raised again: Why did an administration with a Europe-first policy allow itself to be dragged into a Pacific War it hoped to avoid or to delay? See also the Klein-Conroy essay for a further development of this theme. Perhaps Heinrichs' essay provides the most definitive answer.—EDS.]

16. Autobiography, Box 497, Folder 1941, Stankley K. Hornbeck Papers.

17. Hornbeck to Far East Division, 12 August 1941, Box 463, Folder August 1941, Stankley K. Hornbeck Papers.

18. Hornbeck to Sumner Welles, 23 July 1941, Welles File, Stanley K. Hornbeck Papers.

19. Hornbeck's argument of 5 September 1941, *Foreign Relations of the United States: Diplomatic Papers, 1941,* vol. IV, p. 425–26. See also Hornbeck's memorandum of 30 Agusut 1941, ibid., p. 412. [Contrast the views regarding Hornbeck expressed here with those expressed by Barnhart. Graebner sees Hornbeck as consist-

ently wrong, but Barnhart views him as absolutely correct. How can two authors disagree so fundamentally? Perhaps the answer lies in assumptions. If one assumes the war was inevitable because the Japanese could not be detoured from their war of aggression, Barnhart is correct. But if one assumes that the war could have been avoided by greater efforts in Washington, then Graebner's view is correct.—EDS.]

20. Review of the year 1941, Box 497, Folder 1941, Stanley K. Hornbeck Papers.

21. [Note that Graebner's view of Japanese diplomacy is that the major obstacles were not Southeast Asia and the Tripartite Pact but rather American policy toward China, a view different from Utley's. Graebner argues with the contemporary Japanese view that American foreign policy regarding China was a hostage of Great Britain and China. This view is developed further in the Conroy-Klein essay.—EDS.]

22. [We see here raised again the old issues for students of American diplomacy, namely, are moralism-idealism or long-range legalism-realism considerations the proper guide for American foreign policy. Graebner agrees with Best, but for different reasons, that Chinese and American long-range interests were not served by the existing American policy.—EDS.]

23. John K. Emmerson, *The Japanese Thread: A Life in the U.S. Foreign Service* (New York: Holt, Rinehart and Winston, 1978), p. 117.

24. Memorandum, 27 November 1941, *Foreign Relations of the United States: Diplomatic Papers, 1941,* vol. IV, p. 673.

25. Cordell Hull, *The Memoirs of Cordell Hull,* vol. II (New York: Macmillan, 1948), p. 1037.

13. Repulsing the Pearl Harbor Revisionists: The State of Present Literature on the Debacle

ALVIN D. COOX

THE smoke had barely lifted from the blazing hulks at Pearl Harbor on December 7, 1941, when the first American critics began to point accusing fingers at those held responsible for the disaster in Hawaii. Adm. Husband E. Kimmel and Lt. Gen. Walter C. Short, the local commanders on Oahu, were obvious scapegoats. But powerful suspicions of conspiracy, collusion, and perjury also extended in the direction of President Franklin D. Roosevelt; the U.S. Army Chief of Staff, Gen. George C. Marshall; and the Chief of Naval Operations, Adm. Harold R. Stark. These men, in turn, were said to have been abetted by Secretary of War Henry L. Stimson, Secretary of State Cordell Hull, Secretary of Navy Frank Knox and, later, James V. Forrestal. As Senator Tom Connally asked Roosevelt on the day of Pearl Harbor, "How did they catch us with our pants down, Mr. President?" And a senior U.S. Army cryptanalyst supposedly remarked of the American leadership, despairingly, "But they knew, they knew, they knew."[1]

Put simply, the highest American officials, from the President down, were allegedly implicated in a deliberate plot and a massive cover-up designed to drag the reluctant, isolationist United States through the back door to war, by enticing the Japanese into launching a preemptive, surprise operation that would be sufficient to enrage the American people but insufficient to damage American prospects for ultimate victory. In a slim book published privately in 1973 under the revealing title, *The Skeleton in Uncle Sam's Closet,* one American author charged that "Roosevelt traded the military and civilian security of the Hawaiian Islands, for his own political security."[2]

A number of provocative published items have lent new texture to the Devil Theory in recent years.[3] Thus the thrust of the accusations shifted toward Ambassador Joseph C. Grew in the Tokyo embassy and toward certain State Department hands when, in 1976, Frank

Schuler brought out an exposé titled *The Pearl Harbor Cover-up*.[4] Schuler was an experienced foreign service officer whose career spanned the years 1930–1953 and who was personally conversant with matters in both Tokyo and Washington before the attack on Pearl Harbor. It was Schuler's conviction that there had been "a clique within the Department of State that performed their duties in such a manner that, in the light of history, they appear to be guilty of culpable negligence. Subsequently, in order to cover their misdeeds, they undertook actions which, by their nature, condemn the participants of criminal conspiracy and falsification of documents." Specifically, Schuler charged Grew and certain individuals close to him in the State Department with "gross negligence, near criminal oversight, and a tragic display of ugly megalomania." Schuler went on to decry these government officials for their duplicity:

> Despite the enormity of their failings, there is a more ominous and onerous extension that only compounds their guilt, because, in a deviously planned and coordinated effort, Grew and his lackeys formulated a scheme to expunge Department of State records and files in order to delete evidence that would have factually pointed a condemning finger at the people actually responsible for the horror of . . . Pearl Harbor.

When President Roosevelt spoke to Congress about "a date which will live in infamy," Schuler argues bitterly, "he might also have been privately contemplating the infamous blunderings of his Ambassador to Japan. . . ." Because of Schuler's own unique knowledge, he claims, "his life for years was a living hell of frustration and denigration perpetrated by Grew and propagated by Grew's departmental staff."[5]

It is almost refreshing to discern some shifting of the blame away from Roosevelt and, to a lesser degree, from Hull. Still, the majority of the accusers still excoriate the President and his coterie for their part. A former naval officer, Kemp Tolley, revealed in a 1973 book that his practically unarmed little windjammer and two sister ships were ordered out by the President on something like a suicide, or *kamikaze*, mission. In *Cruise of the Lanikai: Incitement to War*,[6] Tolley asserted that the *Lanikai* was commissioned by Roosevelt as a "warship" in late 1941 to join in a three-vessel "defensive information patrol" whose mission was to prowl the waters off Indochina, reconnoiter, and report by radio on Japanese movements in the East China Sea and the Gulf of Siam. Cynics could conclude that the real intention of the President was to invite the Japanese to sink the snooper *Lanikai* or another of the schooners—a very cheap but provocative sinking of an American warship, presumably intended to ignite a declared or even undeclared war between the United States and Japan, not unlike the quasi-war that already existed in the Atlantic between the U.S. Navy and German U-boats. From postwar discussions with senior U.S. naval officers, Tolley became convinced that the *Lanikai* had been "set up to bait an incident, a *casus belli.*" Admiral Kimmel himself told Tolley in 1965 that he had heard about the dispatch of the "defensive information patrol" designed to create an incident. "When that and other moves failed to involve us," Kimmel told Tolley, "the betrayal of the fleet at Pearl Harbor was decided upon."[7]

Presumably Tolley's revelations did not shatter the longstanding cover-up, for he later supplied damning information on the Pearl Harbor affair to John Toland, a veteran writer and winner of a Pulitzer Prize for a book on prewar and wartime Japan. After ploughing through reams of documentation, searching for unpublished materials, and rethinking the whole puzzle, in 1982 Toland brought out the book called *Infamy: Pearl Harbor and Its Aftermath,*[8] which he termed the tenth (and supposedly definitive) investigation. He leveled two main new charges: that American radio operators tracked mysterious signals emanating from Adm. Nagumo Chūichi's Pearl Harbor task force, intercepts that were suppressed by U.S. intelligence, and that the Dutch naval attaché in Washington, Capt. Johan E. Meijer Ranneft, kept a secret diary that revealed that the U.S. Office of Naval Intelligence (ONI) had not "mislaid" the Japanese carrier fleet, as claimed by the authorities in Washington, but had actually detected, in early December 1941, two Japanese aircraft carriers heading east toward Pearl Harbor.

At the time *Infamy* appeared, the press reported that Japanese sources vigorously denied the allegation that Nagumo's flotilla broke radio silence. In 1984, while conducting extensive research in Japan dealing with the period 1941–1942, the author had occasion to interview a number of Japanese respondents, including several ranking survivors of the old Imperial Navy. Nobody had heard of a compromise of Nagumo's orders for radio silence, and indeed nobody could even visualize such an infraction in the tightly disciplined Japanese Navy.[9]

American sources have questioned the solidity of Toland's contentions and his use of evidence, including the masking of the identity of a twenty-year-old American electronics "whiz kid"—"Seaman First Class Z."[10] We now know the identity of this sailor, today a retired businessman who lives in the San Francisco area. In 1983, the U.S. Navy located and interviewed the man. Among others, Professor Telford Taylor of Columbia University has examined the publicly available transcript of the interview with Seaman "Z." Taylor concludes that the sailor's replies "leave him small importance as a witness. He knew nothing at first hand, and little at second or third hand" from the naval lieutenant who was his superior in the intelligence division of the 12th Naval District in San Francisco. Although Toland suggests that "Z" was able to zero in on certain "queer signals that didn't make sense at such frequency" and thus to deduce that the missing Japanese carrier force may have been uncovered, Taylor concludes that, for all the seaman knew, the signals might have come from fishing boats.[11]

Toland's interpretation of the Dutch naval attaché's diary has drawn particularly critical attention. On December 2, 1941, says Toland, the attaché was shown the location of the Japanese strike force steaming "halfway between Japan and Hawaii." But the diary entry refers only to the two carriers having "left Japan on an easterly course." No mention is made of a strike force. On December 6, Meijer Ranneft heard from ONI that the Japanese carriers were now 300 or 400 miles northwest of Honolulu. "No one mentioned anything about a possible attack on Pearl Harbor." According to the diary, however, the two carriers were located *west* of Honolulu, and nobody was talking about a possible *air* attack on Honolulu. "I certainly do not think about it," added Meijer Ranneft, "because I believe that everybody in Honolulu is 100 percent on guard, as is everybody at ONI." ONI's vague explanation that "the Japanese were perhaps interested in 'eventual American intentions,' " Toland asserts, did not make much sense to Meijer Ranneft. Toland's translation of the diary passage reads, "probably in connection with Japanese reports of eventual American action." One can see why the attaché would have been confused by such language. More plausibly, the passage should read, "possibly with respect to Japanese reporting in case of American action."[12]

In short, ONI had learned of the movement of two Japanese aircraft carriers west of Hawaii. The fact itself is not new, for the U.S. Navy has long admitted that, before the attack on Pearl Harbor, two

Japanese carriers had been seen at Kwajalein in the Marshall Islands. The Americans thought the two Japanese carriers were merely a surveillance force, and they certainly did not suspect an air strike against Pearl Harbor. Only after the raid did the erroneous assumption arise that the Japanese strike force had originated from Kwajalein.[13] Toland's overall and unexciting conclusion, however, is the same as that of the classic exponents of the Devil Theory: that Kimmel and Short were innocent patsies for Washington and that, "following the maxim of world leaders," Roosevelt "was convinced that the end justified the means and so truth was suppressed."[14]

Despite these pyrotechnics, there is little fire stirring in the embers of revisionism. The most informed American scholar on Pearl Harbor, the late Professor Gordon W. Prange, demolished the supposed devilry of Roosevelt and company in his book, appropriately titled *At Dawn We Slept* (1981).[15] There are no straw men in the Prange thesis; by 1941, in his view, war between the United States and Japan had become unavoidable, regardless of the point of ignition. After all, it was Adm. Yamamoto Isoroku, the Japanese Combined Fleet Commander, not Roosevelt, who devised the Pearl Harbor raid in utmost secrecy. Even if one accepts the notion that a plot did exist to lure the Japanese into striking first, it was not necessary to leave every U.S. battleship of the Pacific Fleet in port, defenseless at anchor, awaiting massacre on a Sunday morning. Indeed, why not have shared the President's covert intentions and unique information with bright commanders on Oahu, so as to spring a murderous trap on Nagumo's strike force once it had proceeded beyond the point of no return?[16]

As for Secretary Hull's alleged ultimatum (a word used by most Japanese and many Americans to this day), issued to Japanese emissaries in Washington in late November 1941, Hull never stopped insisting that the document was no more than a statement of the American position—a working paper. It *is* a stern statement, but it contains none of the apparatus of an ultimatum, which by definition calls for an end of negotiation and a resort to force.[17]

In his durable history of U.S. naval operations in the Second World War, Samuel Eliot Morison invoked a Homeric allusion when he suggested that at Pearl Harbor ". . . the fates decreed that American pride be humbled. . . ."[18] Apposite to our present examination is Morison's more forensic point: "Nobody in Washington could warn Hawaii of something he neither knew nor suspected."[19]

In Ronald Lewin's final book, published in 1982, on the subject of codes, ciphers, and the conquest of Japan, the British author insisted that "no specific indicator" was available to pinpoint Pearl Harbor as the target of the Japanese aircraft carriers. Indeed, Lewin felt that even the latest researchers had "disinterred . . . nothing convincing." He reminds us that

> the weeks and months preceding [the] ultimate attack represent a phase which, for the historian, makes the most stringent demands on his duty to recall how things looked *at the time*. This is the criterion to apply, and when one does so one sees that, given all the existing circumstances and the extraordinary crackle of 'noise', no intelligence from any other country would probably have reached conclusions different from the Americans'—without the crystal ball of a fortune-teller.[20]

In sum, despite its attraction to suspicious and imaginative minds, the Devil Theory cannot withstand tough historical scrutiny. Among the Americans of December 1941, there was much evidence of human weakness, incompetence, mistakes, and opportunism, but not of provable conspiracy.

NOTES

1. John Toland, *Infamy: Pearl Harbor and Its Aftermath* (New York: Doubleday, 1982), p. 14.

2. Hartford Van Dyke, *The Skeleton in Uncle Sam's Closet* (Vancouver, Washington: Van Dyke Publications, 1973), p. 80.

3. [Coox's allusion here is to the works of such men as Charles Beard and Charles C. Tansill. See suggested readings.—EDS.]

4. Frank Schuler and Robin Moore, *The Pearl Harbor Cover-Up* (New York: Pinnacle Books, 1976).

5. Ibid., pp. v–vi, 1.

6. Kemp Tolley, *Cruise of the Lanikai: Incitement to War* (Annapolis, Md.: Naval Institute Press, 1973).

7. Ibid., p. 279.

8. John Toland, *Infamy, op. cit.*

9. I conducted my interviews mainly at Bōei Kenshūsho, Tokyo, 1984.

10. See David Kahn, "Did FDR Invite the Pearl Harbor Attack?," *New York Review of Books*, 27 May 1982, pp. 36–40.

11. Telford Taylor, "Day of Infamy, Decades of Doubt," *Asia Magazine*, 29 July 1984, pp. 7–10. Professor Iwashima Hisao of Bōei Kenshūsho has already digested and accepted Taylor's gloss. See "Ruuzuberuto wa shitte itaka: Shinjuwan wo

meguru Beikoku no seiji senso" [Did Roosevelt Know? America's Political War Vis-à-vis Pearl Harbor], *Tokyo Shinbun,* 6 December 1984 (P.M. edition).

12. John Toland, *Infamy,* pp. 282–284, 298–299. For assistance with my rudimentary knowledge of the Dutch language, I thank one of my graduate students at San Diego State University, Mr. André Ausems.

13. Samuel Eliot Morison, *History of United States Naval Operations in World War II* (Boston: Little Brown, 1947–62), vol. 3 (1948); *The Rising Sun in the Pacific, 1931–April 1942,* p. 214.

14. John Toland, *Infamy,* p. 324.

15. Gordon W. Prange, in collaboration with Donald M. Goldstein and Katherine V. Dillon, *At Dawn We Slept: The Untold Story of Pearl Harbor* (New York: McGraw-Hill, 1981).

16. See R. J. C. Butow's review of both the Prange and the Toland books in *Journal of Japanese Studies,* Summer 1983, pp. 412–420.

17. As in the case of many primary sources in history, more people talk about Hull's proposals than have consulted them. It is instructive to read or reread *The Memoirs of Cordell Hull* (New York: Macmillan, 1948), vol. 2, pp. 1072–1087; and Joseph C. Grew, *Ten Years in Japan* (New York: Simon and Schuster, 1944), pp. 482–486. John Costello is the latest to be exercised by the question of the background to Hull's statement. See *The Pacific War* (New York: Rawson, Wade, 1981), chap. 38. [Technically, Coox's interpretation is correct, but two questions need to be raised. Did the Japanese not interpret the Hull Note as meaning that no *modus vivendi* was possible? Tsunoda's rendition of Foreign Minister Togo's reaction to the Hull Note is instructive. What was Hull's reaction to his own note? In the Conroy-Klein essay we see that he felt betrayed by the British and Chinese failure to provide him with greater flexibility. Furthermore, he told the secretaries of war and navy that the matter was now in their hands.—EDS.]

18. Samuel Eliot Morison, *Rising Sun,* p. 210.

19. Ibid., pp. 135, 141.

20. Ronald Lewin, *The American Magic: Codes, Ciphers and the Defeat of Japan* (New York: Farrar Straus Giroux, 1982), p. 65. "Whether in terms of cybernetics or of intelligence perception, noise is the buzz set up by competing information signals which prevents the essential message from being heard loud and clear." Ibid., p. 63.

14. Churchill, Roosevelt, and the China Question in Pre-Pearl Harbor Diplomacy

DAVID KLEIN AND HILARY CONROY

IN the aftermath of the aborted *modus vivendi* in late November 1941, Cordell Hull sharply castigated the British for failing, in his estimate, to support his truce initiative. He blamed the British for succumbing to the pressure of Chiang Kai-shek instead of standing firm.[1] The source of Hull's anguish was Winston Churchill's telegram of November 25 to Franklin Roosevelt, drafted in response to the president's personal approach. It was a succinct and abrupt sounding document that emphasized the risks attending the possible collapse of China without mentioning the benefits that Roosevelt had in mind when he sanctioned the search for an interim agreement with Japan. Arriving at a crucial phase of the U.S.-Japanese negotiations, Churchill's response played a significant role in terminating the momentum for a standstill agreement.[2]

How do we decipher Churchill's preoccupation with Chiang Kai-shek when his obsessive concern at the time was the defeat of Hitler and America's entry into the European war? What was the prime minister's intention in composing his terse reply to Roosevelt? Did Churchill, for example, gamble or calculate that a Pacific war would catapult the Americans into the European struggle?

On the basis of circumstantial materials, one is tempted to reply in the affirmative. Upon his repatriation to London in 1942, Britain's ambassador to Japan, Sir Robert Craigie, drafted a secret and extensive memorandum that challenged London's handling of the crisis in the fall of 1941 and rebuked the government for not doing its utmost to bring about a relaxation of the deepening strains in U.S.-Japanese relations.[3] Churchill himself observed in a confidential note to Anthony Eden in September 1943 that it was "a blessing that Japan attacked the United States and thus brought America wholeheartedly and unitedly into the war."[4] Indeed, at a cabinet session as early as October 1940 the prime minister "questioned . . . that it was not in our interests that the United States should be involved in war in the Pacific."[5]

Suspicions about Churchill's intentions did not surface publicly in the post-war era, but they were aired privately. In 1952, for example, Dr. Evatt, Australia's foreign minister at the time of Pearl Harbor, remarked to Ambassador Nishi, Japan's vice foreign minister in the Tōjō cabinet, that in his view Churchill had wanted war.[6]

Although this type of information is circumstantial and the juxtaposition of statements cannot substitute for hard evidence, there are questions about the intentions of the British. Did Chiang Kai-shek maneuver the British into disassociating themselves from Roosevelt's *modus vivendi* efforts, or did the British manipulate the China question for their own ends? Did the British response reflect and reveal how misinformed the government officials were about the high stakes that were being played out in Washington in late November 1941?

We can begin by reducing the subject of the "China question" to a manageable entity. The "China question" emerged as a matter of major concern as a direct consequence of Japan's search for an enlarged military, political, and economic role in Asia. This in itself, however, was never sufficient to bring the Western powers and Japan to the verge of war. Japan's assault on China had been in progress for more than a decade without any country contemplating anything even remotely close to war with Japan in defense of China.

What then radicalized the situation so profoundly that by the late fall of 1941 Japan and the United States stood at the brink of war? The immediate and most provocative issue was not Japan's continuing aggression against China, but rather Japan's expansion beyond China and into Southeast Asia—in particular, Indochina. This was critical, indeed pivotal, as far as Roosevelt was concerned, for it magnified, as no previous expansion had hitherto done, the threat to the British empire in Singapore. It threatened Britain's capacity to survive the struggle with the Nazis, and Roosevelt's overriding concern was to ensure, if not guarantee, Britain's ability to withstand, and ultimately to overcome, the colossal dangers to the West that Hitler, the Nazis, and the Germans represented. In short, it was neither the Japanese invasion of China nor the possibility of Chiang's collapse that moved Roosevelt to initiate comprehensive embargoes against Japan during the summer of 1941. On the contrary, it was the threat to the British empire more than anything else that forged America's stand during that summer.[7] The central issue in Roosevelt's overall appraisal was not the rescue of Chiang Kai-shek but the containment of the Japanese menace to the British in Asia.

America responded to the Japanese invasion of South Indochina with an extension of existing embargoes that eventually culminated in the severing of trade relations between Japan and the United States. The subject of the embargoes is complex and not generally well understood, but an appreciation of how they unfolded is vastly relevant to an understanding of the haphazard diplomacy of this period.[8] It is possible to depict the embargoes, or the freezing order of July 1941, as a bold and decisive move to challenge Japan's bid for Asian hegemony, as a carefully orchestrated or planned maneuver to put teeth into America's bargaining position and ultimately to bring Japan to heel. Such a characterization, while perhaps convenient, grossly distorts what actually transpired. The embargoes may have been bold, and they did indeed prove decisive, but it is questionable whether they were carefully planned.

The embargo decision was not the outgrowth of a carefully conceived policy designed to strengthen America's position at the negotiating table; on the contrary, it emanated from the exhaustion of Roosevelt's options in the search for a way to handle the new crisis. Phrased differently, by the summer of 1941 the administration had left itself little or no choice other than to remain passive in the face of Japan's new challenge or to escalate the existing embargoes. Something had to be done in a hurry, and the only course open was to intensify the existing pressures. In this sense, Washington had become a victim of the spiraling sequence of economic pressures that it had initiated a year earlier.

This, however, is only one aspect of the story, an incomplete picture of that precipitate, agonized period. If the U.S. leaders rushed into the embargo decision as the only viable course left open, they had not clearly resolved among themselves just how far they intended to travel along that perilous path. The evidence seems to suggest, for example, that in approving the freezing order of July 24, Roosevelt left unanswered the question of whether oil was to be totally embargoed. This vacillation was consistent with his management of the crisis both before and after July 1941.

Reduced to essentials, the main issue in the weeks following the freezing decision was not the embargo, but the uncertainty within the administration about how to apply it. The freezing order permitted Japan to apply for export licenses, but neither Roosevelt nor Hull provided guidelines for approving or rejecting the applications. It seems clear, however, that the president did not contemplate a total shutoff.[9]

Nevertheless, in the end trade was brought to a complete standstill. How then do we deal with the discrepancy between Roosevelt's intention to permit a limited oil trade and the emergence of a comprehensive, airtight embargo? Space limitations do not permit the exploration of this question here, but it is important to point out that such a question exists. A brief answer is to be found in the developmental character of the embargo, the ambivalent nature of the instructions, and Roosevelt's preoccupation with the European war and preparations for his historic meeting with Churchill in August. In short, the emergence of a total embargo reflected a process that was more haphazard than it was deliberate—a development that went further than was originally intended but that in the end was accepted by the government. Once the embargo was in place and fully publicized, it became difficult for the president to retreat and at the same time mobilize opinion against Nazi aggression.[10]

Roosevelt recognized all along that a total oil shutdown was likely to precipitate a Japanese move against the Dutch and/or the British rather than to deter aggression. This explains his reluctance throughout July to forge a clear-cut decision on oil sanctions. However, if the president recognized the dangers implicit in a comprehensive embargo, he was also gambling that Japan would forestall a move against the Dutch or the Russians pending a clearer indication of the probable outcome of the German-Russian war. He calculated that Japanese decision makers were closely attuned to the progress of the Soviet-German struggle and that, pending some clarification, Japan would restrain its hand.

That this gamble was ill advised and incorrect soon became apparent; the Magic code intercepts made it increasingly clear during the fall that the embargo was forcing Japan to opt for war.[11]

A Pacific war was not, however, on Roosevelt's agenda—revisionist history notwithstanding. He made it clear that his strategy was structured upon holding the line in the Pacific, gaining time, and averting war in Asia in anticipation of America's entry into the European struggle; he confided this to Churchill at the Atlantic meeting in August, and on this score he enjoyed the full support of the service chiefs. However, the gradual emergence of a complete embargo undercut his strategy. Instead of complementing his Europe-first strategy and orientation, the oil embargoes threatened to disorient and distract the president from what he conceived to be his primary task by forcing Japan to consider war.

It is against this background that we must consider the last-ditch efforts of the administration to disengage itself from the escalating slide towards war, for the evidence indicates that a vacillating Roosevelt moved to simplify the issues to prevent a Pacific confrontation.[12]

Before detailing this important phase and the role of the China question, it is relevant to define Churchill's attitude toward the U.S.-Japanese talks and the risk of a Pacific war. This can be illustrated by referencing London's attitude toward the July oil embargoes and the government's response to Craigie's plea early in November that London intervene to help save the U.S.-Japanese talks from collapse, or, as he phrased it, to place the talks on the rails again. It is perhaps not too much to say that Washington dragged the British along in intensifying the pressures against Japan during the summer of 1941. London clearly understood that a total trade shutdown would bring the question of war to the forefront, but, although Churchill did not want a Pacific war, he wanted even less a crisis in Anglo-American relations. Therefore, he was reluctant to stand up to the Americans, calculating that it was safer to acquiesce to Washington's requests than to risk a breach. Sir Alexander Cadogan of the London foreign office summed up this attitude somewhat pointedly when he noted in May 1941: "And he suffers from the delusion that any cold water thrown on any hare brained U.S. suggestion will stop the U.S. coming into the [European] war."[13] Cadogan's reference to the European war highlights the preeminent thrust of Churchill's efforts as far as Anglo-American relations were concerned, which was the task of bringing the United States into the war against Hitler. It was the dominating challenge to which all other considerations were subordinate.

Why, though, should a candid expression or difference of opinion threaten to estrange relations with Washington? After all, in the instance of the oil embargo, it was the British and Dutch who were the most immediately vulnerable to a Japanese advance. The answer lies in the suspicion and distrust that continued to haunt Anglo-American relations as late as the fall of 1941. It is impossible to do this topic justice in the space allotted here, but the fragile nature of the U.S.-British relationship as it pertained to Britain in the Far East was extremely important. The legacy of Anglo-American discord over Britain's policy during and after the Manchurian Incident remained a significant concern in the minds of key British decision makers. With the stakes as high as they were in the fall of 1941 and with Churchill intent upon converting the Anglo-American relationship into a full-fledged war alliance against Hitler, the prime minister was reluctant to adopt a position that could be construed as an unwillingness to endorse the Americans—even at the risk of a Pacific war. In short, in the paramount interests of preserving the growing unity of the Anglo-American relationship, London was prepared to accept a Pacific war.

This helps to explain London's rejection of Craigie's recommendations in early November that the British intercede to ensure against a collapse of the American-Japanese talks. Apprehensive that Japan was rapidly headed for a military solution, Craigie wired London on November 1, urging the government to participate in the talks that he described as the last barrier to war.[14] Doubting the efficacy of such an approach, however, and clearly concerned over the deleterious impact it might make on the Americans, London opted to ignore Craigie's pleas and to leave the talks, and the responsibility for their outcome, squarely in the hands of the Americans. As a secret foreign office review prepared during the war stated: ". . . to advocate a policy of concessions might have the positive disadvantage of causing misunderstanding with the United States of discrediting Great Britain with her friends generally, at a most critical juncture." London, in other words, calculated that less risk was inherent in accepting war as a political necessity than in trying to help defuse the crisis and thereby endanger a crucial relationship with Washington. Eden may have openly implied this when he told Craigie that Britain considered the "balance of advantage" to reside in letting the Americans play out the talks.

By the late fall, the Magic intercepts were making it abundantly clear that Japan was moving rapidly toward war; the likely outcome of the trade shutdown, this was not the outcome that Roosevelt expected from his efforts to gain time. As such, the comprehensive embargoes ran counter to, were inconsistent with, and undercut the basic thrust of Roosevelt's strategy toward Japan.

It was perhaps in recognition of this dilemma that Roosevelt moved to de-escalate the crisis, to back the United States out of the corner into which her economic diplomacy had pushed her by

November 1941. We might point out that during July Roosevelt had clearly indicated to Lord Halifax, London's ambassador to Washington, that neither the British nor the Americans could fight a war simultaneously in the Atlantic and in the Pacific. If that kind of situation developed, Roosevelt noted, "we should have to say to Japan that we were busy at the moment with Germany and Europe, but that they should make no mistake that when we have finished with our most pressing task we should clear up our differences with them later."[15] It was this perception of global priorities that formed the basis of Roosevelt's efforts to defuse the crisis and to regain control over events that had slid beyond the administration's grasp.

In the remaining space we cannot detail the full efforts of the administration to de-escalate the crisis, but we will explain in some detail the process by which Churchill's advocacy of Chiang Kai-shek's position undercut the search for a standstill agreement with Japan. In contradistinction to Churchill, Roosevelt was now seriously considering downplaying China in the Japanese-American talks. Indeed, proposals drafted both in the White House and in the State Department during this critical search for a workable formula de-emphasized the China question.

Hull first mentioned the possibility of a truce to the British on November 18 when he conferred with Sir Ronald Campbell,[16] but it was not until four days later that the secretary formally introduced the question of America's counteroffer to Japan's proposal of November 20. It was at this meeting, attended by Halifax, the Chinese ambassador, and the Australian and Dutch ministers that Hull outlined the interim arrangement he was contemplating. Halifax's record of this important interview reached London on November 23. It was London's first official indication of the content of the U.S.-Japanese talks. The purpose of the *modus vivendi*, Halifax advised, was to gain time for discussions with a view to securing an overall settlement; unless progress in this direction was reached, the *modus vivendi* was to remain in force no longer than two to three months. The basis of the agreement might be a *quid pro quo*, i.e., the withdrawal of most of Japan's forces from Indochina in exchange for a partial relaxation of the trade pressures resulting from the July embargoes. Before pursuing this any further, Hull made it clear at the November 22 interview that he wanted to know the position of the British, Australian, Dutch, and Chinese governments.[17]

Between November 23 and 24, London reviewed the American

proposal. The foreign office was skeptical of Japan's aims but was willing to support Hull if he considered a truce desirable. Churchill emphasized the China question. Writing to Eden on November 23, he expressed support for a partial relaxation of the pressure provided that it did *not* entail the abandonment of China or the suspension of aid to Chiang Kai-shek and provided that it did not leave Japan free to move against the USSR.

London's position was detailed to Halifax in a dispatch sent on November 24. Intended as a reply to Hull's interview of November 22, the foreign office countered that the Japanese proposal should be regarded as the "opening movement in a process of bargaining" and that Washington should press the Japanese for a hard bargain. Rather than request the removal of the "bulk" of Japanese troops from Indochina, London recommended that the Americans press for the total withdrawal of Japanese forces and equipment, the suspension of military action against Chiang, and assurances against action in Southeast Asia, the northern Pacific, and Russia. In exchange, London was not prepared to concede a relaxation of the embargo pressures insofar as they applied to war-related materials. In short, London's reply moved the China question close to the forefront again while recommending a reduction in the concessions Hull was contemplating.

Hull did not receive this reply until the morning of November 25. On the previous day he had handed the British, Australian, Dutch, and Chinese representatives a copy of the *modus vivendi* that he was planning to deliver to the Japanese. He emphasized the advantages of a truce but was strongly disturbed that the foreign representatives had not yet received replies from their home governments. Characterizing the absence of a reply as a "lack of interest, and lack of disposition to cooperate," he ended the meeting by saying that he was not sure whether to proceed with the truce without some idea of the position of their governments.

Hull was concerned about enlisting a broad consensus of support for his truce initiative, and it is clear that he was highly displeased, if not angered, at the absence of a response. He was not obtaining the prompt, indeed urgent, support that he required and that was, in all probability, a political necessity if he was to be able to sell an agreement to his opponents in the cabinet. This probably explains why Hull approached the president on the evening of November 24, after the meeting with the foreign envoys, and urged Roosevelt to appeal directly to Churchill for an answer.[18]

Roosevelt's letter was drafted on November 24, but before it reached London, Halifax received the foreign officer's dispatch on the morning of November 25. This document contained London's response to the interview of November 22. The British informed Hull that the Japanese proposal was "clearly unacceptable" but that they would support him if he thought it good tactics to have the Japanese advance better terms or to produce a counteroffer himself. If Hull opted for the latter, London advised that he press Japan for very stiff terms and cautioned him that Tokyo was exaggerating "the dangers of delay" to rush him into a decision.

One can well imagine Hull's consternation at this reply, reflecting as it did how hopelessly out of touch the British were with the naked reality of the climaxing crisis. The British reply was re-emphasizing the China issue just when the Americans were downplaying it, and Hull seized upon this in his warning to Halifax that London's recommendation to make the *modus vivendi* conditional upon Japan's cessation of military operations against Chiang Kai-shek "would destroy hope of acceptance." Hull observed that the China issue was one of the major areas of conflict between Japan and the United States and that it would have to be resolved in a general settlement. The truce was to allow for a continuation of the negotiations that would make such a settlement possible. He stressed to Halifax "the utter impracticability of requesting a suspension of further military advances in China." In advocating the *modus vivendi,* Hull was intent upon averting a complete breakdown and upon securing a Japanese commitment that would freeze Japanese movements beyond China even at the temporary expense of acquiescing in continued Japanese operations against Chiang Kai-shek. The British apparently failed to appreciate the overall significance of this strategy in terms of America's global priorities.

It was at this juncture and against this background that Churchill's reply to Roosevelt's telegram reached Washington—sometime during the night of November 25 or the early morning of the next day. It opened with the disclaimer that "of course, it is for you to handle this business and we certainly do not want an additional war." The remaining seven sentences of a remarkably terse statement emphasized Churchill's grave concern about China and the dangers to which the country would be exposed if Chiang's resistance collapsed. "We are sure," the prime minister observed in the penultimate sentence, "that the regard of the United States for the Chinese cause will govern your action." In the end, this phrase contradicted the entire thrust of Churchill's opening disclaimer about not wanting another war; it underscored the China issue precisely when the Americans wished to de-emphasize it.[19]

Arriving at a tense juncture in the U.S.-Japanese talks, this curt statement that stressed, if not exaggerated, China's predicament without affording consideration to the overall picture, was clearly not the support that Hull had hoped to mobilize on behalf of the interim arrangement. Hull interpreted Churchill's reply as an absence of support for a *modus vivendi,* and on the same day he broke off talks with the Japanese. The next day Sumner Welles informed Halifax that "the message sent by Mr. Churchill to the President could hardly be regarded as 'full support' but on the contrary, very grave questioning of the course then proposed."[20] Hull himself was to complain bitterly at the absence of British support and to criticize Churchill for failing to stand up to Chiang Kai-shek's pressure.

Halifax later informed Welles that Churchill's message to the president "had been intended merely to express the objections on the part of the Chinese Government."[21] This is far from clear, however, particularly given that Halifax was not kept informed by London of the prime minister's thinking. Indeed, Sir Alexander Cadogan at the foreign office subsequently wrote to Halifax "that our feelings as regards the *modus vivendi* were in no way dictated to us by the Chinese. We received no representations from them on the subject either in London or from Chungking and we did not take them into consultation here."[22]

What then was in Churchill's mind when he drafted his terse reply to Roosevelt's personal inquiry of November 24? In his postwar account Churchill wrote that in drafting his answer to the president he had to be very careful of the limits to which he could go in commenting upon American policy, and he did not want to encourage the belief that the British were trying to push the Americans into war. As a general description of the direction and tone of British policy-making toward Washington at the time, this characterization is accurate enough, but there are doubts as to whether this explanation fits the circumstances of Churchill's message to Roosevelt. For one thing, the British had already made some detailed and stiff comments in regard to the U.S. counteroffer just two days earlier—a fact that is difficult to reconcile with Churchill's postwar stand that the British had to be guarded in their reply. Second, Roosevelt had personally approached the prime minister to ascertain his attitude about the *modus vivendi.* In contacting Churchill, Roosevelt did not work through the regular diplomatic structure but rather through a secret and private channel of communication that they had developed during the fall of 1939 for matters of pressing importance. By November 1941, Roosevelt and Churchill had developed a certain intimacy in their growing correspondence of matters of vital importance to both countries—a consideration that also argues against the prime minister's postwar explanation.

A second possibility is that Churchill may have been genuinely concerned about the likelihood of Chiang's collapse. Nonetheless, he had no reason to suspect that the United States would sign a truce if it permitted the Japanese to dispose of Chiang Kai-shek. If Cadogan's unpublished account to Halifax is reliable, Churchill received no Chinese representatives in London or Chungking at the time during which the prime minister drafted his reply. Moreover, Hull made it clear that the Americans contemplated an overall China settlement; this would hardly make sense if the United States was prepared to acquiesce in Chiang's defeat. A more likely explanation is that Churchill's emphasis of the China question did not take into account its potential impact on the outcome of the U.S.-Japanese truce talks. It is interesting to record that late in December 1941 Churchill observed that he was shocked at "the extraordinary significance of China in American minds," and that it was "strangely out of proportion," even in official thinking at top levels.[23]

But why emphasize China at this particular juncture? Roosevelt's message to Churchill of November 24, outlining his proposal for an *ad hoc* arrangement with Japan, did not mention the China situation. It is conceivable that Churchill's one-paragraph reply dealing exclusively with Chiang Kai-shek—in complete contradistinction to the president's message—was intended to restore some balance, while failing to anticipate the negative reception it would receive in Washington. If Churchill and the foreign office did not, in fact, anticipate Washington's response, it is difficult to escape the conclusion that the document represented a clumsy and inept display of diplomacy that was dangerously out of touch with the reality of the crisis at hand. The foreign office staff held that this was just the beginning of the bargaining game, not recognizing that the closing stages were upon them.

Not only did the British fail to appreciate the extreme sensitivity of the situation, but they also failed to understand the importance of *modus vivendi* to U.S. efforts to preserve the peace. Furthermore, when the *modus vivendi* was withdrawn, London wholly missed the significance of the decision. Later on during the war the foreign office was to acknowledge secretly that "at the time it was not immediately apparent that not only was the *modus vivendi* dead but that the American-Japanese conversations were virtually at an end."[24] In short, the crisis had overtaken the British before they fully realized what was happening. When the meaning of the aborted *modus vivendi* finally penetrated the foreign office, it was too late for Halifax to inform Hull, as he did on the morning of November 29, that London was "fully prepared to support an interim agreement," or for Churchill to talk of deterrence the following day.[25] The moment, fragile as it was, had passed, and by moving the China question to center stage, Churchill had unwittingly helped to stall the momentum within the American government for a search for an interim agreement to prevent war.

NOTES

1. Cordell Hull, *The Memoirs of Cordell Hull* (New York: Macmillan, 1948), vol. II, p. 1081; U.S. Department of State, *Papers Relating to the Foreign Relations of the United States* 1941, vol. IV (Washington, D.C.: 1956), pp. 685–686 (hereafter cited as *Foreign Relations Papers*); David H. Klein, "Anglo-American Diplomacy and the Pacific War: The Politics of Confrontation" (Ph.D. diss., University of Pennsylvania, 1977), pp. 224–243.

2. Francis L. Loewenheim, Manfred Jonas, and Harold D. Langley, eds., *Roosevelt and Churchill: Their Secret Wartime Correspondence* (New York: Saturday Review Press, 1975), pp. 166–167; David H. Klein, "Anglo-American Diplomacy," pp. 230–232.

3. Craigie to Eden, 4 February 1943, Public Record Office (London), Foreign Office, F821/G, 371/35957. Craigie's published memoirs, *Behind the Japanese Mask* (London: Hutchinson, 1946) gloss over his fundamental disagreement expressed in the memorandum to Eden; David H. Klein, "Anglo-American Diplomacy," pp. 198, 244.

4. Churchill to Eden, 19 September 1943, Public Record Office (London), *Prime Minister's Personal Minutes*, M588/3, PM/43?272 in Foreign Office 371/33957.

5. Public Record Office, *War Cabinet Conclusions,* 264 (40), F4534G, FO 371/24709, 2 October 1940. The Foreign Office was concerned that U.S. involvement in the Pacific would mean a reduction in aid to Britain in the war against Hitler, ibid., 20–21 September 1940.

6. Information from an interview with Nishi.

7. [Klein and Conroy join Utley in seeing the Japanese invasion of Indochina as decisive, but the rationale for their conclusions is different.—EDS.]

8. For a discussion of the embargoes see Diary of Henry L. Stimson (New Haven: Sterling Library, Yale University), especially notes of cabinet meeting, 18 July 1941; Diary of Henry Morgenthau, Jr., (Franklin D. Roosevelt Presidential Library, Hyde Park, New York), especially memorandum of phone conversation between Morgenthau and Harold Ickes, 23 July 1941; Stanley K. Hornbeck Papers (Stanford, Calif.: Hoover Institution), especially memorandum on "Situation in the Far East: Japan's Intention: Our Problem: Summary, 16 July 1941; Harold L. Ickes, *The Secret Diary* (New York: Simon and Schuster, 1955), vol. III, *The Lowering Clouds, 1939-1941,* especially pp. 590–594. For further analysis see David H. Klein, "Anglo-American Diplomacy," pp. 267–288, and Michael A. Barnhart, *Japan Prepares for Total War: The Search for Economic Security, 1915-1941* (Ithaca, N.Y.: Cornell University Press, 1987), pp. 226–231.

9. See *Foreign Relations Papers,* pp. 846–848 for the wording.

10. [Iriye's essay stressed the greater leeway that the Americans had in making foreign policy in the 1930s. The above treatment, however, suggests that by 1941 American foreign policy decision makers enjoyed limited maneuverability because they had become prisoners of past actions and fixed attitudes. In this essay we also see how limited the Americans' options were because of Chinese and British influence. Fujiwara's essay emphasizes the impact that years of Japanese propaganda reaped in preventing any option but war by 1941. He argues that a retreat from Japan's goals would have produced internal revolt.—EDS.]

11. U.S. Congress, *Hearings Before that Joint Committee on the Investigation of the Pearl Harbor Attack,* 79th Cong., 1st sess., vol. 12 (Washington, D.C., 1946), pp. 90–100.

12. [In their interpretation Klein and Conroy not only attack the Beard-Tansill school but also place themselves at loggerheads with Best's assumption that Roosevelt wanted war.—EDS.]

13. David Dilks, ed. *The Diaries of Sir Alexander Cadogan* (London: Putnam, 1971), p. 375.

14. Craigie to Eden, 1 November 1941, Public Record Office (London), Foreign Office, F11672/86/23, FO 371/27911.

15. Halifax to Eden, 7 July 1941, Public Record Office (London), Foreign Office, F5957/5649/G, FO 371/27763.

16. Hull memorandum, 18 November 1941, *Foreign Relations Papers,* pp. 616–617.

17. Foreign office to Craigie, 24 November 1941, Public Records Office (London), Foreign Office, F12544/7883G, FO 371/27912.

18. [The Cordell Hull we see here does reflect the more realistic secretary of state of which Utley wrote. Hull seems to be a more complex man than the simple idealist-moralist characterization allows.—EDS.]

19. Foreign office to Craigie, 26 November 1941, Public Records Office (London), Foreign Office, F12544/7883/G, FO 371/27912; *Foreign Relations Papers,* pp. 655–656; Loewenheim et al., *Roosevelt and Churchill,* pp. 166–167; Winston Churchill, *The Grand Alliance* (Boston: Houghton Mifflin, 1950), pp. 595–596.

20. Welles memorandum, 27 November 1941, *Foreign Relations Papers,* pp. 666–667.

21. Ibid., 666–667.

22. Foreign office to Washington, 2 December 1941, Public Records Office (London), Foreign Office, F12992/86/23, FO 371/27913; Ashley Clarke minute, 1 December 1941; Halifax to Foreign office, 29 November 1941.

23. See William L. Neumann, *America Encounters Japan* (Baltimore: Johns Hopkins University Press, 1963), p. 292.

24. Foreign office to Halifax, 2 December 1941, Public Records Office (London), Foreign Office, F12992/7883/G, FO 371/27913.

25. *Foreign Relations Papers,* pp. 666–667.

15. Indochina: Unplanned Incursion

SACHIKO MURAKAMI

JAPAN'S thrust into French Indochina has often been viewed as part of an ambitious military plan for the conquest of Asia. The Japanese military is said to have accomplished the move by overriding the civilians in the cabinet and bullying the helpless French in Indochina. *In Vietnam: A Dragon Embattled,* for instance, Joseph Buttinger discusses the "fate" of French Indochina as follows:

> The war party in Tokyo had long decided that the lasting material basis for Japan's greatness (one condition of which was the subjugation of China), lay not in Siberia but in Southeast Asia. Japan consequently settled her border conflicts with the Soviet Union and concentrated on liquidating the "China Incident," in preparation of the move that would give her possession of Southeast Asia's resources. Indochina, apart from having a great many of these resources, was a necessary stopping place on Japan's path of conquest. This sealed the fate of French Indochina. It also forced the French to choose between armed resistance and capitulation.[1]

In *The Rising Sun,* which is said to be a history "largely seen from the Japanese point of view,"[2] John Toland expresses sympathy for the military leaders "who had little understanding of political and diplomatic affairs" but gives an opinion of their conduct that is similar to Buttinger's.

> The militarists who had formed this "Don't miss the bus" policy did not want or foresee the possibility of war. With France defeated, and England battling for its own existence, Indochina with its rubber, tin, tungsten, coal and rice was to them "a treasure lying in the street just waiting to be picked up." Within two months Japan forced the impotent Vichy government to sign a convention in Hanoi allowing Japan to set up six bases in northern Indochina and use that area as a jumping-off place for attack on China.
>
> All this was not done without protests from Matsuoka and more

thoughtful men in the Supreme Command who foresaw a collision course
with the Anglo-Saxons in the making. The Army Chief of Staff, Prince
Kanin, resigned in tears.[3]

These views are half-truths at best. Japan's move into northern
French Indochina was not a carefully planned action but was rather a
result of circumstances. In June 1940, many Japanese—politicians as
well as career diplomats—were intoxicated with Germany's victories
in Europe and were demanding a foreign policy that would further
the nation's southward expansion. Japan's move into northern French
Indochina was carried out during this exhilarating time by the South
China army and the operations divisions of the army's general staff,
led by Major General Tominaga, in the face of opposition from most
members of the army's more cautious high command. The resulting
discrepancies between the orders of the high command and those of
the South China army confused and hampered operations in Indochina. The confusion culminated in a disgraceful incident at Lang
Son in September 1940, when Japanese army units in South China,
under an over-eager general, Nakamura Akito, attacked French forces
from their border position just as French Governor-General Decoux
was conceding an agreement to permit the peaceful entry of a limited
number of Japanese troops to monitor secret supply routes to China.
As a result, the Japanese emperor apologized to the French prisoners
who had been taken and declared Japan's respect for French sovereignty in Indochina then and in the future.

Foreign Minister Matsuoka was not overridden by the army. His diplomatic negotiations with the Vichy government, which had been
planned jointly by the foreign office and the military, resulted in the
enactment of the so-called "Matsuoka-Henry agreement" (August
30, 1940), which was much closer to the French counterproposal than
to the original Japanese proposal. Far from being browbeaten by the
Japanese, the French often succeeded in manipulating negotiations
to their advantage. Even the Franco-Japanese Agreements on Joint
Defense of Indochina, which were concluded immediately after the
outbreak of the Pacific War, were "the formula least dangerous to
French sovereignty,"[4] in Governor-General Decoux's words. Finally,
Prince Kanin resigned as army chief of staff, not in protest against the
militarists' abuse of power but as part of the shakeup conducted by
War Minister Tōjō to demonstrate the army's self-criticism of lax military discipline.

At the root of the misinterpretations of Japan's advance toward French Indochina invariably lies a misconception of the character of the Japanese army and its position in society. The attitude of the army leaders on the eve of the Pacific War is often unfairly labeled "reckless," "irrational," or "ignorant"—because of their role in the decision for war against the United States, a country far superior in war potential. Judging the army on the basis of the result of this decision is, however, a questionable historical approach; judgment should be made based on the circumstances under which the decision was made. War potential is certainly an important factor in winning a war, but it is by no means the only or the decisive one. The army's high command at the time of Japan's advance toward French Indochina was neither reckless nor irrational. It was highly realistic in its observation and judgment of domestic and international affairs.

The high command's main concern at that time was to end the war in China and so relieve Japan's strained economy and cope with the turbulent international situation caused by the European war. The decision to secure military bases in northern French Indochina was based on the strategic importance of the bases for operations against Chiang Kai-shek. True, the army was tempted, in its intoxication with German victories, to extend the China war to the South Seas and thereby solve with one stroke two major problems—Japan's strained economy and the seemingly endless war in China. By April 1941, however, the high command had given up its dream of a march on Singapore, after a thorough examination of the effect of such a daring action and of the material resources available. It then reached an agreement with the navy's high command on the "Essentials of the Policy toward the South Seas," which defined the purpose of Japan's South Seas policy at that time as a rapid expansion of the empire's overall defense capacity and which precluded any resort to arms unless the empire was threatened by embargoes or by Allied encirclement. The army took this step with the intention of turning back to its original objectives—the quick conclusion of the China war and the consolidation of defenses against the Soviet Union.

Domestically, the military leaders were striving to influence the nation's economic and political system to support their goal of a strong national defense. Having learned from their own painful experiences in the early 1930s the futility of attempting to force their will on the nation, the military leaders in the late 1930s were trying to achieve their objectives through the political system. They found formidable rivals, however, in the new breed of bureaucrats in the government ministries. Like the military leaders, these bureaucrats were imbued with nationalism of a pan-Asianistic brand and were critical of economic and political conditions at home and of the post-World War I international legal system. At the same time they were determined to take political power away from the military and to secure it in their own hands. Consequently, they cooperated with the military as long as their interests were served. When it came to matters under their respective jurisdictions, however, they were tenacious in defense of or even expansion of their postions.[5]

In the Ministry of Foreign Affairs, for instance, Ministers Hirota, Arita, and Shigemitsu were leaders of the renovationist faction organized by the new bureaucrats. They maintained that Europe and the United States must abandon their positions in East Asia and recognize Japan as the stabilizing power in that area. They therefore believed that Japan should adopt strong measures toward China. The vanguard of this renovationist faction was the so-called Shiratori group, whose members were younger and more radical than others in the faction who did not favor a reckless course. Foreign Minister Arita was forced by this group to declare Japan's determination to fulfill her "mission" as the stabilizing power in East Asia. Also, Foreign Minister Matsuoka, a renovationist of different pedigree, refused to accept the meddling of the army in diplomatic negotiations with the Vichy government and concluded the aforementioned Matsuoka-Henry agreement that limited Japan's use of military facilities in Indochina strictly to operations against Chiang Kai-shek.

The army leaders had another rival within the army itself. The leadership of the 1936–1941 years, the so-called "Control Faction" *(Tōsei-ha)*, was first organized around 1933 by mid-level staff officers who were concerned about Army Minister Araki's political ineptitude.[6] With the downfall of the "Imperial Way Faction" *(Kōdō-ha)*, led by Generals Araki and Mazaki, shortly after the February 26 Incident (1936), the Control Faction rapidly rose to power. Its efforts to build a strong national defense state inevitably involved the new leadership more deeply in internal politics. In 1938, the Control Faction, in cooperation with renovationist bureaucrats with socialist leanings, began a series of political moves to transform the free economy of the nation into a controlled one. This caused profound anxiety and fear in financial circles and among the ruling class. The Imperial Way Faction saw an opportunity to recapture the power it had lost. By branding the Control Faction Marxist it tried to stir up anxiety and fear. The Imperial Way Faction, which included many regimental officers, advocated strong measures against the Soviet Union and strongly opposed Japan's southward advance and the establishment of the Greater East Asia Co-Prosperity Sphere. In addition to the Imperial Way Faction, there was an influential group led by Generals Ugaki and Minami, whose rational renovationism was demonstrated by the famous Ugaki arms reduction of 1925.[7] They were critical, however, of the Control Faction for its reckless handling of the Manchurian and Mongolian problems. This group was, in a way, the successor of the once all-powerful "Chōshū Faction" of the Japanese army and was therefore still regarded as the mainstream of the army. Many non-political generals belonged to this group. Compared to this faction and the Imperial Way Faction, the leaders of the Control Faction were younger and consequently lower in rank, although they held important positions in both the army's general staff and the war ministry. The tormenting indecision of the army's high command at every step of the move into northern French Indochina can best be understood in the light of this three-way internal division.

The army's high command in the early 1940s was not in a position to impose its will on the rest of the nation, as it had been at the time of the Manchurian Incident. Japan's southward advance was, rather, a national policy supported by the majority of her leaders, military as well as civil. The ultimate reason for the southward advancement lay in the rapidly growing tension between the United States and Japan after the outbreak of the China war.

Despite the U.S. government's declaration of the celebrated "Stimson doctrine of non-recognition" in the wake of the Manchurian Incident, U.S.-Japanese relations continued, albeit uneasily. Despite the Japanese violations of the Nine-Power Treaty and the Kellogg-Briand Pact in Manchuria and Mongolia, the U.S. government tried to avoid armed conflict with Japan so long as America was preoccupied with internal economic conditions and its military preparedness was inadequate. Besides, isolationist sentiment was strong in the Congress and in business circles. As for Japan, no matter how objectionable the American loans to the Chiang Kai-shek regime were, the government had to retain commercial relations with the United States as a basic tenet of its foreign policy as long as Japan was dependent on raw materials, especially oil and iron, imported from the United States.

With the outbreak of the China incident, however, this situation began to change. On October 5, 1937, President Roosevelt delivered his famous "quarantine" speech in Chicago, indicating a departure from the principle of neutrality. As the war expanded in China, U.S.-Japanese relations became increasingly tense, and on October 6, 1938, the United States lodged with the Japanese government an extremely comprehensive and sharp protest against infringements on American rights in China.

By this time Japanese leaders, both military and civil, had given up hope for peace with the Chiang Kai-shek regime and were determined to reorganize China as part of their program for a "New Order in East Asia." In this setting Japan's reply to the American note was cutting. On November 18, Foreign Minister Arita stated that invoking principles that might have been applicable before the outbreak of the China incident but that had no relation to the new situation emerging in East Asia would be futile not only for resolving present problems but for establishing lasting peace in that area as well.[8] This statement, which was in effect a flat rejection of the Nine-Power Treaty and the Kellogg-Briand Pact, enjoyed the backing of officials at or above the level of bureau chief within the foreign ministry. The Japanese press, too, gave their full support.

Arita's reply, however, merely stiffened the U.S. attitude. Roosevelt's friends and advisors now urged him to consider some form of coercion to stop Japan. It was assumed that economic sanctions would compel the Japanese to capitulate. By the summer of 1939, the isolationists' influence in Congress was weakened to the extent that on July 18, Senator Arthur Vandenberg, a powerful Republican spokesman, demanded the abrogation of the U.S.-Japanese Treaty of Commerce and Navigation of 1911. The Gallup poll, too, indicated that the nation supported the hard-liners in the administration. Responding to this strong domestic pressure, the U.S. government, on July 26, 1939, formally notified the Japanese government of its intention to terminate the treaty in six months.

This was a blow for Japan. In consternation, the foreign ministry established in early August a committee to deliberate policies toward the United States. This committee, headed by Matsumiya Jun, a zealous renovationist of the Shiratori group, was convinced that the establishment of the New Order in East Asia required the dissolution of the "Washington Conference System" and that, since the United States insisted on its preservation, conflict was inevitable. Shortly thereafter, however, the Hiranuma cabinet fell, due to the sudden announcement of the German-Soviet nonaggression pact. It was replaced by the Abe cabinet on August 30. The new Foreign Minister, Nomura Kichisaburō, was convinced that the policy his predecessor had adopted toward the United States must be modified and that Japan should normalize its relations with the United States by ensuring respect for foreign rights and interests in China and for the principles of the Open Door. The renovationist members of the committe to deliberate policies toward the United States were vehement in their criticism of the foreign minister and proceeded to plan his downfall. They feared that with Nomura as foreign minister, Japan's efforts to establish the New Order in East Asia would end in disaster. Unfortunately for Nomura, the United States maintained that it would not enter into a new commercial treaty unless Japan's policy toward China underwent a fundamental change. Nomura's attempt to improve U.S.-Japanese relations ended in failure.

In January 1940, the Abe cabinet was replaced by the Yonai cabinet, and Arita was again appointed foreign minister. In the same month the U.S.-Japanese commercial treaty was abrogated. Under the circumstances, the renovationist members of the cabinet planning board became increasingly vociferous in demanding that Japan cease to rely on the United States for war materials and instead try to establish a self-sufficient economy. They advocated that Japan push ahead with the economic development of Manchuria and China and at the same time seek strategic resources in Southeast Asia. During 1940, the Yonai cabinet concentrated its efforts on a peaceful southward advance. The Japanese army moved to northern French Indochina in late September, in conformity with the Franco-Japanese Agreement on Joint Defense of Indochina.

Meanwhile, in the United States the hard-liners around President Roosevelt, such as Harold L. Ickes and Henry Morgenthau, were pressing for an embargo and no-compromise. In July, Roosevelt strengthened this group immeasurably by appointing Henry Stimson secretary of war and Frank Knox secretary of the navy. With Stanley Hornbeck in the State Department, the Roosevelt administration's policy toward Japan was now leaning strongly toward no-compromise. In the same month the U.S. Congress adopted the National Defense Act, which included a provision authorizing the president to prohibit or limit the export of any material he considered essential for national defense. On July 20, the president signed a bill to create a two-ocean navy. The administration hoped that the United States would be able to confront Japan in the Pacific without deserting Britain in the Atlantic.

Japan concluded the Tripartite Pact on September 27, 1940, with the intention of deterring President Roosevelt from interference in European and Asian affairs by virtue of the powerful entente. There was hope that the Soviet Union would join. The pact would provide Japan, Foreign Minister Matsuoka envisioned, with the best opportunity for pursuing a vigorous expansion into Southeast Asia by diplomatic means. This was a fatal miscalculation. No other action could so directly or effectively have seemed to bear out the contention of the hard-line faction in Washington that Japan's southward drive was part of a vast Axis plan for world conquest that would eventually reach America unless she acted immediately to stop it.

Americans began to sell Japanese securities. *Business Week* estimated on October 26, 1940, that "many [U.S.] investors in Japanese national, municipal, and corporate bonds (totaling about $500,000,000 last April 1st) have recently unloaded to Japanese buyers." Kuhn, Loeb & Company, which was instrumental in sending the two Catholic priests Fathers Walsh and Drought to Japan for a peace initiative, was one of the few financial concerns still interested in Japanese investments. On July 24, 1941, when a report reached Washington that Japanese warships had appeared off Cam Ranh Bay, the Roosevelt administration decided to freeze all Japanese assets in the United States. The freeze particularly hurt Japanese oil imports. In less than six months the United States and Japan were at war.

In the last analysis, therefore, French Indochina was caught in an inevitable collision of the opposing policies of the United States and Japan concerning China and the Pacific. This would explain in part Japan's scrupulous respect for French sovereignty in Indochina throughout the period of their collaboration and Japan's curious lack of sympathy towards Annamese nationalism. Japan in 1941 was not really prepared to launch a military conquest of Southeast Asia.

NOTES

1. Joseph Buttinger, *Vietnam: A Dragon Embattled,* vol. 1 (New York: Praeger, 1967), p. 234.
2. John Toland, *The Rising Sun: The Decline and Fall of the Japanese Empire, 1936–1945* (New York: Random House, 1970), p. xxxiii.

3. Ibid., pp. 62–63.

4. Admiral Jean Decoux, *A la Barre, de le Indochine* (Paris: Plom, 1949), pp. 157–160.

5. After the May 15 Incident of 1932, which demonstrated a strong military opposition to party cabinets, a series of so-called national unity cabinets were formed. These cabinets were dominated by the military and the bureaucracy. During this period a new breed of bureaucrat emerged in response to a rising demand for a strong political leadership that would enable Japan to cut through the internal and external crises of the mid-1930s. They were aiming at an administrative reform that was to integrate the functions of all government ministries under unified command so that a coherent national policy could be formed and carried out. Among the most active were Yoshida Shigeru and Matsui Haruo of the Ministry of Home Affairs and Baba Eiichi and Ogawa Gōtarō of the Ministry of Finance.

6. There were two major factions within the army at this time, namely the Imperial Way Faction *(Kōdō-ha)* and the Control Faction *(Tōsei-ha)*. The Imperial Way Faction was led by Generals Araki and Mazaki, who emphasized spiritual Nipponism and anti-communism. The Control Faction was led by Nagata Tetsuzan, Tōjō Hideki, Mutō Akira, and others, who advocated the establishment of a strong national defense state.

The founding father of the Japanese Imperial Army was Yamagata Aritomo, who had organized a new volunteer army for the lord of Chōshū to fight for the emperor during the Meiji Restoration. Naturally the Japanese Imperial Army was dominated for a long time by the officers from Chōshū, causing profound disatisfaction and resentment among officers from other provinces, particularly Satsuma, Tosa, and Saga, that were known for their meritorious services to the Meiji Restoration. After Yamagata's death in 1922, the predominance of the Chōshū faction gradually weakened and new factions emerged, advocating reform. Reflecting the army's involvement in internal politics at this time, these factions differentiated themselves not so much by the home provinces of the officers as by the policies they advocated.

7. In compliance with the retrenchment policy of the Kato cabinet (June 1924–January 1926), Army Minister Ugaki agreed to abolish four divisions on the condition that the expenditure saved by the abolition be used for modernization of armaments.

8. Usui Katsumi, "Nitchū-sensō no Seijitaki Tenkai," *Taiheiyō sensō e no michi* 6 (1962), p. 170.

16. The Road to Pearl Harbor

Fujiwara Akira

During the 1980s Japan has been leaning to the right, and her military strength has been building. In this atmosphere, voices defending Japan's position during the World War II have become louder. In 1982, approval by the Ministry of Education of certain history textbooks became a serious political and diplomatic issue, with the Ministry of Education taking a negative stance toward any emphasis on Japan's war responsibility. They argued that Japan in 1941 had no intention of starting a war with the United States. Her leaders—the emperor, Konoe, and even Tōjō—wanted to maintain peace with the United States. What drove Japan into the war was the U.S. embargo. The economic blockade by the ABCD (Americans, British, Chinese, and Dutch) forced Japan into a corner. Then, in the U.S.-Japanese negotiations, the Americans demanded that Japan withdraw her forces from the Chinese continent. This was one point Japan simply could not yield. Finally, the so-called Hull Note of November 26, 1941, forced Japan to declare war against the United States. Therefore, the defenders of Japan's position contend, the United States should bear the responsibility of pushing Japan into war.

Such contentions, however, are not based on an empirical study of the actions taken by the military leaders of Japan before they selected the road to the Pacific War. The military leaders deliberated carefully before concluding that war was their only alternative. It was a meticulously studied and planned decision. In the history of modern Japan, the will to go to war had never been so clearly and deliberately defined.[1]

The decision to enter into the Pacific War, unlike the Manchurian Incident of 1931 or the war with China of 1937, was a reflection of the nation's will. The Manchurian Incident was started by a Kwantung army plot that eventually dragged the entire army and the gov-

Translated by Takahashi Noboru and Taeko Wellington

ernment into war. The 1937 war with China was never officially
declared. When the firing started no one expected it to spread far or
last long. In contrast, the Pacific War was declared with a full awareness that the country would be thrust into a great war that would
decide her fate. All the steps necessary to make it a national policy
decision were taken, as a formality at least.

On July 27, 1940, the Japanese government issued a document
called "The Outline of Action to Deal with the Situation Brought
about by the Development in World Affairs," which delineated a
southward expansion policy that might involve the use of military
force. It was an ambitious policy that took advantage of German tri-
umphs in Europe, and that did not preclude the possibility of war
with the United States. This southward expansion policy came to a
temporary halt due to the failure of the Germans to land in England
coupled with the export control measures on scrap iron and petroleum taken by the U.S. government.

In June 1941, Japan was faced with another decision—whether to
move north or south—that was brought about by the outbreak of
hostilities between Germany and the USSR. On July 2, at the liaison
conference between imperial headquarters and the civilian government held in the presence of the emperor, it was decided to prepare
for war against the USSR and simultaneously to maintain the southward expansion policy that "does not preclude a war with the United
States and Great Britain." These policies were formulated into an
"Outline of the Imperial Policy to Meet with the New [World] Situation."

As a consequence of the policy adopted at this conference, the
U.S.-Japanese relationship became increasingly strained. In this
atmosphere, another imperial conference was held on September 6.
At this conference an "Outline of the Execution Plan of the Imperial
Policy" was adopted. It contained two principles: (1) "With the possibility of a war with the United States (Great Britain, and Holland)
in mind, complete all preparations for the state of war by the end of
October," and (2) "In the event that no possibility of realizing our
requests is evident in early November we resolve to open war immediately against the United States (Great Britain and Holland)."

At the imperial conference on November 5, after the Tōjō cabinet
came into power, another "Outline of the Execution Plan of the
Imperial Policy" was adopted. This plan clarified Japan's resolve "to
open war against U.S.-Britain-Holland." The outline set a time limit

of December 1, 0:00 hour, for negotiations with the United States. It also specified that Japan would resort to military action at the beginning of December and that all the necessary preparations were to be completed by then. Thus, the war against the United States did not result from an unexpected turn of events at all. It was a deliberate and active decision made by the government and the military leaders after long and careful consideration.

On October 5–6, 1941, imperial headquarters completed the plan of operations against the United States and Great Britain and ordered the army and navy to be in operational readiness. On November 5, the army and navy were ordered to be on alert, awaiting a directive giving an exact date to start the offensive. On November 26, a task force left a port in the Kurile Islands for Hawaii. Troops with missions to attack the Philippines and Malaya started to assemble, and some were already on the move. Secretary of State Hull's note arrived after all these activities had started. Although it is true that the final decision to begin war with the United States and Great Britain was officially made at the imperial conference on December 1, this conference was a formality and very brief. The outbreak of war was already a *fait accompli.*

Thus it is clear that Japan's decision to begin the war had been reached before the arrival of Hull's Note.[2] An astonishing fact is that the Japanese leaders took the plunge into war with little hope of victory against the United States while simultaneously making preparations for a war against the USSR and continuing hostilities against China. On what ground did the Japanese leaders arrive at a decision to initiate war even though they were cognizant of the unlikelihood of victory and the distinct possibility of defeat? How did they rationalize their decision?

It is well known that the top-level navy leaders had serious misgivings about the prospect of a protracted war based on their knowledge of the disparity in national strength between Japan and the United States. Some of the staff officers in naval headquarters held the radical opinion that it would be better to gamble on an aggressive war than to wait to be squeezed into a corner by a shortage of petroleum. The top-level leaders, however, were considerably more cautious. On September 29, in the last days of the third Konoe cabinet, Yamamoto Isoroku, commander-in-chief of the combined fleet, is said to have given his assessment of the prospect of the outcome of war to Nagano, chief of the general staff. He felt that Japan would be able

to achieve a measure of success at the onset but that the war would
inevitably turn into a long one. He clearly foresaw the difficulties that
lay ahead:

> If I may express my opinion as an impartial observer, it is obvious that the
> Japan-American war will be a protracted one. As long as Japan remains in
> a favorable position, the United States would never stop fighting. As a
> consequence, the war would continue for several years, our supplies
> would be exhausted, our ships and arms would be damaged, and ulti-
> mately we would not be able to escape defeat. Not only that, as a result of
> the war, people of this nation would be reduced to abject poverty. The
> residents on the main islands may endure such a condition but the people
> in Korea, Manchuria, or Taiwan would be malcontent and numerous
> unrests that would undoubtedly occur would be difficult to quell. We
> should not venture on such an imprudent attempt that offers little hope
> of success.[3]

Like Yamamoto, many naval officials who would be in the forefront of the war were pessimistic about the outcome if a war were to
go on beyond three years since the U.S. defense industry would be
operating at full power by then. Okada Keisuke and Yonai Mitsumasa, two greatly revered senior leaders in the navy, and fleet commanders on active duty such as Kondō Nobutake and Inoue Shigeyo-
shi reportedly took a position opposing the war.[4] Even Nagano
Osami, chief of the general staff, who was closest to the war faction in
the navy, would only go so far as to say, "We cannot forecast beyond
the third year."[5]

From the evidence cited above, the political responsibility for the
decision to start a war rests squarely on the army leaders who advocated the hard-line policy. However, some critics hold the navy
responsible for not taking a stronger stand against the war, especially
since the naval leaders were fully aware of the futility of such a war.

What kept the naval leaders from asserting that there was no
chance of winning? In the U.S.-Japanese negotiations, the final point
of disagreement between the two countries was on the withdrawal of
Japanese forces from China. If war was to be prevented, Japan had to
yield on this point. Why couldn't Japan come to terms with the
United States on the China issue and avoid rushing headlong into the
fateful war against the United States?

The central issue of the U.S.-Japanese negotiations held in Washington, D.C., in 1941 was the withdrawal of Japanese forces from the Chinese continent.[6] Since the turn of the twentieth century, when Japan began her imperialistic aggression in China, the United States and Japan had been opposed on the China issue. In an attempt to stop Japan's expansion of her sphere of influence in China during World War I, the United States succeeded in having nine countries sign the Nine-Power Treaty at the Washington conference in 1922. After Japan occupied Manchuria by force, Secretary of State Stimson announced the Stimson Doctrine of January 7, 1932, "to disapprove Japanese operations." As the official U.S.-Japanese negotiations began on April 16, 1941, Secretary of State Hull announced his four fundamental policies: territorial integrity and respect of sovereignty; no interference in the domestic affairs [of China]; equal opportunity; and maintenance of status quo in the Pacific. The United States did not recognize the Japanese occupation of China, but Japan insisted on the approval of Japan's occupation. As long as neither side made any change in its fundamental principle, there was no possibility of reaching an agreement.

From 1937 on, hostilities between Japan and China grew more and more widespread. In the face of fierce resistance by the Chinese people, Japan could no longer expect an easy victory. The Japanese economy deteriorated under the heavy burden of war expenses. As a result, in 1940, Japan decided to adopt a southward expansion policy to gain access to the vast natural resources of Southeast Asia. Even though the likelihood of a successful conclusion of the war with China grew increasingly remote, Japan did not attempt to withdraw all of her forces from the Chinese continent. Japanese leaders feared that such an action would be tantamount to an admission of failure and might invite the ire of malcontent citizens who had paid dearly for the war effort.

The army leaders agreed to negotiate with the United States provided Japan could continue to station her troops in China. When it became clear, during the negotiations, that the withdrawal of Japan's troops from China was the central issue, the army leaders were unyielding. They would never agree to a withdrawal. Other Japanese officials, including Prime Minister Konoe, also opposed a withdrawal.

The army-navy draft of the "Outline of the Execution Plan of the Imperial Policy," which was drawn during the chief of staff meeting on September 2, enumerated items of "minimum request which must be granted to Japan." One of them was that the United States and Great Britain were not to interfere with or obstruct Japan's "treatment of the China incident." A special note attached to this item added: "Concerning the matter of stationing Japanese troops under the terms of the new agreement between Japan and China, we will adhere to these terms at all costs."[7]

This note remained in the "Outline of the Execution Plan" adopted at the imperial conference on September 6. During the imperial conference, Minister of Foreign Affairs Toyoda remarked on the note attached to the "Outline." A "Sugiyama Memo"[8] recorded Toyoda's remarks as follows: "The matter of stationing Japanese troops under the terms of the new agreement between Japan and China, mentioned in Note No. 1, Item No. 1, means future stationing of the troops under a yet to be signed agreement between Japan and China. This does not depart from the principle we have already indicated to the United States in Our N Scheme. (This explanation is worthy of particular attention.)"[9] As long as this was the prevailing attitude among the Japanese leaders, there was no hope of a successful conclusion of the U.S.-Japanese negotiations. Not only the army but also the national leaders, including Minister of Foreign Affairs Toyoda, were united on keeping the troops in China.

In October 1941, the disagreement between Tōjō, the minister of war, and Prime Minister Konoe became apparent. Tōjō opposed the withdrawal of Japanese troops from China and believed that Japan should stop negotiating with the United States and resolve to enter into a war. Konoe, on the other hand, felt that Japan could acquiesce to the American demand of withdrawal and still could find a way to keep her troops in China.[10] During the cabinet meeting on October 14 Tōjō stated:

Furthermore, troop withdrawal is the heart of the issue. How dare you think of it so lightly. We, the Army, attach utmost importance to this point. To capitulate to American demands is to destroy all the fruits of the China Incident. Such an action would endanger the existence of Manchukuo and Japan's control of Korea. In view of our objectives of waging a sacred war, we have not annexed any territory nor have we demanded reparations. We have lost hundreds of thousands of fellow soldiers, leaving many times that number of bereaved families. Hundreds of thousands of men have been wounded and several million servicemen as well as one hundred million civilians have long endured hardships. The national expenditure has amounted to tens of billions of yen. If any of the world powers were to experience hardships such as we have, they surely would seek a concession that would include territorial cession. However, this country has maintained a magnanimous attitude. We believe that it is quite right to station our troops on Chinese soil in order to bring this Incident to a conclusion. We should not feel constrained by the criticism of other nations. Nor should we be intimidated by the pressures from the United States."[11]

Tōjō's view was that to acquiesce to the withdrawal of Japanese troops was to admit that the war with China was a failure. Such an admission would be unjustifiable in the face of the long-suffering military, the families of those lost in the war, and the spirit of the departed heroes. Worse yet, the lower ranks might not accept the defeat and might resort to a coup d'etat or a riot.

In the letter that Konoe submitted to the emperor notifying His Majesty of the general resignation of the cabinet, he stated: "The Minister of War, although he was fully aware of the efforts and intentions of the Prime Minister, insisted that the idea of troop withdrawal was something he just could not accept from the standpoint of maintenance of the troop morale."[12] Thus, the issue of the withdrawal of troops from China became far larger than an operational consideration of the military. It became a problem of internal control in the armed forces. It further escalated into a political issue involving the trust of the people and colonial control. What motivated the army to resolve to end negotiations with the United States and to go to war was a fear that troop withdrawal from China might anger the citizens enough to cause a revolution.

It was not the army leaders alone who insisted on keeping the troops in China. Even Prime Minister Konoe held a similar view. On October 12, Konoe summoned Minister of War Tōjō, Minister of the Navy Oikawa, Minister of Foreign Affairs Toyoda, and President of Planning Agency Suzuki to his private residence in Ogikubo for a conference. This conference became in substance the last opportunity to choose between war and peace. Here again Tōjō insisted that he could not yield his ground on the troop withdrawal issue. Konoe's idea was to "yield in form and take the substance." He urged, "Let us accept the American demand formally. We can still keep our troops in China in reality through other arrangements."[13] He thought that Japan could recognize China's territorial integrity and respect her sovereignty nominally and could still continue to station Japanese troops in China by an agreement with China.

Fukudome Shigeru, who was the chief of operations in the navy at the time and later became chief of staff of the combined fleet, recalled statements made to him by Koga Mineichi and Yamamoto Isoroku, both commanders-in-chief of the combined fleet. Koga said, "An internal disturbance would have been inevitable had the effort to avert war succeeded at that time. However, in looking back over history, no nation has ever ceased to exist because of internal unrest. What annihilates a nation is a war with another nation. Therefore, those who were at the helm of the nation should have avoided going to war at all cost without giving heed to a possibility of a revolt." Yamamoto said, "We, at this very moment, stand no chance of victory in the war. We should wait at least until we build our air strength substantially. We may be able to restrain the jingoists once. But such an action surely would induce a coup d'etat and the revolutionary government would rush head-on into war. I cannot think of any sure way to prevent such an eventuality."[14] These remarks indicate that the two top naval leaders did not dare take a firm stand against war, despite their own convictions, for fear of an internal uprising.

One of the reputedly most radical jingoists in the navy, Ishikawa Shingo, who was the chief of the first service section in the Bureau of Naval Service, wrote in his memoirs:

As long as we adhere to the policy of 'accomplishing the objectives of the China Incident,' waves in the Pacific Ocean will rage more and more regardless of changes of Foreign Ministers, formation of new cabinets, or whatever might come. Can we make a fresh start by acceding to American demands? Even suppose we can do such a thing, how are we going to justify such an about-face to our 600,000 or more fallen soldiers? How can we face their bereaved families or over one million wounded men? How can we assume the responsibility of having thrust our nation into a war of more than four years? Were we to abandon the cause of the China Incident, how could we suppress our people's indignation? It is difficult to predict what might happen when people's anger spills over.[15]

Similarly, Prime Minister Konoe and Imperial Household Minister Kido hesitated to change the national policy for fear of an outburst of rebellion or revolution. Following the general resignation of the third

Konoe cabinet, Konoe consulted Kido, who agreed that Tōjō should be Konoe's successor. Kido explained their reasoning in his memoir:

> In those tense moments it was almost impossible to form a cabinet which would indicate a sudden change in national policy. If someone not famil-iar with what had been going on behind the scene tried to form a cabinet, he would have difficulties even to get enough people willing to serve in the Cabinet. He might suffer a similar fate with the abortive effort of the Ugaki cabinet in which Mr. Ugaki failed to form his cabinet as he could not get anyone to serve as the Minister of War. And, since our men had been deployed as far south as French Indochina, in the event that the Army leaders lose control there was no telling what kind of critical situa-tion might occur in those far off places. The Army units might choose to invoke the 'right of self-defense.' We also felt that if the cabinet could not be formed quickly, depending on who the Prime Minister designate was, the nation might be thrown into chaos or even a state of civil war.[16]

In other words, they felt that the negotiations could not be success-fully concluded without a drastic change in national policy and that such a change would lead to internal unrest or revolution. In those days of 1941, Japan was under a strict news control policy. The news media added more and more fuel to the nation's fervor for war in accord with government and military orders. Any pacifism or anti-war sentiment was severely suppressed. Both printed pages and air waves were filled with the propaganda of military victories in China as well as news of the German victories in Europe. Anti-American and anti-British articles were numerous. In this atmosphere, the lead-ers felt, a major concession in the U.S.-Japanese negotiations and the withdrawal of military forces from China would cause people to lose trust in their leaders. The leaders chose to continue the policy they had taken thus far—the road to war.

On the eve of the Pearl Harbor attack in 1941, there were only two alternatives left to prevent war: (1) for the United States to ignore the Japanese violations of the Non-Aggression Pact of 1928 and the Nine-Power Treaty of 1922 and to retract Hull's four principles, or (2) for Japan to abandon the control of China, stop the war of aggression on the Chinese continent, and withdraw her troops. As far as Japan was concerned, it was impossible to take the option open to her with-out a drastic change in her internal political structure. Since 1937 and the start of the war with China, Japan was under a national mobiliza-tion system with the military leadership. Unless Japan freed herself of

160 FUJIWARA AKIRA

the military dominance, she could not choose the road to peace. Even
a summit conference with Roosevelt would have only postponed the
inevitable war.

NOTES

1. [Fujiwara joins Murakami in dismissing those who argue that the Pacific War
occurred because of irrational, unplanned foreign policy. Japan's decision to undertake a war with the United States may have been irrational, but they argue that the
steps taken by Japan leading to that decision were exhaustively and deliberately
planned.—EDS.]
2. [Note the significance of Fujiwara's comment. His answer to those Japanese
who say that the Hull Note drove Japan to war is to say that Japan already had
decided to initiate the war before the Hull "ultimatum" had been received. By
inference his argument diminishes those essayists in this volume who still think there
was a chance to avoid the war had the Hull and Kurusu-Nomura talks of late November succeeded.—EDS.]
3. Bōeichō Bōei Kenshūjo Senshi Shitsu hen (Defence Agency, Military History
Office, ed.), Senshi sōsho: daihon'ei rikugunbu daitōa sensō kaisen keii (Military
history series: particulars on the greater East Asia war), vol. 5, 1966, quoted in Sawa-
moto Nikki (p. 88).
4. Fukutomi Shigeru, Kaigun no hansei (A self examination by the navy) (Tokyo:
Nihon Shuppan Kyōdō, 1951); Takagi Sōkichi, Yamamoto Isoroku to Yonai Mitsumasa (Yamamoto and Yonai) (Tokyo: Bungei Shunjūsha, 1950); Ogata Taketora, Ichi
Gunjin no Shōgai (Life of a soldier) (Tokyo: Bungei Shunjūsha, 1955); Okada
Keisuke, Kaikoroku (Remembering the past) (Tokyo: Mainichi Shimbunsha, 1950).
5. Nihon Kokusai Seiji Gakkai (Japan International Politics Assoc.), Taiheiyō
Sensō Gen'in Kenkyūbu hen (Pacific War Origins Study Group), Taiheiyō Sensō e
no michi (The road to the Pacific war) 8 vols. (Tokyo: Asahi Shimbunsha, 1967–8);
Hattori Takushiro, Daitōa sensō zenshi (Complete history of the greater East Asia
war), vol. 1 (Tokyo: Masu Shobo, 1981) 206 pp.
6. [See the Utley essay for a different view and the Conroy-Klein and Graebner
essays for a similar view.—EDS.]
7. Daihon'ei Rikugunbu (Imperial Headquarters, Army), Daitōa sensō kaisen keii
(Particulars on the greater East Asia war) vol. 4 (Tokyo: Japan Defense Agency,
1974), p. 201.
8. Bōeichō Senshi Shitsu Shozoku (Defense Agency, Military History Office, ed.)
Daihon'ei seifu renraku kaigi gijiroku (Record of proceedings of Imperial Headquarters, government joint meetings) (Tokyo: Japan Defense Agency, 1974).
9. Senshi sōsho: daitōa kaisen keii (Military history series: particulars on the
greater East Asia war) vol. 4, 1974, 550 pp. "This material is what Chief of staff Sugiyama and Deputy Director Tsukuda (probably) said. 20th Section Chief Arimatsu's
opinion not clear" as for N Policy regarding US-Japan Understanding—Secret memo
of negotiations.
10. [Fujiwara elaborates on this statement later. The Konoe statement seems to

contradict completely the view of Tsunoda and Ikei that Konoe "sincerely" planned a summit meeting with Roosevelt that would result in substantive concessions on China. This issue is indeed murky, however, for we see that Konoe's decision to resign occurred in part because Tōjō would not agree to a withdrawal of Japanese troops form China.—EDS.]

11. Sanbō honbuchō (General Staff Headquarters), ed. *Sugiyama Memo I* (Tokyo: Hara Shobo, 1967), pp. 49–50.

12. Konoe Fumimaro, Ushinawareshi seiji (Politics that Failed) (Tokyo: Asahi Shimbunsha, 1946), pp. 137–138.

13. Oka Yoshitake, *Konoe Fumimaro: A political biography* (Shumpei Okamoto and Patricia Murray, trans.) (Tokyo: University of Tokyo Press, 1983) p. 155. Yabe Teiji, *Konoe Fumimaro II* (Tokyo: Kobundo, 1952).

14. Fukutome Shigeru, *Shikan Shinjuwan kōgeki* (Historical view of the attack on Pearl Harbor) (Tokyo: Ajiasha, 1955), pp. 128–129.

15. Ishikawa Shingo, *Shinjuwan made no keii* (Particulars on Pearl Harbor) (Tokyo: Jiji Tsushinsha, 1960), p. 201; cf. Oka, *op.cit.* pp. 156–157.

16. Kido Kōichi, *Sensō kaihi e no doryoku* (Efforts to avoid war) (Tokyo: Kido Kōichi Kankei Bunsho, Tokyo University Shuppankai, 1966).

17. The Russian Factor in Japanese-American Relations, 1941

WALDO HEINRICHS

DESPITE all we know about the road to Pearl Harbor, it is still hard to fathom why the United States brought matters to a head with Japan in July–August 1941 when it was supposedly pursuing a strategy of concentration against Germany and strict defense in the Pacific.[1] In particular, it is difficult to understand why the United States imposed a total embargo on the shipment of petroleum products to Japan when officials from the president on down recognized that such an act might propel Japan into a grab for Dutch East Indies oil, the very southern advance the United States hoped to prevent. The various explanations at hand—sentimentalism over China, naive hopes about the deterrent capacity of air power in the Philippines, a coup by hawkish bureaucrats while the president was at the Atlantic Conference, chaotic decision making in the Roosevelt administration —simply do not alone or together provide satisfying answers.

Perhaps we are looking in the wrong direction. It is true that East Asia-Pacific policy had its own parameters, as did Atlantic-European policy, and that American policies East and West tended to be the reciprocals of one another. Yet this was not the only framework of policy. The great question for world leaders in the first half of 1941 was whether Hitler would attack the Soviet Union, and the great question in the latter half was whether he would succeed. This was the central dynamic of world politics from which hung in large measure the strategic decisions of Japan, Great Britain, and the United States, not to mention the USSR, which had its own East-West reciprocals, standing as it did between Germany and Japan.

A chain of reciprocals encircled the globe, and every link was relevant to Roosevelt and his advisers; their framework of policy was truly worldwide by 1941. So we may hypothesize that the German-Soviet conflict had a direct bearing on Japanese-American relations. Within this wider canvas we may find better answers to nagging questions.

A decisive change—one needing greater emphasis—occurred in American foreign and strategic policy in mid-1941. It occurred at the time of, and partly as a result of, the Atlantic Conference between Churchill and Roosevelt but was not bounded by the time frame or agenda of that conference.

From January until well into July of 1941 Roosevelt's policy had been extremely cautious and hesitant. Fear of encouraging isolationist sentiment during the Lend-Lease debate was undoubtedly one factor. So was a scarcity of military resources. The U.S. Atlantic Fleet simply did not have the ships and readiness to make an important contribution to the Battle of the Atlantic before mid-summer. Japan's threat of southward advance, reinforced by the Soviet-Japanese neutrality treaty, delayed the transfer of reinforcements from the Pacific Fleet to the Atlantic.

What most worried Roosevelt, however, was uncertainty about Hitler's intentions. The United States did not, as we thought was the case, receive an unambiguous warning early in 1941 of the forthcoming German attack on the Soviet Union.[2] In these months an invasion of England remained the most likely possibility. From April on German troop movements to the East made a decisive outcome of Soviet-German tensions seem inevitable, but the overwhelming belief was that the German concentration was for the purpose of intimidation, that Hitler would finally present an ultimatum demanding concessions, and that Stalin would bow. The German blitz in the Balkans in April and the seizure of Crete in May pointed the way to Suez and the Middle East, and at all times intelligence flowed into Washington, which was especially sensitive on the score, of a possible German southwestern drive through Spain and Gibraltar to northwestern Africa and Dakar.

Roosevelt and his advisers were truly uncertain about which set of reports to believe until early June. No possible vector of German advance seemed sure enough to build policy on, and so the tendency was to guard against the worst case and protect the Atlantic. After a year of devastating events, a German attack on Russia looked too good to be true. Even if an attack occurred, the war was not expected to last longer than four to eight weeks, allowing time for further campaigning that year. The aura of German power before the Russian campaign was little short of overwhelming.

Beginning with the Japanese acquisition of bases in southern Indochina at the end of July, American policy changed dramatically. It is hard to imagine how Roosevelt could have avoided some demonstration of firmness in the face of this latest Japanese move, obviously penultimate to an attack on Malaya and the Dutch East Indies and taken despite American warnings and mounting trade curbs stopping just short of oil. What is difficult to account for solely in an East Asian or any other regional context is the sweeping nature and boldness of his moves. He ordered a suspension of petroleum exports to Japan before leaving for the Atlantic Conference and converted it into an embargo upon his return. At the conference he established that no significant secret agreements yet existed between Britain and the USSR and worked out with Churchill a set of war aims that were congruent with American Wilsonian values and that formed a basis for risking or waging war. He agreed to undertake an escort of convoys in the western Atlantic. He ordered maximum assistance to the Soviet Union before winter set in and pushed for a conference in Moscow to arrange for further deliveries in amounts acceptable to the Soviets. He agreed to Churchill's plea for a warning to Japan that any further move would lead to war, and he gave it, although in diluted form. Finally, he began reinforcement of the Philippines, especially with air power.

The assertion that Roosevelt temporarily suspended oil exports contradicts the conclusion of well-accepted, independent studies of the question and requires an explanation. Jonathan Utley and Irvine Anderson have been most helpful in showing the extent to which shipments of petroleum products had already been virtually halted by various means such as the withdrawal of tankers and a ban on shipment of oil in drums. They contend that despite Roosevelt's declared intent of permitting the shipment of some kinds and amounts of petroleum products, Dean Acheson and other second-level officials managed to discover bureaucratic devices to shut the tap completely while the president was away at the Atlantic Conference.[3]

On the point of presidential knowledge and intent, I disagree. Declarations to the contrary notwithstanding, Roosevelt left for the Atlantic Conference determined to withhold further shipments of oil until he had discussed this and related questions with Churchill. Sumner Welles, acting secretary of state and long-time confidant of Roosevelt, told Assistant Secretary Acheson on July 29 that the "happiest solution" would be to withhold action on Japanese applications for dollars to buy oil for the "next week or so." Evidence suggests that the time frame he meant was in fact two weeks, or not far short of the time during which Welles and the president would be at the Atlantic Conference.[4]

It is difficult to imagine Welles not speaking for Roosevelt or Acheson acting without authorization on so sensitive an issue. Acting on orders fits with Acheson's account in his memoirs and with his discontent at his own performance eight years earlier when, as undersecretary of the treasury, he had refused to sign an order legalizing the devaluation of the dollar and had been fired for it. The lesson he drew and undoubtedly applied on this his second chance was that an assistant to the president must be "very alert and watchful" of the president's position and interests, indeed "twice as much as your own."[5] Acheson was under orders to stall and found ways to comply.

The president was temporizing but moving in a direction he knew entailed great risk. Why would he do so just when he was about to enter into the Battle of the Atlantic? Surely the logic of Plan Dog and Rainbow 5, of concentration against Germany and defense in the Pacific, would argue against so severe an oil policy.

We begin to understand Roosevelt's intent if we consider an event that coincided with the Japanese move into southern Indochina and was at least as significant: a pause in the German advance on Moscow beginning July 19 and lasting into mid-August, occasioned by the need for resupply and a disagreement among Hitler and his generals about a strategy for the next stage.[6] While Roosevelt was considering what to do about Japan he was seeing the first evidence that the Soviet Union might, after all, survive the German onslaught until winter and so into 1942. The press reported "Nazi drives halted," "blitzkrieg braked." On July 29 the *Washington Post* described the German invasion timetable as "completely upset." The same day Hanson Baldwin, under a headline, "Winter looms as Red Ally," wrote: "The future history of the world is being written in the struggling melee of tanks and planes and men on the 2,000 mile front." Diplomatic reports reinforced the emerging optimism. The American embassy in Berlin learned that German plans were awry due to the discovery of a second Soviet defense line of more than 100 fresh divisions east of the so-called Stalin Line. The general feeling in Germany now was that the war would go into another winter.[7] At his conference with Churchill, Roosevelt heard Harry Hopkins' encouraging report of his meeting with Stalin.

From the depths of despair, morale bounded higher than circumstances at the moment justified, but even the possibility of Russian survival made all the difference. The reversal of fortunes from as late as March 1941 when an alignment of the Axis with the Soviet Union seemed quite possible was near miraculous. A coalition of the United States, Great Britain, and the Soviet Union had the power to defeat Germany. This was the time to get Hitler, said Treasury Secretary Henry Morgenthau. "We will never have a better chance. . . . [W]e can't count on the good Lord and just plain dumb luck forever."[8] Roosevelt began pressing his aides to allocate and speed shipments of arms to the Soviet Union in the strongest possible way, as a matter of vital national safety.[9]

Support for the Soviet Union and the grand coalition to defeat Hitler had serious implications for American East Asian policy. The question before the Japanese government in the wake of the German attack was whether to join Germany, as requested, in attacking the Soviet Union or to pursue its southward advance. The decision of the Imperial Conference of July 2 was to move into southern Indochina but to prepare in the north and to attack if circumstances favored it, that is, if the Germans were clearly winning and the Soviets transferred enough of their Far Eastern forces to the western front. Preparing in the north meant mobilizing 850,000 men, causing an inflow of troops carefully monitored by American consuls in Manchuria. It was difficult to decide whether Japan would go north or south, or when and under what conditions, but an attack on Russia became a distinct possibility.

Opposite were thirty tough, experienced Soviet divisions, three cavalry brigades, sixteen tank brigades, and 2,000 tanks and aircraft. A great deal depended on whether a crisis in the west would compel Stalin to withdraw these forces. American leaders undoubtedly asked themselves what conditions would provide Stalin with sufficient assurance about Siberia to withdraw enough of these forces to survive in the west. Foreign Minister V. M. Molotov sought an American warning that the United States would come to Russia's assistance if it were attacked by Japan.[10] Roosevelt was not prepared to offer such a commitment, to join the war and send an army to the Russian front, as invited, to provide more than token aid in 1941. What could he do to help?

To do nothing regarding Japan would not only leave the resources of southeast Asia and Britain's connections to Australia and New Zealand at Japan's mercy but would offer no discouragement to a Japanese attack on the Soviet rear. To pursue diplomacy might prevent or delay a southward advance, but any agreement at China's expense was likely to weaken China's will to resist and permit further redeployment of Japanese forces north or south or both. Furthermore, any evidence of American appeasement was likely to undermine American credibility and reliability in the eyes of the anti-Hitler coalition. Any security Japan might gain in the south by an agreement with the United States could well encourage Japan to strike northward. Any assurance of American petroleum supplies, a probable requirement of agreement, would provide the wherewithal. Even reducing allocations to Japan's peacetime levels would allow the import of more than five million barrels of crude oil and nearly half a million barrels of gasoline in the remainder of 1941.

Roosevelt could also apply maximum pressure: not a drop of oil. Let Japan's oil supplies dry up and its capacity for military operations anywhere shrink. Seek closer collaboration with the British, Dutch, and Australians and provide further assistance to the Chinese. Reinforce the Philippines, especially with long-range bombers capable of raiding Japanese cities. Create such uncertainty and concern among Japanese decision makers regarding the south and relations with America that they did not dare go north. This was a line of argument advanced by an officer in the Far Eastern division of the State Department a few days after the German attack on the Soviet Union.[11]

Containment was Roosevelt's preferred way of dealing with Japanese aggression. Victory in any struggle between the two nations, he wrote in 1923, was bound to lie with the United States, which had vast economic superiority. In 1937 he had commented approvingly on a suggestion by the U.S. Asiatic Fleet commander, Admiral Harry Yarnell, that the way to fight Japan was to form a common front with Britain, France, the Netherlands, and the Soviet Union to cut off all trade with Japan, simply attacking Japanese commerce from distant encircling bases, while China tied down Japanese troops. The result would be the "strangulation" of Japan without the cost of huge armies or Jutland-style naval battles.[12]

Containment on this order, of course, remained only an idea as the threat of Hitler supervened and conceivable Asian partners fell by the wayside, weakened or turned in other directions. Now, however, the British-American alignment with the Soviet Union, even if only implicit as far as Japan was concerned, the growing possibility of establishing a British Eastern Fleet, and the availability of B-17 bombers and their success in flying the longest hop to Hawaii in a possible ferry route to the Philippines revived the idea of containment.

July was a wonderful clarifying month for Roosevelt and his advisers. Hitler's attack on the Soviet Union together with the first evidence of the Russians' ability to sustain resistance made it conceivable, realistic, and calculable to marshall forces sufficient to defeat Nazi Germany. On July 9 the president ordered the services to estimate how much total production would be required to defeat the nation's potential enemies.

The incalculable component of this global scheme was Japan. The Soviet-German war had intensified Japanese expansionism, opportunism, and unpredictability. Whether Japan went north or south—and who could tell which?—it threatened to upset the improving balance of forces. This careening expansionism must be stopped. Japan must be boxed in, contained, immobilized. Embargo, coalition diplomacy, military aid, demonstrations of firmness, and air and naval deployments would, it was hoped, keep Japan within bounds. The risks of war would increase, but the risks of inaction, in the global calculus, seemed greater. Roosevelt could see the whole picture now. He was forceful, impatient of delay, pressing upon events, so different from the reserved, withdrawn president of the spring.[13]

Let no one mistake the severity of American policy toward Japan. Acheson reported to Welles upon the latter's return from the Atlantic Conference that none of Japan's applications for funds had been approved. No countervailing directive came down; Roosevelt had promised Churchill to maintain his economic measures in full force, and he did. Utley and Anderson have shown that Acheson and his colleagues, by insisting that the Japanese pay from sequestered funds before dollars could be unblocked and by other devices, managed to bring trade to a halt without any formal order. They could point out, Acheson explained with relish to a British diplomat, that the Japanese had "imposed [an] embargo upon themselves by their lack of loyalty" to the American order to freeze their dollars.[14]

Roosevelt's dilution of the war warning was not a weakening but a means of delay. The Japanese suggestion of a leaders' meeting provided too good an opportunity of stringing out talks while reinforcement of the Philippines proceeded and the de facto embargo took hold. Careful examination of the American documents and negotiating position reveals not a whit of evidence that Roosevelt or Hull intended compromise or summit.[15] Somewhat like Acheson and his

trade officials, the Far Eastern officers of the State Department questioned, compared, and criticized Japanese terms, asking always for
further clarification and explanation without registering progress or
impasse. The object was, as Roosevelt had told Churchill, to gain a
delay of thirty to sixty days. Upon the fall of the Konoe cabinet in
October he wrote Churchill that he had gained "two months of respite in the Far East."[16]

Before meeting Churchill at the Atlantic Conference, Roosevelt
met with his military advisers and authorized sending thirty-six B-
17's to the Philippines. "That was a distinct change of policy," General H. H. Arnold later reminisced. "It was the start of a thought to
give General MacArthur weapons for offensive operations." As General George Marshall, chief of staff, explained, these planes would act
as a "serious deterrent" to Japan, especially in the winter months that
were suitable for high altitude bombing.[17]

After the Atlantic Conference, from the middle of August through
September, news from the Russian front was dismal; the Germans
besieged Leningrad and encircled Kiev, capturing two-thirds of a million Soviet troops. The Ukraine and Odessa were lost, the Crimea cut
off, the crossings of the Dnieper seized. Beyond lay the riches of the
Donetz Basin and the Caucasus. Every major city of European Russia
except, for the moment, Moscow, was imperiled. Stalin admitted in a
letter to Churchill that the Soviet Union was in "mortal menace" and
would be defeated or rendered useless as an ally unless the British
mounted a second front in the Balkans or France and provided large
quantities of aluminum, aircraft, and tanks. The Soviet ambassador,
in conveying the message, Churchill informed Roosevelt, used language implying a separate peace if Soviet demands could not
be met.[18]

A second front was out of the question, but Roosevelt and
Churchill were determined to do what they could by way of supply.
They hastened a conference in Moscow and cobbled together a commitment of 500 tanks per month, which meant stretching out the
equipping of the U.S. Third, Fourth, and Fifth Armored Divisions
and fifteen independent tank battalions, and postponing the activa-
tion of the Sixth Armored Division. They also promised 1,800
planes. Roosevelt supplied the three largest U.S. troop transports to
take a British division to Basra, Iraq, from where it might reinforce
the Russians in the Caucasus or, in case they collapsed, defend against
a German thrust from that direction.

On September 5, the day Roosevelt received Stalin's message, besides approving arrangements for the first escort of convoys and the Basra transports, the president saw Hull, who converted Acheson's undercover stalling tactics into a de facto embargo. On that same day nine B-17's departed from Hawaii for the Philippines, and twenty-seven more received orders to depart in October. As Churchill had informed Stalin on August 28, Roosevelt "seemed disposed . . . to take a strong line against further Japanese aggression whether in the South or in the Northwest Pacific." General Marshall urged the president to authorize a buildup of air power in the Philippines to restrain Japan "from advance into Malaysia or Eastern Siberia."[19] On September 12, when the first nine B-17's arrived safely, the army ordered thirty-five more across in December, totaling seventy, together with dive bombers, more fighters, and command, air warning, reconnaisance, ordnance, and engineering units for the air force as well as tanks, antiaircraft, and artillery. About this time, according to the British ambassador Lord Halifax, Roosevelt sent a verbal message to Stalin (possibly through Averell Harriman) advising that in case of an acute crisis in the west he should withdraw his troops from Siberia and not worry about what the Japanese did, because any incursion could be corrected later.[20] Support for the Soviet Union correlated with a stiffening policy toward Japan.

In October a powerful, concentrated German assault on Moscow made the Russian situation even more precarious. The question returned of how to get Japan "off Russia's back," as one diplomat put it. An army intelligence estimate of October 2 warned against any agreement with Japan that would permit Japan to withdraw the bulk of its army from China. Any liberation of Japanese forces "for action against Russia's rear in Siberia would be foolhardy." The Army War Plans Division advised a continuation of existing pressures "with a view to rendering Japan incapable of offensive operations against Russia or against possessions of the associated powers in the Far East."[21]

The fall of the Konoe cabinet on October 16 and the appointment of General Tōjō as premier increased fears of Japanese aggression. Some signs pointed south, but the balance of opinion in October, including the president's, was that Japan would strike to the north.[22] With the embargo now complete, with persistent warnings already given to Japan against an attack to the north as well as to the south, the only further means of pressure was to strengthen American military power in the region. With the president's approval the army had increased the number of B-17's planned for the Philippines to 170. The dispatch of these aircraft, however, was scheduled over many months, and the force would not be complete until October 1942. On October 16, 1941, in the wake of the fall of the Konoe cabinet and after an emergency meeting of the president and his military advisers, the dispatch of the bombers was accelerated so that 165 would arrive by March 1942.[23] Now also for the first time the army committed an additional ground combat unit, an infantry regiment, and another tank battalion, an antiaircraft regiment, and a field artillery brigade. The navy dispatched Submarine Squadron Two, twelve newly commissioned boats, pushing the Asiatic Fleet's submarine force to twenty-nine, the largest in the navy.

As the establishment of American air power in East Asia progressed, the American military leadership warmed to the idea. The Army War Plans Division argued that "strong offensive air forces" in the Philippines, prepared to operate from British and Dutch bases, would provide a crucial deterrent to Japanese expansion southward. Deterring a Japanese attack on Siberia would be American, British, and Dutch forces in Japan's rear, as well as the possibility of American entry into the war and the use of Russian bases for bombardment of Japan's cities.[24]

Secretary of War Henry Stimson was enthusiastic about the capability of the B-17's to deter an attack on Singapore. He was skeptical about northward deterrence but nevertheless advised the president that Vladivostock was crucial for the supply of Russian troops because the Archangel route was in jeopardy from the German advance and the Persian corridor was undeveloped. He presented an exciting picture of these long-range bombers sweeping from the Philippines across Japan to Soviet bases on the Kamchatka Peninsula and onward to Alaska and back, after the fashion of the German Condors shuttling between bases in western France and Norway.[25]

General Marshall showed unaccustomed enthusiasm in describing the new possibilities. In a phone conversation he pointed out that the B-17's could operate from Australia, New Britain, Singapore, and the Dutch East Indies, "possibly even Vladivostock." They could cover the whole area of possible Japanese operations and "exercise a more determining influence on the course of events right now than anything else." This force, he said, "practically backs the Japanese off and would certainly stop them on the Malaysian thing. It probably would make them feel they didn't dare take the Siberian thing and I think it has a better than 50 percent chance of forcing them to practically drop the Axis." By acting quickly the United States might give Japan "a complete pause."[26]

Similar thinking was occurring in London. The fall of the Konoe cabinet and what Foreign Minister Anthony Eden described as the "Russian defeats," and the Admiralty as "the deterioration of the Russian situation," precipitated a decision pressed by Churchill and Eden to send H.M.S. *Prince of Wales* with the new carrier *Indomitable* to join the battlecruiser *Repulse* in the Indian Ocean. "The firmer your attitude and ours," Churchill wrote Roosevelt, "the less chance of their taking the plunge."[27]

In early November it appeared that the threat to the survival of Russia had passed, and a change occurred. The German offensive against Moscow bogged down in bad weather at the end of October. Winter seemed to have finally arrived. Optimism about Russia's ability to survive reemerged. Now the Soviet problem could be disengaged from Japanese-American relations. This was fortunate, too, because evidence was now accumulating about a Japanese attack to the south. Plan Dog thinking revived, and the president and Hull seriously attempted to reach a temporary accommodation with the Japanese that would permit the completion of the reinforcement of the Philippines. This foundered on Chinese and British objections, and the road then led directly to Pearl Harbor. Confidence that the Russian campaign was over for the winter lasted only briefly. The German offensive resumed on November 15, and by November 25, the day the *modus vivendi* project was cancelled, Moscow was imperiled. The Red Army was said to be fighting "one of the most critical battles of its history." The Russian situation looked "awful" to Roosevelt; Moscow, he said, was "falling."[28] The time called for solidarity and steadfastness. Critical in the final defense of Moscow and the Russian counteroffensive launched December 4 were the Siberian troops withdrawn from the Far East.

It was not a case of Roosevelt's saving Moscow. Stalin withdrew half his Far Eastern forces on information gathered in October by his spy Richard Sorge in the German embassy in Tokyo that the Japanese were headed south not north. The Japanese decided on August 9, at the time of the Atlantic Conference and before Roosevelt had settled on a full-scale embargo, not to attack Siberia unless the Soviets collapsed. The embargo did not contain; it precipitated a decision to attack southward.[29] Only a small portion of the air-power deterrent arrived in time and was soon wiped out. Submarine Squadron Two's torpedoes did not work. The *Indomitable* went on reef in Jamaica, the *Prince of Wales* and *Repulse* to the bottom of the South China Sea. Fallacies about air power, confusion between deterrence (the B-17's) and coercion (the embargo), gross underestimation of Japanese military capability and desperate determination, and racist notions of firmness in dealing with Asians: all these errors occurred.

Yet what other reasonable courses lay open to Roosevelt and his advisers? Was serious negotiation possible with a Japanese government that was so opportunistic, unpredictable, and given to force?[30] What would be the consequences of negotiation in light of information available to the American government, which by no means ruled out an attack northward? Circumstances can outpace men's ability to avoid war.

However one judges the wisdom of the containment of Japan, the Russian factor goes a long way toward answering the questions raised here. Roosevelt engaged in an oil embargo to immobilize Japan and prevent any attack north or south. This entailed a risk—more than he knew—of an attack southward but less of a risk than a Japanese attack northward because the survival of the Soviet Union was crucial to a victory over Germany. Roosevelt rejected negotiation with Japan except to gain time because any measure of stability Japan might secure in the south might encourage an attack northward. It pays to think beyond Plan Dog and the Atlantic-Pacific options and to see the problem the way FDR saw it, in a global perspective.

NOTES

1. This essay is derived from a book-length study of the American entry into World War II, prepared for publication by Oxford University Press. It was originally presented on April 7, 1987, at a memorial symposium for my colleague at Temple University, Shumpei Okamoto. Research and writing for this study were made possible by a fellowship from the Woodrow Wilson International Center for Scholars as well as by grants from the Earhart Foundation, the American Philosophical Society, and Temple University.

2. Waldo Heinrichs, "President Franklin D. Roosevelt's Intervention in the Battle of the Atlantic, 1941," *Diplomatic History* 10 (Fall 1986): 311–332.

3. Jonathan G. Utley, "Upstairs, Downstairs at Foggy Bottom: Oil Exports to Japan, 1940–41," *Prologue* 8 (Spring 1976): 17–28; Irvine H. Anderson Jr., *The*

Standard-Vacuum Oil Company and United States East Asian Policy, 1933-1941 (Princeton, N.J.: Princeton University Press, 1975).

4. Memorandum for Secretary's files, 30 July 1941, Henry J. Morgenthau Diary, Franklin D. Roosevelt Presidential Library, Hyde Park, New York; memorandum by George F. Luthringer, 30 July 1941, U.S. Department of State, *Papers Relating to the Foreign Relations of the United States,* 1941, vol. IV, Washington, D.C.: 1956–63), pp. 844–845 (hereafter cited as *Foreign Relations Papers*).

5. As quoted in David S. McLellan, *Dean Acheson: The State Department Years* (New York: Dodd, Mead & Co., 1976), p. 28.

6. [We see here, and throughout Heinrichs' essay, the argument that the Soviet connection was intimately connected with American foreign policy in 1941.—EDS.]

7. Chargé in Germany (Leland Morris) to Secretary of State, 6–7 August 1941, radioed to president 7–8 August 1941, Department of State General Records, Record Group 59, 740.0011 European War 1939/13649D–E, National Archives, Washington, D.C.; Martin Van Creveld, "Russian Roulette," in *Supplying War: Logistics from Wallenstein to Patton,* ed. Martin Van Creveld (London: Cambridge University Press, 1977), pp. 142–180.

8. As quoted in John Morton Blum, ed., *From the Morgenthau Diaries: Years of Urgency, 1938-1941* (Boston, Mass.: Houghton Mifflin, 1965), p. 265.

9. [How much do Heinrichs' views of Roosevelt's thinking in regard to the relationship between the Soviet Union and the defeat of Germany qualify Best's criticisms of Roosevelt's foreign policy?—EDS.]

10. [A question for further research is how much did the Soviet military presence and the possibility of a Soviet-Japanese war play a role in the American miscalculation that the Japanese would not dare attack the United States.—EDS.]

11. Walter Adams memo, 25 June 1941, *Foreign Relations Papers,* pp. 278–280.

12. Waldo Heinrichs, "The Role of the U.S. Navy," in *Pearl Harbor as History: Japanese-American Relations, 1931-1941,* ed. Dorothy Borg and Shumpei Okamoto (New York: Columbia University Press, 1973), pp. 211–213.

13. [How much of Roosevelt's thinking regarding the Soviet Union was conveyed to other policymakers? Why have previous historians overlooked this issue? Are the perspectives of historical researchers limited only to what we are looking for? Obviously Heinrichs has opened up a new area of research; specialists will be driven back to their files to see what they may have overlooked in order to refute or support Heinrichs' interpretation.—EDS.]

14. Acheson memo to Welles, 16 August 1941, *Foreign Relations Papers,* pp. 858–860; Sir Ronald Campbell to Foreign Office, 27 September 1941, Public Record Office (London), Foreign Office, 371/27982, F9976/1299/23.

15. [This view does not contradict the essays by Tsunoda, Ikei, and Emmerson that the Americans failed badly in avoiding the summit, but it is at loggerheads with the conventional view that Roosevelt intially showed active interest in one. Heinrichs provides no substantiation in this essay for his view.—EDS.]

16. Roosevelt to Churchill, 15 October 1941, R-63x, in *Churchill and Roosevelt: The Complete Correspondence,* vol. 1, ed. Warren F. Kimball (Princeton, NJ: Princeton University Press, 1984), p. 250. Kimball sees Roosevelt looking ahead to two months of respite, but although the president's language is unclear, he was almost certainly looking back on time gained. It was two months since Argentia.

17. Arnold's long-hand notes of the Argentia Conference, Box 181, General Henry H. Arnold Papers, Library of Congress, Washington, D.C.; Henry H. Arnold, *Global Mission* (New York: Harper and Row, 1949), pp. 249–250; record of discussion between Marshall, General Sir John Dill, and Brigadier Dykes, 11 August 1941, Public Record Office (London), PREM 3/485/5, Prime Minister's Office records.

18. Ambassador John G. Winant to Secretary of State, 5 September 1941, Department of State General Records, Record Group 59, 740.0011 European War 1939/14752 1/6, National Archives; Churchill to Roosevelt, 5 September 1941, C-114x, in *Churchill and Roosevelt: The Complete Correspondence,* vol. 1, p. 238.

19. Churchill to Stalin, 28 August 1941, CAB 120/681, Cabinet records, Public Record Office; Marshall memorandum for president, "Information Used by Chief of Staff at Conference with President, 22 September 1941" folder, Box 885, Entry 31, Chief of Staff Secretariat Files, Records of the War Department General and Special Staffs, 1920–1941, Record Group 165, National Archives. On the reinforcement of the Philippines: Carl Spaatz memorandum for Marshall, 12 September 1941, 320.2 Philippines folder, Box 88, Arnold papers, Library of Congress; transcript of phone conversation between Marshall and Arnold Vanaman, 12 September 1941, Box 185, Arnold papers, Library of Congress; Marshall to General Douglas MacArthur, 3 October 1941, Philippines folder, Box 11, Stimson safe file, Record Group 107, National Archives; Daniel F. Harrington, "A Careless Hope: American Air Power and Japan, 1941," *Pacific Historical Review,* vol. 48 (May 1979): 217–238.

20. Halifax to Foreign Office, 11 October 1941, Public Record Office, Foreign Office, 371/27910, F10639/86/23.

21. Col. Hayes A. Kroner memorandum for Marshall, 2 October 1941, U.S. Congress, *Hearings before the Joint Committee on the Investigation of the Pearl Harbor Attack,* 79th Cong., 1st sess., 1946, 14:1357–1358; War Plans Division strategic estimate, October 1941, 4510, War Plans Division numerical files, Record Group 165.

22. Roosevelt to Churchill, 15 October 1941, R-63x, in *Churchill and Roosevelt: The Complete Correspondence,* vol. 1, p. 250.

23. Adams to MacArthur, 21 October 1941, and Chief of Air Staff to Commanding General Air Force Combat Command, 22 October 1941, 452.1 Philippines folder, Box 129, Arnold papers, Library of Congress.

24. "Strategic Concept of the Philippine Islands," Brigadier General Leonard Gerow memorandum for Stimson, 8 October 1941, Philippines folder, Box 11, Record Group 107.

25. Henry L. Stimson Diary, 12 September 1941, 21 October 1941, Henry L. Stimson Papers, Yale University Library, New Haven, Conn.

26. Transcript of telephone conversation between Marshall and Lt. Cdr. W. R. Smedberg III, aide to Admiral Harold Stark, 25 September 1941, Office of Naval Operations telephone records, 1941–1942, U.S. Navy Operational Archives, Navy Yard, Washington, D.C.

27. Special Naval Observer at London to Naval Operations Office, Washington, D.C., 26 October 1941, Pacific-Far East U.S. Joint Staff correspondence #2, Box 117, Strategic Plans Division Records, ibid.; Churchill to Roosevelt, 2 November 1941, C-125x, in *Churchill and Roosevelt: The Complete Correspondence,* vol. 1, p. 265; Arthur J. Marder, *Old Friends, New Enemies: The Royal Navy and the Imperial Japanese Navy; Strategic Illusions, 1936-1941* (Oxford: Clarendon Press, 1981),

chap. 8. [Heinrichs' view severely qualifies the Klein-Conroy argument that Churchill and the British foreign office misread American intentions in late 1941; however, on the next page we see that Heinrichs retreats somewhat from this position.—EDS.]

28. *New York Times,* 25 November 1941; Henry J. Morgenthau Diary, 26 November 1941.

29. [Implicitly, Heinrichs supports the view that a hard-line American policy did encourage further Japanese aggression. A key question is whether Sorge's information was passed on to the United States by the Soviet Union. Chalmers Johnson has been studying this question for an epilogue to a forthcoming reprinting by Stanford University Press of *An Instance of Treason* (1964).—EDS.]

30. [Heinrichs joins Barnhart and Fujiwara in seeing an inevitability of war given the Japnese attitude and actions in 1941.—EDS.]

18. Concluding Remarks

Hilary Conroy, with Peter Yong-Shik Shin

As will readily be observed by the careful reader of this volume, most of the essays show ways in which diplomacy was somehow short-circuited in the profusion and confusion of words and events preceding Pearl Harbor. In general, since Ambassador Nomura and others in the Japanese government, probably including Premier Konoe and even the emperor himself, wanted peace, or at least a *modus vivendi* with the United States, it should have been possible for American diplomats, who presumably wanted peace also, to find a way to at least postpone hostilities, perhaps indefinitely.

Only two essays (Barnhart and Fujiwara's) really argue that "Hornbeck was right" in assuming that the Japanese were so much on the warpath that nothing Washington's diplomacy could do was likely to deflect them. They assert that even though there may have been many mistakes in diplomacy, these were only of secondary importance. Japan wanted war and brought it about by direct attack. B2

As an historian of diplomacy and an advocate of peace research both my mind and my emotions urge me not to accept this, saying that no war is "inevitable," that there must have been a peaceful way out in 1941. This is not to say that Japanese intransigence and war-mindedness were figments of American imagination. Fujiwara Akira makes an important point in his essay when he shows that there was a fundamental Japanese intransigence on the China question; thus neither "war-man" Tōjō nor "peace-man" Konoe was willing to withdraw Japanese military forces from China. Tōjō would challenge the United States to war on the issue. Konoe would pretend to agree to withdraw but would find undercover ways to avoid carrying out any withdrawal agreements. Oka Yoshitake, in his biography of Konoe,[1] shows him to have been a "quitter;" unfortunately, that did not apply to the situation in China. Thus both Japanese premiers of the crucial year 1941 were determined to rule China.

Moving further down the level of leadership to the acknowledged doves in the Japense political-military establishment, we come to Ambassador (Retired Admiral) Nomura and Admiral Yamamoto, who voiced the navy's general concern that Japan could not win a war against the United States. Despite Nomura's no-doubt sincere peace-making efforts (admitted to be sincere by Cordell Hull himself), he never faced the problem of Japanese troop withdrawal from China as a condition for peace. Indeed, what expressions we have from him indicate that he was almost as uncompromising as Tōjō in "justifying" Japan's presence there.[2]

As for Yamamoto, although he issued dire warnings against the army's easy willingness to enter into war with the United States, having done so he set about planning the greatest war game of them all —Pearl Harbor. Also, as John Stephan has shown, once the die for war was cast Yamamoto and other Japanese navy leaders were soon busily concocting plans for the seizure and occupation of Hawaii as part of an "Eastern Operation" that they advocated in the face of some army opposition.[3]

Before reaching not a conclusion but perhaps an inference on the inevitability of the Pacific War, however, let us hear from a truly neutral party, Peter Yong-Shik Shin, a Korean who was raised in prewar and wartime Japan, who repatriated to Korea for college, and who then pursued in the United States a long career of graduate study of modern Japan's international history. Prewar Japanese is his first, Korean his second, and English his third language, so the following will be a paraphrase of his thoughts on the subject. He begins with the observation that "Japanese understand power." Every nuance of the Japanese language is indicative of this. Rooted in Japan's feudal past, linguistic deference to power in the most minute and sensitive gradations certainly remained true into the post-Pacific-war era and is by no means eradicated even today. On this point Shin contrasts Japanese and Koreans, whose "understanding of power is not so clear, and whose language of power is merely formalized politeness."

Many important Japanese scholars have studied the long- and short-range causes of the Pacific War. Shin would, in general, divide them into three groups: Marxists, Greater Asia Nationalists, and Moderates. Marxists and near Marxists argue that the war was an inevitable imperialist war, with the Japanese leadership from Meiji times onward seeking the profits of imperialism and getting into wars. Scholars like Tōyama Shigeki, Inoue Kiyoshi, Ienaga Saburō, and Shinobu Seizaburō are of this school. These scholars are not "Communist party Marxists" but rather Japanese "intellectual Marxists who do not care about the 'realities' of politics and who concentrate instead on theory," concerning which they have "arguments and refinements." For example, Tōyama and Inoue regard Japanese military and civilian leadership as so closely intertwined as to be indistinguishable, or not worth distinguishing, but Shinobu and Ienaga find the military significantly worse than the civilians, although the latter cooperated with them at crucial points and times in promoting Japanese aggression. The record of imperialism and aggression is also long and consistent, from the Meiji era's Sino- and Russo-Japanese wars and the annexation of Korea through the Manchurian crisis, the China "Incident," and on to the Pacific War. Such arguments appear most consistently in *Rekishigaku kenkyū* (Journal of Historical Science).

Peculiarly, Greater Asia nationalist historians, of whom Hayashi Fusao is the most famous and most prolific,[4] also regard the Pacific War as having a very long history. Like the Marxists they do not regard the "Taishō democracy" of the 1918–1930 era or Japan's years of membership in the League of Nations or her participation in the Washington and London conferences as anything very significant. The Pacific War, says Hayashi over and over in sixteen articles published in *Chūō Kōron* (Central Review) between September 1963 and June 1965, was "justified." It was a hundred years' war to liberate Asia, beginning when Perry led the Western world into Japan and when Western imperialism pushed into China. It was not the Meiji leaders, who sought to (and did) strengthen Japan by imitating the West, but Saigō Takamori, the great samurai hero of Satsuma, who, rejecting "western-style" modernization sought to move Japan to leadership on the continent of Asia, first by conquering Korea, which he advocated in the famous "Conquer Korea" (Seikan) argument that split the new Meiji government in 1873. Saigō lost the argument to the "peace party" returnees from the Iwakura mission, who had traveled abroad, seen, and feared the West, and he died in 1877 leading an abortive samurai (Satsuma) rebellion against the accommodationist Meiji government he had come to detest for failing to uphold traditional samurai values. Although Saigō failed and died, his memory lived on, glorified by "secret" patriotic societies—the Genyōsha (Black Ocean) and the Kokuryūkai (Black Dragon-Amur River)—and by ultranationalists like Tōyama Mitsuru, Uchida Ryōhei, and Ōkawa Shūmei who through their influence on "young officers," patriotic reservists, and other dissatisfied elements of Japan's burgeoning population made Japan realize that her destiny was to lead Greater East Asia in the struggle against Western imperialism. That, to them, was the meaning of the Pacific War.

Such "Marxist" and Asia Nationalist arguments are attractive theoretically perhaps but are of insufficient interest on the question of the war's inevitability. Of course, the war was inevitable if the causes were as deep as these schools of thought would have it. In the center are the less theoretical, more analytical "moderate" scholars, who try to zero in on specific matters. For example, Seki Hiroharu of Tokyo University, in an article published in 1963 in the *Taiheiyō sensō e no michi* collection, showed that those who plotted the Manchurian takeover in 1931 included ranking generals, such as Ugaki, Sugiyama, and Koiso, and not merely lower-level colonels, as the Tokyo War Crimes Tribunal presumed.[5] Fujimura Michio "rediscovered" this in 1980, without referring to Seki,[6] and Eguchi Keiichi wraps this point up in his article on "The Manchurian Incident and the Military" (in Japanese in *Rekishigaku kenkyū*, October 1982).[7]

The Manchurian Incident, of course, set off the "Fifteen-Year War," the final stage of which was initiated by the Pearl Harbor attack. Imai Seiichi, Fujiwara Akira, and others in their "Criticisms" of "The Course toward the Pacific War" *(Taiheiyō sensō e no michi)* published in *Rekishigaku kenkyū* in June 1964[8] emphasized that its editor Tsunoda Jun and others had placed the responsibility for the war on Japan's "Naval Command," who allowed themselves to be persuaded by subordinates. In so doing they missed several chances to avoid the confrontation with the United States, as when Germany invaded the USSR, with whom Japan had a neutrality pact. Japan could have backed off from Germany then. In addition, the emperor's desire to avoid war somehow was never utilized.

Thus most of the scholars in Japan's "moderate" school would find points at which or ways in which the Pacific War could have been avoided or at least postponed, and most of the contributors to this volume, whether Japanese or American, do or could do so as well. But we should at least pose the question of whether there is also a psychological factor, deeply imbedded in Japan's samurai heritage, that made taking a "suicide leap" into the Pearl Harbor attack so exciting and dramatic a war game that once it was proposed as a possibility it had to be tried. This was certainly an element in the psychology of General Tōjō. Brought up by samurai values, his entire schooling and adult life spent on military "duty," he had once admonished an ambivalent Konoe that there might come a time in a man's life when he must take a huge risk and, with his eyes closed, jump "from Kiyomizu temple" (a high temple in Kyoto) into the ravine below. Admiral Yamamoto, although admitting to and even cautioning overly daring military colleagues that victory over the United States might not come until peace "could be dictated in the White House," nonetheless could launch the Pearl Harbor attack. In addition, although Konoe may have been softer in tone and policy, it should be remembered that his father, Konoe Atsumaro, was an admirer and sometime patron of the Black Dragon Society. In the end he took the samurai way out, suicide, when named as a war criminal suspect in postwar Japan—not by the sword, it is true, but by poison, on December 16, 1945.

Such were the men who controlled the triggers of Japanese militarism. With no swell of anti-war sentiment from below to give them pause, it must still be considered uncertain whether, in the setting of their leadership, diplomacy had much chance. Certainly, it behooves humankind not to allow any samurai mentalities to control the triggers of nuclear war.[9]

The above remarks point only at the Japanese side. Did the Americans really want peace? Charles Beard's famous (or infamous) *President Roosevelt and the Coming of the War*[10] opined that FDR indeed wanted war with Japan, even including the attack on Pearl Harbor. Although this has been dismissed by mainline scholars as a polemic against FDR and even ridiculed as "history through a beard,"[11] it should be observed that in addition to Japanese scholars Hosoya and Ikei, and Emmerson, who may be called anti-Hornbeck, at least two of the other American scholars whose essays are presented in this volume have indicated obliquely, if not directly, that persons higher than Hornbeck, including Hull and Roosevelt, were not very interested in Japanese peace overtures, whatever they were.

Thus Jonathan Utley shows Hull insisting on a *public* renunciation of Japan's alliance with Germany and a "humiliating" Japanese withdrawal from China. Face-saving assurances were not enough, not enough even to be discussed at a Pacific conference between Konoe and Roosevelt. Waldo Heinrichs argues that Assistant Secretary of State Dean Acheson's seeming misunderstanding or negligence, which resulted in an "unintended" complete freeze on Japanese assets, was in fact deliberate; it was President Roosevelt's way of bringing trade with Japan to a complete halt without any formal order—and thereby keeping Japan at risk of war with the United States so she could not attack the USSR. These are high-risk politics indeed, and persuasively presented.[12]

However, before we accept intransigence of either or both sides, it should be observed that postwar history would seem to mock an inevitability theory of whatever kind. Japan has learned to live (very well) without controlling China or Southeast Asia, and the United States learned not only to do without its Open Door policy in China but also to favor a strong Japan as a good balance in Asia. So why the war at all?

Another postwar change for the better, which had it come earlier might have made peace more possible, lies in the realm of social change, specifically with regard to racism. As John Dower has pointed out, the Pacific War was in many ways a *race* war between the Japanese and the Americans.[13] Happily such intense racism seems absurd today. Whether less racism would have tipped the scales for peace must remain a moot point. In the preface we promised no definitive answer on the inevitability of the Pacific War, so on this note we shall close this volume.

NOTES

1. See Oka Yoshitake, and Shumpei Okamoto and Patricia Murray, trans., *Konoe Fumimaro: Unmei no seijika* (Konoe Fumimaro: A Political Biography) (Tokyo: Iwanami, 1972; Tokyo: University of Tokyo Press, 1983). Reviews of these books appear in the *Journal of Asian Studies*, vol. 34 (February 1975): pp. 473–476 and vol. 43 (May 1984).

2. Nomura Kichisaburō, "Beikoku no Yūjin ni Atau" (To Friends in the United States), *Gaikō Jihō (Diplomatic Review)*, vol. 84 (1937): pp. 233–236.

3. John J. Stephan, *Hawaii under the Rising Sun* (Honolulu: University of Hawaii Press, 1984).

4. Hayashi Fusao, "Daitōa Sensō Kōteiron" (Justification of the Greater East Asia War), *Chūō kōron (Central Review)*, no. 911 (September 1963), pp. 294–307; no. 912 (October 1963), pp. 257–269; no. 913 (November 1963), pp. 233–252; no. 914 (December 1963), pp. 234–250; no. 918 (April 1964), pp. 168–185; no. 919 (May 1964), pp. 177–187; no. 920 (June 1964), pp. 284–295; no. 921 (July 1964), pp. 300–317; no. 922 (August 1964), pp. 112–123; no. 923 (September 1964), pp. 169–183; no. 924 (October 1964), pp. 122–138; no. 925 (November 1964), pp. 266–285; no. 926 (December 1964), pp. 290–305; no. 930 (April 1965), pp. 222–244; no. 931 (May 1965), pp. 212–227; no. 932 (June 1965), pp. 196–208.

5. Seki Hiroharu, "Manshū jihen zenshi, 1927–1931" (Before the Manchurian

Incident, 1927–1931) in *Taiheiyō sensō e no michi* (The Road to the Pacific War), vol. 1, ed. Kokusai Seiji Gakkai (Tokyo: Asahi Shinbunsha, 1962), pp. 287–440. Professor Seki has since become a leading advocate and practitioner of peace research at the Institute of Oriental Culture, University of Tokyo, the Institute of Peace Science, Hiroshima University, and the United Nations University, Tokyo.

6. Fujimura Michio, "Iwayuru jūgatsu jiken no saikentoō: Nihon Fuashizumu Ron no Oboegaki" (A Reexamination of the So-called October Incident—Remembering Japanese Fascism) *Nihon rekishi,* no. 393 (February 1981), pp. 52–65.

7. Eguchi Keiichi, "Manshū jihen to gumbu" (The Manchurian Incident and the Military), *Rekishigaku kenkyū,* no. 509 (October 1982), pp. 16–23.

8. Imai Seiichi, Fujiwara Akira, Arai Shinichi, and Nozawa Yutaka, "Taiheiyō sensō no rekishiteki igi" (The Meaning of the Pacific War): "Asahi Shinbunsha taiheiyō sensō e no michi hihan" (Criticism of the Asahi Shimbun publication on The Road to the Pacific War), *Rekishigaku kenkyū,* no. 289, (June 1964), pp. 1–5 (Imai), pp. 5–7 (Fujiwara), pp. 8–11 (Arai), pp. 11–13 (Nozawa).

9. Konoe's suicide was reported in the *Nippon Times* (Tokyo) issue of 17 December 1945 under the heading "Konoye Kills Self on Eve of Arrest in Surprise Action: Poison Vial Found at Bedside—Last Days Said Full of Worry." Concerning Japanese blame for the war it may be noted that Professor and former ambassador to Japan Edwin O. Reischauer, whose lifelong dedication to the cause of Japanese-American friendship is well known and exemplary, nonetheless in his memoirs published in 1986 expresses no doubt that he was correct in "vigorously supporting American aims to block Japanese aggression in East Asia" in 1941. See his *My Life between Japan and America* (New York: Harper and Row, 1986), p. 87. A trip he made to Japanese-controlled Korea helped to convince him. Ibid., pp. 67–70. Regarding the importance of a Korean perspective in understanding prewar Japan, see Chong-sik Lee, *Japan and Korea: The Political Dimension* (Stanford, Calif.: Hoover Institution, 1985), espec. p. 4, citing the great Japanese liberal educator, Fukuzawa Yukichi.

10. New Haven, Conn.: Yale University Press, 1948.

11. Harvard Professor Samuel Eliot Morrison challenged Yale-man Beard in "Did Roosevelt Start the War—History Through a Beard," *Atlantic Monthly,* August 1948.

12. See the essays in this volume by Jonathan Utley and Waldo Heinrichs. See also the facinating "my full authority" and "step on it" order from FDR to Wayne Coy, dated August 2, 1941 (FDR Letters 2:1195–1196), Franklin D. Roosevelt Presidential Library, Hyde Park, New York.

13. John Dower, *War without Mercy: Race and Power in the Pacific War* (New York: Pantheon Books, 1986). Part 1, chapter 1, is entitled "Patterns of a Race War." Evidence that the common people of Japan had little or no understanding of the path on which their leaders had embarked abounds in Thomas R. H. Havens, *The Valley of Darkness: The Japanese People and World War Two* (New York: W. W. Norton, 1978).

Suggested Readings

English-Language Sources

Barnhart, Michael A. *Japan Prepares for Total War: The Search for Economic Security, 1915-1941.* Ithaca, N.Y.: Cornell University Press, 1987.

Beard, Charles. *President Roosevelt and the Coming of the War, 1941: A Study in Appearances and Realities.* New Haven, Conn.: Yale University Press, 1948. (Reprint by Shoe String, 1968.)

Borg, Dorothy, and Shumpei Okamoto, eds. *Pearl Harbor as History: Japanese-American Relations 1931-1941.* New York: Columbia University Press, 1973.

Boyle, John Hunter. *China and Japan at War, 1937-1945.* Stanford: Stanford University Press, 1961.

Burns, Richard Dean, and Edward M. Bennett, eds. *Diplomats in Crisis: United States-Chinese-Japanese Relations, 1919-1941.* Santa Barbara, Calif.: ABC-CLIO Press, 1974.

Butow, Robert J. C. *The John Doe Associates: Backdoor Diplomacy for Peace, 1941.* Stanford: Stanford University Press, 1974.

————. *Tōjō and the Coming of the War.* Princeton: Princeton University Press, 1966.

Conroy, Hilary. "The Strange Diplomacy of Admiral Nomura," *Proceedings American Philosophical Society* 114, no. 3 (June 1970): pp. 205-216.

Coox, Alvin, and Hilary Conroy, eds. *China and Japan: Search for Balance.* Santa Barbara, Calif.: ABC-CLIO Press, 1978.

Crowley, James B., ed. *Modern East Asia: Essays in Interpretation.* New York: Harcourt Brace and World, 1970.

————. *Japan's Quest for Autonomy.* Princeton: Princeton University Press, 1966.

Dower, John. *War Without Mercy: Race and Power in the Pacific War.* New York: Pantheon Books, 1986.

Feis, Herbert. *The Road to Pearl Harbor: The Coming of the War between the United States and Japan.* Princeton: Princeton University Press, 1953.

Grew, Joseph C. *Ten Years in Japan.* New York: Simon and Schuster, 1944.

Heinrichs, Waldo H., Jr. *American Ambassador: Joseph C. Grew and the Development of the United States Diplomatic Tradition.* Boston: Little Brown, 1966.

————. *Threshold of War: Franklin D. Roosevelt and American Entry Into World War II.* New York: Oxford University Press, 1988.

Hinton, Harold B. *Cordell Hull, A Biography.* Garden City, N.Y.: Doubleday, 1942.

Hosoya, Chihiro. "Japan's Decision for War, 1941," *Peace Research in Japan,* I, no. 1 (1967): pp. 41-51.

Hull, Cordell. *The Memoirs of Cordell Hull.* 2 vols. New York: Macmillan, 1948.

Ienaga, Saburō. *The Pacific West: World War II and the Japanese, 1931–1945.* New York: Pantheon Books, 1978.

Ike, Nobutaka. *Japan's Decision for War: Records of the 1941 Policy Conferences.* Stanford: Stanford University Press, 1967.

Ikle, Frank W. *German-Japanese Relations, 1936–40.* New York: Bookman Association, 1956.

Iriye, Akira. *Power and Culture: The Japanese-American War.* Cambridge: Harvard University Press, 1981.

————. *The Origins of the Second World War in Asia and the Pacific.* Essex, England: Longmen Group, 1987.

Jansen, Marius. *Japan and China from War to Peace, 1894–1972.* Chicago: Rand McNally, 1975.

Johnson, Chalmers. *An Instance of Treason.* Stanford: Stanford University Press, 1964.

Langer, William L., and S. Everett Gleason. *The Undeclared War, 1940–1941.* New York: Harper and Row, 1953.

Lord, Walter. *Day of Infamy.* New York: Henry Holt, 1957; Bantam Books, 1958.

Lu, David J. *From the Marco Polo Bridge to Pearl Harbor.* Washington, D.C.: Public Affairs Press, 1961.

————, ed. *Perspectives on Japan's External Relations.* Lewisburg, Pa.: Center for Japanese Studies, Bucknell University, 1982.

Meskill, Johanna. *Hitler and Japan: The Hollow Alliance.* New York: Atherton, 1966.

Mishima, Yukio. *Sun and Steel.* Translated by John Bester. New York: Grove Press, 1970.

Morley, James B., ed. *Deterrent Diplomacy, Japan, Germany, and the USSR, 1935–1940: Selected Translations from Taiheiyō sensō e no michi: Kaisen gaikō shi* (Studies of the East Asian Institute, Japan's Road to the Pacific War Series). New York: Columbia University Press, 1976.

Morison, Samuel Eliot. *History of United States Naval Operations in World War II.* Boston: Little Brown, 1947–62.

————. "Did Roosevelt Start the War—History Through a Beard." *Atlantic Monthly* (August 1948).

Nish, Ian, ed. *Anglo-Japanese Alienation.* Cambridge: Cambridge University Press, 1982.

Prange, Gordon W. (Donald M. Goldstein and Katharine V. Dillon, eds.). *At Dawn We Slept: The Untold Story of Pearl Harbor.* New York: McGraw Hill, 1981.

————. *Miracle at Midway.* New York: McGraw Hill, 1982.

————. *Pearl Harbor: The Verdict of History.* New York: McGraw Hill, 1986.

Pratt, Julius W. *Cordell Hull, 1933–1944.* 2 vols. New York: Cooper Square, 1964.

Presseisen, Ernst L. *Germany and Japan: A Study in Totalitarian Diplomacy, 1933–1941.* The Hague: Martinus Nijhoff, 1958.

Sato, Kyozo. *Japan and Britain at the Crossroads, 1939–1941.* Tokyo: Senshu University Press, 1986.

Schroeder, Paul W. *The Axis Alliance and Japanese-American Relations, 1941.* Ithaca, N.Y.: Cornell University Press, 1958.

Stephan, John J. *Hawaii under the Rising Sun*. Honolulu: University of Hawaii Press, 1984.

Takemoto, Tōru, and Hilary Conroy. "An Ounce of Prevention: A New Look at the Manchurian Incident." *Peace and Change* II, no. 1 (Spring 1974): pp. 42–46.

Tansill, Charles Callan. *Back Door to War: The Roosevelt Foreign Policy, 1933–1941.* Chicago: Henry Regency Co., 1952.

Thorne, Christopher. *Allies of a Kind: The United States, Britain, and the War Against Japan, 1941–1945*. New York: Oxford University Press, 1978.

—————. *The Issue of War: States, Societies and the Far Eastern Conflict of 1941–1945*. New York: Oxford University Press, 1985.

Toland, John. *Rising Sun: The Decline and Fall of the Japanese Empire, 1936–1945*. New York: Random House, 1970.

—————. *Infamy: Pearl Harbor and Its Aftermath*. New York: Doubleday, 1982.

Utley, Jonathan G. *Going to War with Japan, 1937–1941*. Knoxville: University of Tennessee Press, 1985.

Waller, George M., ed. *Pearl Harbor, Roosevelt and the Coming of the War*. Lexington, Mass.: D. C. Heath, 1976.

Wohlsetter, Roberta. *Pearl Harbor: Warning and Decisions*. Stanford: Stanford University Press, 1962.

Wray, Harry, and Hilary Conroy, eds. *Japan Examined: Perspectives on Modern Japanese History*. Honolulu: University of Hawaii Press, 1983.

Japanese-Language Sources

Arita Hachirō. *Bakahachi to hito wa iu: Ichi Gaikōkan no Kaisō* (They call me Hachi the Fool: A diplomat's memoirs). Tokyo: Kowado, 1959.

—————. *Hito no Me no chiri o miru: Gaikō mondai kaisōroku.* (I saw dust in their eyes: A recollection of diplomatic problems). Tokyo: Kōdansha, 1948.

Fujiwara Akira et al. "Historical significance of the Pacific War: Critique of Taiheiyō sensō e no michi" (in Japanese). *Rekishigaku kenkyū* (June 1964); *Gunjishi* (History of the Japanese Military), 1961.

Fukutome Shigeru. *Kaigun no hansei* (A self-examination by the navy). Tokyo: Nihon Shuppan Kyōdō Kabushikikaisha, 1951.

—————. *Shikan Shinjuwan kōgeki* (Historical view of the attack on Pearl Habor). Tokyo: Ajiasha, 1955.

Haga Takeshi. *Tōakyōeiken to Nanyō Kakyō* (The Greater East Asia co-prosperity sphere and the overseas Chinese in the South Seas). Tokyo: Toko shoin, 1941.

Hagihara Nobutoshi. *Tōgō Shigenori* (Biography). 2 vols. Tokyo: Genshobō, 1985.

Hattori Takushirō. *Daitōasensō Zenshi* (A History of the Greater East Asia War). Tokyo: Masu shobō, 1953.

Harada Kumao. *Saionjikō to seikyoku* (Prince Saionji and politics). Tokyo: Iwanami Shoten, 1950–1956.

Hata Ikuhiko. *Taiheiyō kokusai Kankei-shi* (History of the international relations of the Pacific area). Tokyo: 1972.

—————. "Kōdō-ha to Tōsei-ha" (The Imperial Way faction and the Control faction). *Jiyu* (Freedom) 3, no. 5 (1961): pp. 78–90.

Hayashi Fusao. "Justification of the Great East Asian War" (in Japanese). *Chūō Kōron* September, October, November, December 1963; April, May, June, July, August, September, October, November, December 1964; April, May, June, 1965.

Hoshina Zenshirō. *Daitōasensō hishi* (A secret history of the Greater East Asia War). Tokyo: Hara Shobō, 1975.

Hosoya Chihiro, Saitō Makoto, Imai Seiichi, and Royama Michio, eds. *Nichi-Bei kankeishi: kaisen ni itaru jūnen* (A history of Japanese-American relations: The decade preceding the war) 4 vols. Tokyo: Tokyodaigaku Shuppankai, 1971.

Ikeda Kiyoshi. 1966–1967. *Nihon no kaigun* (The Japanese navy). 2 vols. Tokyo: Shiseido.

Inoue Kiyoshi. "Taiheiyō sensō shikan." *Gendaishi kenkyū* (December 1961).

Iriye Akira. *Kyokutō Shinchitsujo no Mosaku* (The search for a new order in the Far East). [Kindai Nihon Gaikōshi Sōsho (Series on modern Japanese diplomacy), vol. 8.] Tokyo: Hara Shobo, 1968.

Iwakuro Hideo. "Heiwa e no arasoi" (A dispute for the cause of peace). *Bungei Shunjū* (August 1966): pp. 220–240.

Kaneko Takansuke. *Kosei futsuryō Indoshina no zenbō* (The New French Indochina). Tokyo: Aikoku Shinbunsha, 1941.

Kase Toshikazu. *Mizuri-gō e no dōtei* (Journey to the U.S.S. Missouri). Tokyo: Bungei Shunjū Shinsha, 1951.

———. *Nichibei kōshō* (The Japanese-American negotiations). [*Nihon Gaikōshi* (A diplomatic history of Japan), vol. 23.] Tokyo: Kajima Kenkyūjo Shuppankai, 1970–1980.

Kazami Akira. *Konoe Naikaku* (The Konoe cabinet). Tokyo: Nihon Shuppan Kyōdō Kabushikikaisha, 1951.

Kiba Kōsuke, ed. *Nomura Kichisaburō*. Tokyo: Nomura Kichisaburō Denki Kankōkai, 1961.

Kido Kōichi. *Kido Kōichi kankei bunsho* (Kido Kōichi papers). Tokyo: Tokyo Daigaku Shuppanbu, 1966.

———. *Kido nikki* (Diary of Koichi Kido). Tokyo: Tokyo Daigaku Shuppanbu, 1966.

Konoe Fumimaro. *Heiwa e no doryoku* (My struggle for peace). Tokyo: Nihon Denpō Tsūshin-sha, 1946.

———. *Ushinawareshi seiji* (Politics that failed). Tokyo: Asahi Shinbunsha, 1946.

Kugai Saburō, ed. *Shiryō: Betonamu sensō* (Documents: The war in Viet Nam). Tokyo: Kinokuniya Shoten, 1969.

Kuzuu Yoshihisa. 1933–1936. *Tōa senkaku shishi kiden* (Biographical sketches of pioneer patriots in East Asia). 3 vols. Tokyo: Kokuryukai Shuppanbu.

Kurusu Saburō. *Hōmatsu no sanju-go-nen* (Thirty-five years of vain endeavor). Tokyo: Bunka Shoin, 1948.

Matsui Iwane. "Shinajihen no Kaiketsu to Beikoku Mondai" (The settlement of the China Incident and the problem of the United States). *Dai Ajiashugi* (July 1941). (International Military Tribunal for the Far East [IMTFE], International Prosecution Section [IPS] Doc. # 2397.)

Matsumoto Shunichi. *Nanpō mondai* (The question of the southward advance) (*Nihon gaikōshi* Vol. 22). Tokyo: Kajima Kenkyūjo Shuppankai, 1970.

Matsuoka Yōsuke. *Kōa no taigyō* (A great work of developing Asia). Tokyo: Daiichi Kōronsha, 1941.

————. *Sūjikukoku ni tsukaishite* (My mission to the Axis countries). Tokyo: Katsuragi Shoten, 1941.

Minami Manshū tetsudō kabushiki-kaisha Tōa Keizai Chōsakyoku (South Manchuria Railway Company, East Asia Economic Research Bureau). *Futsuin Gyōsei-seido Gaikan* (The administrative system of French Indochina). Tokyo: 1943.

————. *Waga Nanshin-seisaku wo meguru Futsuryō Indoshina no Seiji Keizai Dōkō* (The political and economic activities in French Indochina relative to Japan's policy of southern expansion). Tokyo: 1941.

Nihon Gaikō Gakkai (Japanese Society for the Study of Diplomacy). *Taiheiyō-sensō geninron* (Origins of the Pacific War). Tokyo: Shimbun Gekkansha, 1953.

Nihon Kokusaiseiji Kenkyūkai (Japanese Society for the Study of International Politics). *Taiheiyō-sensō e no michi* (Road to the Pacific War). Tokyo: Asahi Shimbunsha, 1960–1963.

Nomura Kichisaburō. *Beikoku ni Tsukaishite: Nichi-Bei Kosho-no Kaiko* (Ambassador to the United States: Reminiscences of the Japanese-American negotiations). Tokyo: Iwanami Shoten, 1946.

Ōhashi Chūichi. *Taiheiyō-sensō yuraiki* (Origins of the Pacific War). Tokyo: Kaname Shobō, 1952.

Oka Yoshitake. *Konoe Fumimaro: "Unmei" no seijika* (Konoe Fumimaro: A Political Biography). Translated by Shumpei Okamoto and Patricia Murray. Tokyo: Iwanami, 1972; Tokyo: University of Tokyo Press, 1983.

Rekishigaku Kenkyūkai (Society for the Study of History). *Taiheiyō-sensōshi* (History of the Pacific War). Tokyo: Yomiuri Shinbunsha, 1955.

Shigemitsu Mamoru. *Gaikō kaisōroku* (Diplomatic memoirs). Tokyo: Mainichi Shinbunsha, 1953.

Tanaka Naokichi. "Nichi-Bei gaikō kankei no gaiken" (A General view of Japanese-American diplomatic relations). *Kokusai Seiji* (International Politics) 1961.

Tanemura Sakō. *Daihonei kimitsu nissi* (Confidential journal of Imperial General Headquarters). Tokyo: Daiamondosha, 1952.

Tōgō Shigenori. *Jidai no ichimen* (An aspect of the times). Tokyo: Hara Shobō, 1952.

————. *Gaikō shuki* (Diplomatic memoirs). Tokyo: Hara Shobō, 1969.

Tsunoda Jun, ed. *Taiheiyō no sensō e no michi* (The road to the Pacific War). 8 vols. Tokyo: Asahi Shimbunsha, 1962.

Yabe, Teiji. *Konoe Fumimaro*. Tokyo: Jiji Tsūshinsha, 1953.

Contributors

Michael Barnhart is associate professor of Japanese history at the State University of New York, Stony Brook. He is author of *Japan Prepares for Total War: The Search for Economic Security 1915–1941* and editor of *Congress and United States Foreign Policy: Controlling the Use of Force in the Nuclear Age.*

Gary Dean Best, professor of American History at the University of Hawaii, Hilo, is author of *The Politics of American Individualism* and *Herbert Hoover: The Post Presidential Years.*

Hilary Conroy is professor of Far Eastern history at the University of Pennsylvania. He has published numerous books and articles on Japanese foreign relations, among them *China and Japan: Search for Balance.* He is coeditor, with Harry Wray, of *Japan Examined: Perspectives on Modern Japanese History* and, with Roy Kim, of *New Tides in the Pacific.* He is past president of the Council on Peace Research in History.

Alvin D. Coox is professor of Japanese history and chair of the Japanese Studies Institute at San Diego State University. Among his numerous publications are *The Soviet-Japanese Struggle for Changkufeng/Khasan, 1938* and *Nomohan: The Soviet-Japanese War of 1939.* In 1987 he was awarded the Samuel Eliot Morison Prize by the American Military Institute for distinguished career contributions to the field.

John K. Emmerson (deceased) was a U.S. Foreign Service officer assigned to the American Embassy in Tokyo during the pre-Pearl Harbor ambassadorship of Joseph Grew. After his retirement from the foreign service, he was a senior scholar at Stanford University. Among his publications is *The Japanese Thread.*

Fujiwara Akira is a specialist in military and political history. Retired from the faculty of Hitotsubashi University in 1987, he currently teaches at Rikkyō University and Nihon Joshi University. Widely published, his most recent works are *Nihon gunji shi* (A military history of Japan) and *Okinawa sen, kokudo ga senjō ni natta toki.*

Norman A. Graebner is emeritus professor of American history at the University of Virginia. He is the author of numerous books and articles focusing on American diplomacy, among them *Cold War Diplomacy, Ideas and Diplomacy,* and *The Age of Global Power.*

Hata Ikuhiko is professor of history at Takushoku University. From 1971 to 1976 he served as chief historian at the Ministry of Finance. His publications include *Shiroku Nippon saigunbi* (History of Japan's rearmament) and *Nanking jiken* (Nanking atrocities).

Waldo Heinrichs is professor of American history at Temple University. He is author of *Joseph C. Grew and the Development of the U.S. Diplomatic Tradition* and *Threshold of War: Franklin D. Roosevelt and American Entry into World War II* and is coeditor, with Dorothy Borg, of *Chinese-American Relations, 1947–1950.*

Hosoya Chihiro has published extensively on international relations. He retired from Hitotsubashi University to become vice-president of the International University of Japan. He is coeditor, with Honma Nagayo, of the widely used college textbook *Nichibei kankei shi* (A history of Japanese-American relations).

Ikei Masaru is a specialist in international relations at Keiō University who writes on scholarly topics and popular aspects of American culture. His *Gaisetsu Nihon gaikoshi* (A survey of Japanese diplomatic history) is the most widely used college textbook on the subject.

Akira Iriye is the author of many books and articles on American-Japanese relations, including *Pacific Estrangement, Power and Culture: The Japanese-American War,* and *The Origins of the Second World War in Asia and the Pacific.* He is professor of American history at the University of Chicago, and past president of the American Historical Association.

David Klein received his Ph.D. in history from the University of Pennsylvania. He is currently working as a consultant in Osaka, Japan.

Sachiko Murakami (deceased) received her Ph.D. in history from New York University.

Peter Yong-Shik Shin received his Ph.D. from the University of Pennsylvania. He specializes in modern Japanese history.

Tsunoda Jun, who retired from his position of professor of history at Kokushin University in 1988, was formerly the research director and senior diplomatic historian of the National Diet Library and adviser on foreign affairs to several Japanese prime ministers and foreign ministers. He is editor of the eight-volume work *Taiheiyō no sensō e no michi* (The Road to the Pacific War).

Jonathan G. Utley, associate professor of American history at the University of Tennessee, is the author of *Going to War with Japan, 1937–1941,* as well as numerous articles on Japanese-American relations.

Taeko Wellington teaches Japanese language at Kamehameha School in Honolulu and frequently acts as a simultaneous interpreter and translator.

Harry Wray, formerly associate professor of history at Illinois State University, is currently on the faculty of Japanese language and culture at the University of Tsukuba, Japan. He is coeditor, with Hilary Conroy, of *Japan Examined: Perspectives on Modern Japanese History* and coauthor, with Takahashi Shirō, of *Senryoka no kyoiku kaikaku to kenetsu* (Postwar educational reform and censorship).

Index

Production Notes

This book was designed by Roger Eggers.
Composition and paging were done on the
Quadex Composing System and typesetting
on the Compugraphic 8400 by the design
and production staff of University of
Hawaii Press.

The text and display typeface is Garamond #49
and the display typeface is ITC Garamond.

Offset presswork and binding were done by
Vail-Ballou Press, Inc. Text paper is
Writers RR Offset, basis 50.